Second Edition

The
Legal
Research
Manual

A Game Plan for
Legal Research and Analysis

Published and distributed by Adams & Ambrose Publishing,
1274 South Park Street, P.O. Box 9684, Madison, Wisconsin 53715.
Tel. (608) 257-5700.

Additional copies may be ordered from Adams & Ambrose Publishing.

*Acknowledgment of permission to reprint previously published
material appears on page iv.*

Printed in the United States of America

Printing: 20 19 18 17 16 15 14 13 12 11

Library of Congress Cataloging in Publication Data

Wren, Christopher G., 1950 —
  The legal research manual:
  a game plan for legal research and analysis
  Second Edition

  Reprint. Originally published: Madison, Wis.:
A-R Editions, c1986.
  Includes bibliographical references and index.
    1. Legal research — United States. I. Wren,
Jill Robinson, 1954 —   II. Title.
KF240.W7 1988   340'.072073   88-14437
ISBN 0-916951-16-2 (previously ISBN 0-89579-210-9) (pbk.)

Second Edition

The Legal Research Manual

A Game Plan for Legal Research and Analysis

Christopher G. Wren
J. D., Harvard Law School
Member, Massachusetts and Wisconsin Bars

Jill Robinson Wren
J. D., Boston University School of Law
Member, Wisconsin Bar

Adams & Ambrose Publishing, Madison, Wisconsin

Permissions

The following materials are reprinted with the kind permission of the copyright holders.

INTRODUCTION

About This Book

The key to successful legal research is organization. You have to gather your facts, find the relevant law, and then weave the law and facts into a pattern that conveys a story. The story might be one you tell to a judge or jury (or law school professor), or perhaps one you tell to a city council or state legislature. But whatever your story and whoever your audience, your goal is to persuade somebody to agree with you.

You will develop an effective presentation most quickly and with the least effort if you gather your facts and do your legal research methodically. As with any complex task, you need a "game plan" that helps you comprehend and complete the job as quickly, efficiently, and thoroughly as possible. For legal research, the best game plan simplifies the research process by breaking it down into its basic steps because at that point, legal research becomes an easily comprehended process.

This manual, which presents a basic research procedure suitable for any legal research project, breaks legal research down according to its component phases. By reading this book, you will become familiar with all the steps involved in analyzing and researching a legal problem: gathering and evaluating facts; identifying the legal issues raised by the facts; organizing your problem for research; finding the law; reading and analyzing the law; determining whether the law you've located is still valid; taking effective notes; and determining when to stop your research. If you follow the tips included here, neither legal research techniques nor the vast array of books used in legal research will bewilder, intimidate, or overwhelm you.

How to use this book. The structure of legal research will make sense to you when you understand the relationship between the sources of law (courts, legislatures, and administrative agencies) and the books in which you will find the law they create. Therefore, in Part I, we explain the fundamentals of this relationship. Nonetheless, in order to avoid bogging you down in a maze of unnecessary detail, we have limited the discussion in Part I to only the amount of information we believe is necessary to appreciate the significance, for the purposes of doing legal research, of the relationship between law books and their sources.

Part I also sets law and legal research in their essential framework—that is, the facts, which provide the starting point in every problem requiring legal research.

Consequently, reading Part I before turning to the explanation of the legal research processes in Part II will shed light on the purposes underlying the various research steps, which will in turn take the "mystery" out of them.

Part II covers the mechanics of legal research, with the steps placed in an easy-to-follow analytical framework of, *first*, finding the law; *second*, reading the law; and *third*, updating the law. This framework helps to keep the overall legal research process in focus. Still, the nature of legal research requires anyone who sets out to do it to master a degree of detail. So, Part II also covers the essential details of the research process.

You don't need to absorb all the points covered in Part II immediately, however. Because Part II arranges the specifics of legal research according to *function,* you can skim through that portion of the book to get an overview of the legal research steps, then simply take this book with you to the library as a "roadmap" to which you can refer as questions arise while you actually do your research.

The appendices in Part III augment Parts I and II by providing selected supplemental reference materials to further expedite your legal research efforts.

A final note. Many other books have been written about legal research. These other volumes typically devote themselves almost exclusively to minutely detailed descriptions of the various law books used in legal research. We do not consider that format helpful to people learning how to conduct legal research. Instead, we believe a legal research manual should concentrate on explaining to the reader *when* to use which type of law book and then *how* to use it.

Therefore, our explanation of legal research is based on the purposes for which particular law books are used. It avoids unnecessarily exhaustive descriptions of law books, providing instead only as much description as you need to understand the law books' functions and uses. We believe the beginning legal researcher's critical need is to know how to draw effectively on the research books essential to conducting thorough and efficient research, including understanding how to select from the myriad of law books the one book required at any given point in legal research. In our view, it makes no sense to know what a law book looks like if you don't know when and how to use it.

In short, this book synthesizes the essentials of conducting legal research and presents them in a function-oriented package—including charts, diagrams, tables, and checklists of research and analysis steps—that gets the beginner as quickly as possible from reading about legal research to actually doing it.

This is the legal research manual we wish we'd had when we were law students. We hope it will spare you many of the frustrations we—and thousands of law students before and after us—have experienced.

Preface to the Second Edition

The enthusiastic response to our first edition from students, teachers, and others in the legal community has confirmed our view that, because legal research is a process, the most effective way of learning how to do legal research is through a process-oriented research guide. Therefore, in preparing this edition, we have retained the same functional organization and approach as the first edition.

Most of the changes in the second edition briefly amplify points covered in the earlier edition and reflect subtle shifts in style and emphasis. The major change is the addition of an appendix on legislative history research. Comments from readers persuaded us of the desirability of an expanded discussion of legislative history as an aid in interpreting statutes. Consequently, our new Appendix K expands substantially on the discussion of statutory interpretation found in Chapter 5. Placing the new coverage in a separate appendix permits a presentation of the details unique to legislative history research without disrupting the discussion in Chapter 5 of how, in general, to read and interpret legal authorities.

In keeping with our overall process-oriented approach, the new appendix does not stop with descriptions of the publications used in legislative history research; the appendix also explains the techniques for conducting this kind of research. In addition, to help researchers employ their research results most effectively, we summarize the divergent views about how lawyers and courts should use legislative history when analyzing statutes.

As with our first edition, we hope this new edition will help researchers learn, as efficiently and painlessly as possible, how best to draw on the law library's vast resources to meet their specific research needs.

Madison, Wisconsin   C.G.W.
March 1986   J.R.W.

Acknowledgments

Our most pleasant task in preparing this book is to thank the people who, in a variety of ways, have assisted in the project. We wish to acknowledge the opportunities given us by the judges in whose service we learned much about doing legal research: Judge James E. Doyle of the United States District Court for the Western District of Wisconsin; Judge Angela B. Bartell of the Dane County (Wisconsin) Circuit Court; and Judge P. Charles Jones of the Dane County Circuit Court. We would be remiss if we did not also thank Philip Robbins and Robert Willson, professors of journalism at George Washington University, who years ago instilled in us a desire to communicate clearly and concisely. We hope we have not fallen too far short of the example they set.

For their support and constructive comments on the manuscript for the first edition, we are indebted to our friends and colleagues who reviewed our text at various times. Ann Kerns' meticulous review of our draft at an early stage provided especially useful feedback at an important turning point. Our gratitude for their thorough and thoughtful review of the original manuscript goes also to Roberta ("Mimi") Berry, William Berry, Jeffrey Gallagher, Betty Hertel, and Kenneth Vandevelde.

In connection with the second edition, we thank the following people for their generosity in reviewing our manuscript for the appendix on legislative history: Stanley Hammer, Assistant Professor of Law and Associate Law Librarian at Campbell University School of Law; Louise Jellings, M.L.S., law librarian for the law firms of Michael, Best & Friedrich and Quarles & Brady; Michael J. Remington, Chief Counsel, House Judiciary Subcommittee on Courts, Civil Liberties, and the Administration of Justice; and Sharon Ruhly, an Assistant Attorney General with the Wisconsin Department of Justice. We appreciate their advice and gratefully acknowledge that the new appendix has significantly benefited from the incorporation of many of their suggestions.

Finally, we also appreciate the wealth of advice and expertise provided us by everyone at Adams & Ambrose Publishing who assisted in the publication of this book.

Table of Contents

Table of Figures and Illustrations

PART I

Background: Understanding the Tools

Part I covers the following subjects:

- the relationship between law books and the institutions that create law (Chapter 1)

- citations (Chapter 2)

- fact gathering and analysis, and identification and organization of issues for legal research (Chapter 3)

CHAPTER 1

Before You Start: Sources of the Law

Legal research makes more sense when you understand how particular law books relate to the political and legal institutions that create law. Therefore, this chapter focuses on these institutions and their relationships to legal research.

Most of us are generally familiar with the structure of American government: the United States Constitution as the supreme law of the land; the federal nature of the political system, with a national government existing alongside state governments; and the three branches of government—the executive, the legislature, and the judiciary. Figure A depicts these relationships.

Although this depiction of American government may satisfy a fledgling political scientist, it's not adequate for someone doing legal research. Another kind of government organization (not shown in Figure A) has burgeoned in this century, and this entity—known as the administrative agency—often looms larger and more directly in legal research than do the three customarily recognized branches of government.

At the federal level, administrative agencies are created by statutes passed by Congress. Generally, the President, with the consent of Congress, appoints high-ranking agency officials. To carry out a federal agency's functions, its officials usually make rules (also called "regulations") that have the force of law throughout the country, and interpret and enforce these rules through administrative hearings and decisions. These federal administrative rules and decisions are subject to review by the federal courts.

Federal agencies fall into two basic categories. *Executive agencies* are agencies located within the executive branch. Federal cabinet departments, such as the Department of State, the Department of Justice, and the Department of Defense, are examples of executive agencies. High-ranking executive agency officials are appointed by the President,

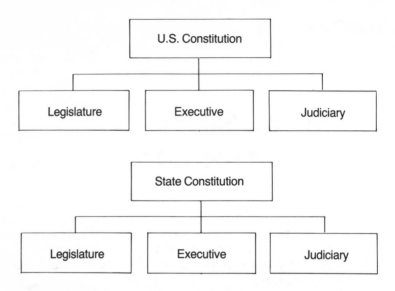

Figure A. Basic Organization Charts of Federal Government and State Governments

subject to the Senate's consent, and can be removed from office at any time by the President.

Independent agencies, on the other hand, sit outside all three branches. The Federal Reserve Board is an example of an independent agency. As with executive agencies, high-ranking officials of independent agencies are also appointed by the President, with Senate approval. However, these independent agency officials are usually appointed for fixed terms and generally cannot be removed from office except under special circumstances, and then often only with congressional approval. This arrangement is designed to insulate these agencies and officials from the political whimsy of either the President or Congress. This insulation is supposed to allow these agencies to pursue their statutory goals independent of political shifts or trends, hence their informal designation as "independent agencies," *i.e.*, independent of politics.

At the state level, a similar pattern prevails—but with two major differences. First, in many states, some agencies are created by the state constitution rather than by statute. Second, some agency officials are elected rather than appointed. For example, many states have elected attorneys general or treasurers. (At the federal level, the President would appoint these officials.) But whether their officials are elected or appointed, agencies at the state level perform essentially the same role as agencies at the federal level: implementation of particular government policies or functions through administrative rules and decisions subject to review by state courts.[1]

The existence of agencies thus adds another element to the earlier, simplified diagram. Figure B incorporates this refinement.[2]

The significance of government structure to legal research

Returning to the "civics course" introduction to American government, another axiom holds that legislatures make laws, courts interpret laws, and executives execute (*i.e.*, enforce) laws. As the foregoing discussion of administrative agencies may already have suggested to you, this view vastly oversimplifies the functions of each branch.

In fact, for the legal researcher there are three branches of government that make law, but they are not the three on which civics courses focus. Instead, a legal researcher sees these three branches:

(1) the legislature
(2) the administrative agencies
(3) the judiciary

Each of these "branches" makes a different kind of law. Legislatures create *statutory law* by passing bills, which become law when signed by the executive. Agencies create *administrative law*, consisting of rules and decisions issued by the agencies. Finally, the judiciary makes *common law*, sometimes informally referred to as judge-made law, which is found in court decisions. Federal statutory, administrative, and common law apply throughout the United States; a state's statutory, administrative, and common law apply only in that state.

At this point, then, government (for a legal researcher) consists of legislatures, agencies, and courts, which make—respectively—

---

[1]For a good overview of administrative agencies and administrative law, see K. DAVIS, BASIC TEXT ON ADMINISTRATIVE LAW (3d ed. 1972), and B. SCHWARTZ, ADMINISTRATIVE LAW (2d ed. 1984). For a more in-depth (and sometimes controversial) treatment of the subject, see Professor Davis's multi-volume ADMINISTRATIVE LAW TREATISE (2d ed. 1978–84).

[2]*The United States Government Manual* provides detailed descriptions and organization charts for each federal administrative agency, along with such information as each agency's purposes, its statutory authority, and its publications. The *Government Manual* is published by the U.S. Government Printing Office and is revised periodically.

Each state also publishes a comparable manual containing information about its own administrative agencies.

statutory law, administrative law, and common law. This perceptual re-organization of government brings greater coherence to legal research because each of these bodies of law is collected in separate kinds of law books.

Statutory law. Statutory law is found in two kinds of collections: (1) *session laws,* which collect the statutes in the chronological order of

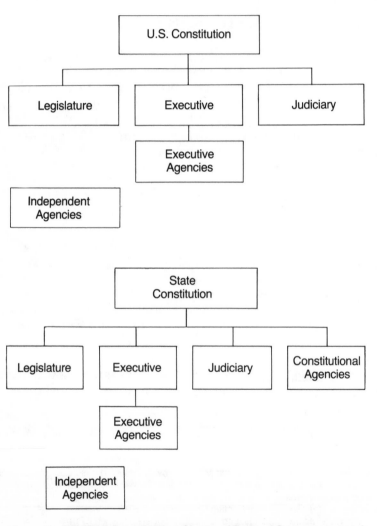

Figure B. Modified Organization Charts of Federal Government and Typical State Government

their enactment, and (2) *statutory codes,* which rearrange these statutes according to subject matter so that, for example, all criminal laws are grouped together regardless of the dates on which the individual criminal statutes were passed. At the federal level, the session laws are found in the series called *Statutes at Large* (abbreviated as "Stat."); the codified version is found in the *United States Code* ("U.S.C.") and in two commercially published editions, *United States Code Annotated* ("U.S.C.A.") and *United States Code Service* ("U.S.C.S."). Session laws and statutory codes also exist at the state level, but states vary in their practices in organizing and publishing these.[3]

Administrative law. As with statutes, administrative rules are often arranged in two ways: chronologically in *administrative registers,* and also according to subject matter in *administrative codes.* Federal administrative rules, regardless of which agency issues them, are collected chronologically in the *Federal Register* (abbreviated "Fed. Reg."); they are also rearranged according to specific regulatory topics in the *Code of Federal Regulations* ("C.F.R."). At the state level, many states do not publish their administrative rules; in such a case, the best (or perhaps only) source of state administrative rules are the agencies themselves. In some instances, a commercial publisher may have filled the gap. Where states do routinely publish their administrative rules, their publication formats and the adequacy of indexing vary widely.

Federal administrative agency decisions (which interpret and enforce administrative rules) are available from the agencies themselves. These decisions may also be compiled and published by the government and, occasionally, by commercial publishers as well. Publishing practices at the state level vary. Often, the state agency that issues the administrative decision will be the only source from which a copy of the decision can be obtained.

---

[3] Because they can be analytically viewed as special types of statutes, two other kinds of law—constitutions (federal and state) and local ordinances—should be mentioned in connection with statutes.

Constitutions. A constitution is a written document setting forth the organization, functions, and powers of government. Constitutions are written in a style similar to that used for statutes. Also, like statutes, constitutions prescribe standards according to which the government and citizens must conduct themselves, and they are subject to revision or repeal. In fact, constitutions are normally reprinted in statutory compilations at both the federal and state levels. Constitutions, however, address broader, more fundamental, and timeless matters of government structure and power, whereas statutes respond to specific problems as they arise.

The United States Constitution sets the standards against which *all* federal and state law is ultimately measured, and it applies throughout the country. Each state has its own constitution, which applies only within that state's boundaries.

Ordinances. Statutes passed by local governments (such as cities) to regulate local matters (such as health or zoning) are referred to as ordinances. These may be compiled in ordinance codes.

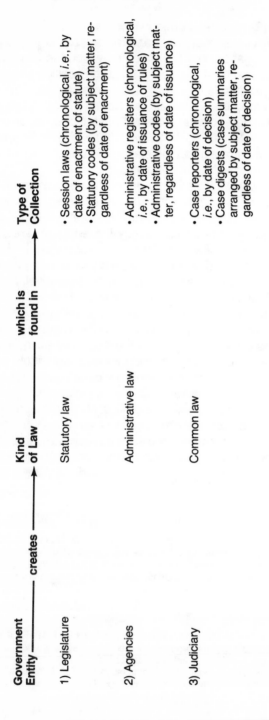

Government Entity	—— creates ——>	Kind of Law	—— which is found in ——>	Type of Collection
1) Legislature		Statutory law		• Session laws (chronological, *i.e.*, by date of enactment of statute) • Statutory codes (by subject matter, regardless of date of enactment)
2) Agencies		Administrative law		• Administrative registers (chronological, *i.e.*, by date of issuance of rules) • Administrative codes (by subject matter, regardless of date of issuance)
3) Judiciary		Common law		• Case reporters (chronological, *i.e.*, by date of decision) • Case digests (case summaries arranged by subject matter, regardless of date of decision)

Figure C. Relationships of Government Entities to the Kinds of Law They Create and the Books in Which the Law Is Found

Common law. Court decisions are collected chronologically in volumes called *case reporters*, and summarized by subject matter in reference works called *case digests*. Because the structure of the court system requires more detailed discussion (which follows shortly), case reporters and digests are treated more fully later in this chapter.

At this point, then, the relationship between governmental structure and legal research sources is illustrated in Figure C.

A further refinement: the structure of the courts

Effective legal research requires a further refinement of governmental structure with respect to the judiciary. Within the court systems there are usually several levels, each of which performs a specific function. The federal courts have three levels, as do many state courts: a trial level, an intermediate appellate level, and a final appellate level. Figure D illustrates this arrangement.

At the federal level, the trial courts are called United States District Courts. Each state has within its boundaries at least one federal judicial district, and some states have several. The number of districts in a state is determined primarily by population and the geographic size of the state. For example, Massachusetts has only one federal judicial district, which covers the whole state and is called the United States District Court for the District of Massachusetts. California, on the other hand, has four federal judicial districts, each of which covers a discrete geographic region of the state. California's four districts are known as the U.S. District Court for the Northern District of California, the U.S. District Court for the Central District of California, the U.S. District Court for the Southern District of California, and the U.S. District Court for the Eastern District of California.

Federal intermediate appellate courts are known as United States Courts of Appeals. There are 13 federal Courts of Appeals, each of which covers a particular geographical area known as a "circuit." There are 11 numbered circuits (First Circuit, Second Circuit, etc.), a circuit for the District of Columbia, and a circuit known as the Federal Circuit. Except for the D.C. Circuit, each Court of Appeals circuit encompasses several states. For example, the Tenth Circuit embraces Colorado, Kansas, New Mexico, Oklahoma, Utah, and Wyoming. The Federal Circuit hears appeals from *all* U.S. District Courts in certain specialized kinds of cases. The map in Figure E shows the geographical organization of the United States Courts of Appeals.

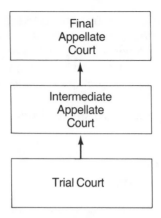

Figure D. Typical Court Structure

When a party to a lawsuit in a U.S. District Court wants to appeal that court's decision, the appeal normally goes to the U.S. Court of Appeals covering that district. For example (as Figure E shows), if you were involved in a lawsuit in a U.S. District Court in California and you wanted to appeal the decision in your case, you would take your appeal to the U.S. Court of Appeals for the Ninth Circuit. Similarly, a party in a lawsuit in a U.S. District Court in Oklahoma would take an appeal to the U.S. Court of Appeals for the Tenth Circuit.

The final appellate court in the federal court system is the Supreme Court of the United States. The U.S. Supreme Court hears appeals from decisions of the U.S. Courts of Appeals; from the highest appellate court of each state (when a federal question is involved); and (on extremely rare occasions) directly from U.S. District Courts. In certain limited cases, the U.S. Supreme Court also has original jurisdiction and then acts as a trial court.

State court structures vary from state to state. Many states have three levels, like the federal system, although some have only two (a trial level and one appellate level). The names of the state courts differ among the various states, too. For example, the highest court in Massachusetts is called the "Supreme Judicial Court"; in New York, it's known as the "Court of Appeals"; and in California, it's called the "Supreme Court."

Regardless of the courts' names, though, they perform essentially the same functions at both the state and federal levels. Trial courts decide what the facts in a given dispute are, and what those facts mean in terms of the law—for example, whether they mean guilt or innocence, and if guilt, what the penalty should be. Appellate courts review to see if

The Thirteen Federal Judicial Circuits

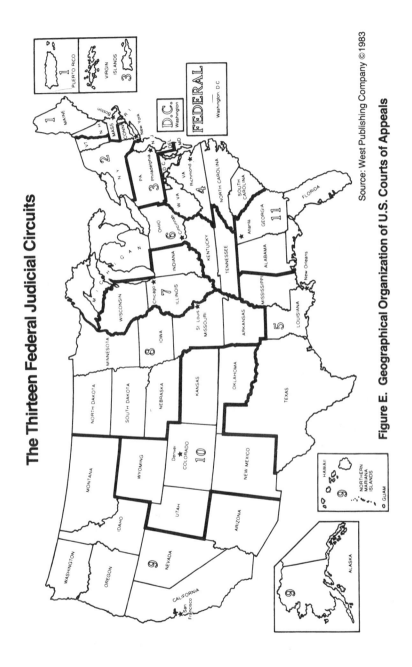

Source: West Publishing Company © 1983

Figure E. Geographical Organization of U.S. Courts of Appeals

Typical Court Structure	Federal (example)	State (example)
Final Appellate Court	U.S. Supreme Court	Wisconsin Supreme Court
↑	↑	↑
Intermediate Appellate Court	U.S. Court of Appeals for the 9th Circuit	Wisconsin Court of Appeals
↑	↑	↑
Trial Court	U.S. District Court for the Central District of California	Dane County Circuit Court

Figure F. Comparative Examples of Federal and State Court Structures

the trial judge correctly applied the relevant points of law to the facts determined at the trial level; except in rare cases, appellate courts do not re-evaluate or re-determine findings of fact made at the trial level.

The structure of the federal court system and many state court systems is shown schematically in Figure F.

Case reporters

Court decisions are compiled chronologically by date of issuance and published in volumes called case reporters.

Federal courts. Each level of the federal courts has at least one case reporter for its decisions. Cases decided by the United States Supreme Court are collected and published in a series of books called *United States Reports* (abbreviated "U.S."), which is the *official, i.e.,* government-approved, reporter of these decisions. In addition, there are two *unofficial* reporters: West Publishing Company publishes the *Supreme Court Reporter* ("S. Ct."), and Lawyers Cooperative Publishing Company publishes the *United States Supreme Court Reports, Lawyers' Edition* ("L. Ed." and "L. Ed. 2d").[4] These unofficial reporters contain everything in the official reporter, plus some helpful editorial features added by the publishers' in-house staffs. Strictly speaking, *United States Reports* is the only official, authoritative reporter of U.S. Su-

---

[4] "L. Ed. 2d" refers to the second series of this Lawyers' Cooperative publication. Legal publishers frequently divide continuing lines of publications into consecutively numbered series, simply to break them into more manageable sets of books.

preme Court opinions; the unofficial reporters, however, are highly reliable and widely used by lawyers and judges.[5]

United States Court of Appeals decisions from all circuits are found in the *Federal Reporter,* published by West. The first series of this reporter contains opinions issued from 1880 to 1924 and is abbreviated as "F.". The second series covers the period from 1924 to the present and is abbreviated "F.2d".

From 1880 to 1932, United States District Court opinions were reported along with U.S. Court of Appeals decisions in the first and second series of *Federal Reporter.* Since 1932, U.S. District Court opinions have been collected in a reporter known as *Federal Supplement* ("F. Supp."). In addition, since 1938, certain kinds of District Court opinions (those dealing with procedural rules that apply in the United States District Courts) have been published in *Federal Rules Decisions* ("F.R.D.") instead of *Federal Supplement.*

In 1894, West published *Federal Cases* ("F. Cas.") as a retrospective supplement to *Federal Reporter. Federal Cases* collects opinions of the United States Courts of Appeals and District Courts issued between 1789 and 1880, when West began publishing *Federal Reporter.* Editorial exigencies compelled West to arrange the opinions in *Federal Cases* alphabetically by plaintiffs' names rather than by the date of a decision's issuance.

Finally, there are other, specialized federal courts—such as the United States Court of International Trade—whose opinions are also reported in the federal reporters. But the District Courts, Courts of Appeals, and the Supreme Court are the federal courts whose opinions the majority of lawyers and judges rely on most frequently. For easy reference, a list appears at the beginning of each volume of the federal reporters indicating all the courts whose decisions are reported in that volume.

Figure G shows the relationship between federal courts and their respective reporters.

State courts. Decisions of state courts are collected in state case reporters. Each state has at least one official reporter for its highest court, and some states have more than one official reporter. Some states also have separate reporters for their intermediate appellate courts, and a few states have reporters for trial level courts. In general, the larger a state's population, the greater the number of reporters that

---

[5]In addition to these reporters, the full texts of U.S. Supreme Court decisions are reprinted in *United States Law Week* and *Supreme Court Bulletin,* both of which are a type of publication known as "looseleaf services." See Chapter 6 for more about looseleaf services.

Federal Court	Opinions Found in	Reporter Abbreviation	Dates of Coverage
U.S. Supreme Court	U.S. Reports	U.S.	1790–present
	Supreme Court Reporter	S. Ct.	1882–present
	U.S. Supreme Court Reports, Lawyers' Edition, Second Series	L. Ed. 2d	1956–present
	U.S. Supreme Court Reports, Lawyers' Edition	L. Ed.	1790–1956
U.S. Courts of Appeals	Federal Reporter, Second Series	F.2d	1924–present
	Federal Reporter	F.	1880–1924
	Federal Cases	F. Cas.	1789–1880
U.S. District Courts	Federal Supplement	F. Supp.	1932–present
	Federal Reporter, Second Series	F.2d	1924–1932
	Federal Reporter	F.	1880–1924
	Federal Cases	F. Cas.	1789–1880
	Federal Rules Decisions (decisions on procedural rules only)	F.R.D.	1938–present

Figure G. Table of Federal Courts and Their Respective Case Reporters

Regional Case Reporter	States Covered
Atlantic	Connecticut, Delaware, D.C., Maine, Maryland, New Hampshire, New Jersey, Pennsylvania, Rhode Island, Vermont
North Eastern	Illinois, Indiana, Massachusetts, New York, Ohio
North Western	Iowa, Michigan, Minnesota, Nebraska, North Dakota, South Dakota, Wisconsin
Pacific	Alaska, Arizona, California, Colorado, Hawaii, Idaho, Kansas, Montana, Nevada, New Mexico, Oklahoma, Oregon, Utah, Washington, Wyoming
South Eastern	Georgia, North Carolina, South Carolina, Virginia, West Virginia
South Western	Arkansas, Kentucky, Missouri, Tennessee, Texas
Southern	Alabama, Florida, Louisiana, Mississippi

Figure H. Table of Regional Case Reporters

state has. For example, as a highly populous state, New York has reporters all the way down to its trial level courts. Less populous Nevada and New Hampshire, on the other hand, have reporters only for their highest courts. A standard reference book called *A Uniform System of Citation*[6] lists the reporters for each state and the courts whose opinions are contained in each reporter.

Many state court opinions are also published by West Publishing Company in a series of reporters called *regional reporters,* each of which reprints the full text of opinions from courts in a specific geographical region of the country. Some states have designated as official reporters for their jurisdictions the regional reporters containing their courts' opinions. Figure H shows the arrangement of the regional reporter system.

Case digests

As discussed in the preceding section, case reporters at both the federal and state levels compile court decisions chronologically, *i.e.*, by date of the decisions' issuance. As with statutory and administrative law, though, common law is also collected according to its *topics* or subject matter. The topical arrangements of court decisions are published

[6]See Chapter 2 for more about *A Uniform System of Citation*.

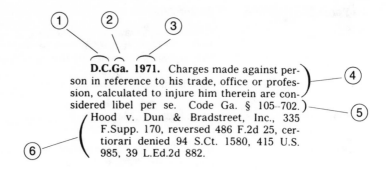

D.C.Ga. 1971. Charges made against person in reference to his trade, office or profession, calculated to injure him therein are considered libel per se. Code Ga. § 105–702. Hood v. Dun & Bradstreet, Inc., 335 F.Supp. 170, reversed 486 F.2d 25, certiorari denied 94 S.Ct. 1580, 415 U.S. 985, 39 L.Ed.2d 882.

Source: West Publishing Company ©1977

Figure I. Elements of a Case Digest Summary

Explanation of Figure I

1) *Court which decided the digested case*—Here, "D.C." indicates that a federal District Court decided the case from which this point of law was digested. ("C.A.", "C.C.A.", or "U.S.C.C.A." would indicate a decision coming from a U.S. Court of Appeals. "U.S." would designate an opinion from the U.S. Supreme Court.)

2) *State in which the digested case originated*—Here, the state is Georgia.

3) *Year in which the digested case was decided.*

4) *Digest (or "blurb") summarizing a point of law in the digested case.*

5) *Citation* to statute (if any) involved in the digested case.*

6) *Citation* of the digested case*—The citation may include, as this one does, the case's subsequent history (appeals, reversals, etc.).

*Citations are discussed in Chapter 2.

---

in multi-volume collections known as *case digests*. In effect, the digests serve as grand indexes to the case reporters.

Each digest collection breaks the law into hundreds of legal topics.[7] Because any given court opinion typically deals with several different legal topics (unlike statutes and administrative rules, which generally deal with just one subject at a time), a court opinion usually cannot be classified under only one topic. Moreover, reprinting the full opinion un-

[7] The topics used by West Publishing Company in its digests, for example, are listed in Appendices G and H in Part III of this book.

der each appropriate legal topic in a digest would be unmanageable. Therefore, each digest publisher's editorial staff analyzes published opinions, determines which legal issues each opinion deals with, and summarizes in a one-paragraph "digest" (often referred to colloquially as a "blurb") the opinion's ruling on each issue. Each one-paragraph summary (or "blurb"), along with the citation to the case from which it is drawn, is assigned to and published under an appropriate topical heading in the digest. As a result, a single case may appear digested under several topics.

Figure I shows and explains a typical case summary selected from a West digest of federal cases.

For federal courts, there are several digests. *United States Supreme Court Digest* (published by West) and *United States Supreme Court Digest, Lawyers' Edition* (published by Lawyers Cooperative) contain digests of *only* U.S. Supreme Court cases. West also publishes a series of digests containing summaries of decisions of *all* federal courts: *Federal Digest* covers cases decided during the period from 1789 to 1939; *Modern Federal Practice Digest* covers from 1939 to 1961; *West's Federal Practice Digest 2d* covers 1961 to 1975; and *West's Federal Practice Digest 3d* covers 1975 to the present.

For state courts, West publishes separate digests for nearly every state plus the District of Columbia, as well as digests tied to five of West's seven regional case reporters. In some states, there are also case digests available from publishers other than West.

In addition, West publishes a continuing series of digests collecting all the one-paragraph case summaries contained in both its state *and* federal digests during consecutive ten-year periods. Known as *Decennial Digests,* these multi-volume publications follow the format of West's individual federal and state digests, arranging each ten-year collection of summaries according to West's digest topics. *Decennial Digests* are supplemented by a series of periodically issued non-cumulative paper-bound and hardbound volumes called *General Digests.* In effect, the *Decennial Digests* (and *General Digests*) use chronological criteria in selecting which summaries to include, whereas state and federal digests use jurisdictional or geographical standards for selection. For most research purposes, using a federal digest or the digest for just the state whose law you are researching will be sufficient, but the *Decennial Digests* permit researchers to compare how federal and state courts throughout the country have ruled on particular points of law.

Figure J summarizes the structure of the common law (*i.e.*, court decisions) for legal research purposes.

Court	Chronological Compilation (with cases reprinted in full)	Topical, *i.e.*, Subject Matter, Compilation (with case summaries arranged under topic headings)
U.S. Supreme Court	*U.S. Reports* ("U.S.") *Supreme Court Reporter* ("S. Ct.") *U.S. Supreme Court Reports, Lawyers' Edition, Second Series* ("L. Ed. 2d") *U.S. Supreme Court Reports, Lawyers' Edition* ("L. Ed.")	*U.S. Supreme Court Digest* *U.S. Supreme Court Digest, Lawyers' Edition* *West's Federal Practice Digest 3d* *West's Federal Practice Digest 2d* *Modern Federal Practice Digest* *Federal Digest* *Decennial Digests*
U.S. Courts of Appeals	*Federal Reporter, Second Series* ("F.2d") *Federal Reporter* ("F.") *Federal Cases* ("F. Cas.")	*West's Federal Practice Digest 3d* *West's Federal Practice Digest 2d* *Modern Federal Practice Digest* *Federal Digest* *Decennial Digests*
U.S. District Courts	*Federal Supplement* ("F. Supp.")* *Federal Reporter, Second Series* ("F.2d")** *Federal Reporter* ("F.") *Federal Cases* ("F. Cas.") *Federal Rules Decisions* ("F.R.D.")***	*West's Federal Practice Digest 3d* *West's Federal Practice Digest 2d* *Modern Federal Practice Digest* *Federal Digest* *Decennial Digests*
State Courts	State reporters Regional reporters	State digests Regional digests *Decennial Digests*

*Since 1932
**Until 1932
***Decisions on procedural rules only

Figure J. Table of Federal and State Courts and Their Related Chronological and Topical Compilations of Reported Court Decisions

Conclusion

With an awareness of the relationship between the structure of government and legal research sources, you should find your legal research proceeds more methodically and efficiently. Viewed as a whole, the relationships discussed in this chapter for all three of the major law-creating branches of government (courts, agencies, and legislatures) can be illustrated as shown in Figures K through M.

Government Entity	Chronological Compilation	Topical (*i.e.*, Subject Matter) Compilation
FEDERAL:		
• Courts		
U.S. Supreme Court	*U.S. Reports* ("U.S.") *Supreme Court Reporter* ("S. Ct.") *U.S. Supreme Court Reports, Lawyers' Edition, Second Series* ("L. Ed. 2d") *U.S. Supreme Court Reports, Lawyers' Edition* ("L. Ed.")	*U.S. Supreme Court Digest U.S. Supreme Court Digest, Lawyers' Edition West's Federal Practice Digest 3d West's Federal Practice Digest 2d Modern Federal Practice Digest Federal Digest Decennial Digests*
U.S. Courts of Appeals	*Federal Reporter, Second Series* ("F.2d") *Federal Reporter* ("F.") *Federal Cases* ("F. Cas.")	*West's Federal Practice Digest 3d West's Federal Practice Digest 2d Modern Federal Practice Digest Federal Digest Decennial Digests*
U.S. District Courts	*Federal Supplement* ("F. Supp.")* *Federal Reporter, Second Series* ("F.2d")** *Federal Reporter* ("F.") *Federal Cases* ("F. Cas.") *Federal Rules Decisions* ("F.R.D.")***	*West's Federal Practice Digest 3d West's Federal Practice Digest 2d Modern Federal Practice Digest Federal Digest Decennial Digests*
• Agencies (independent and executive branch agencies)	*Federal Register* ("Fed. Reg.")	*Code of Federal Regulations* ("C.F.R.")
• Congress	*Statutes at Large* ("Stat.")	*United States Code* ("U.S.C.")
STATE:		
• Courts	State reporters Regional reporters	State digests Regional digests *Decennial Digests*
• Agencies (independent, executive branch, and constitutional agencies)	Administrative registers†	Administrative codes†
• Legislatures	Session laws	Statutory codes††

*Since 1932
**Until 1932
***Decisions on procedural rules only
†Some states may not issue this publication.
††Some states have not yet codified their statutes.

Figure K. Comprehensive Table of Government Entities and Their Corresponding Legal Research Sources

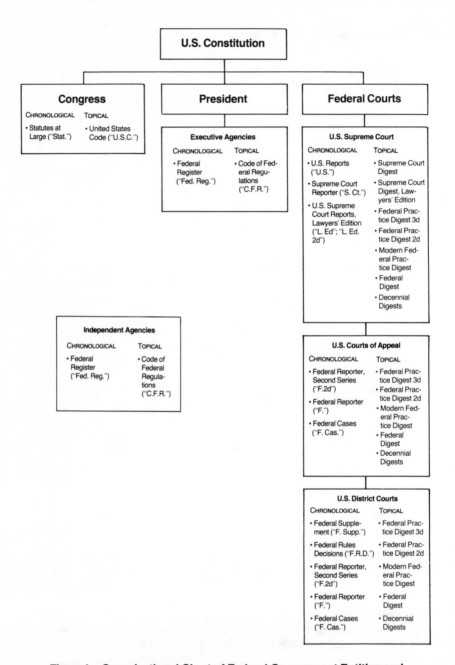

Figure L. Organizational Chart of Federal Government Entities and Their Corresponding Legal Research Sources

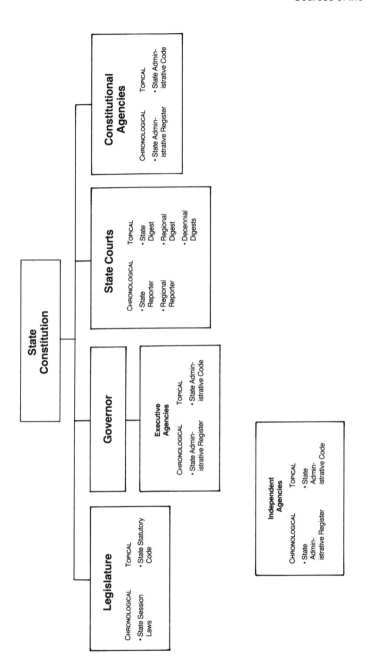

Figure M. Organizational Chart of State Government Entities and Their Corresponding Legal Research Sources

CHAPTER 2

About Citations

A *citation* identifies a legal authority or reference work, such as a constitution, statute, court decision, administrative rule, or treatise. In order to find the legal authority or precedent you need, you must know how to read and understand citations. Thus, citations play an essential role in legal research. It isn't necessary to remember all the details, but to do legal research you will need to have a basic working familiarity with citation form.

The standard publication on citations is *A Uniform System of Citation* (often nicknamed "the Blue Book"), a joint publication of the law reviews at Columbia, Harvard, the University of Pennsylvania, and Yale.[8] The *Blue Book* contains scores of technical rules about citation form. In this chapter, however, only the basic *Blue Book* rules about citing cases, statutes, administrative rules, books, legal encyclopedias, and law reviews are introduced because most of your beginning research will be in those sources.

Some courts have issued rules for citation form that modify some of the *Blue Book* rules. Because these modified rules would control citation form in those courts, you should check to see if your jurisdiction's rules of court contain such modifications. Otherwise, the *Blue Book* generally remains the standard reference on citation form.

Cases. A standard case citation contains:

(1) the name of the case;
(2) the published sources in which you can find the case;

---

[8]If unavailable in local bookstores, the *Blue Book* can be purchased by mail from the Harvard Law Review Association, Gannett House, Harvard Law School, Cambridge, Massachusetts 02138.

(3) information in parentheses indicating
   (a) the year the decision was issued, and
   (b) when not apparent from the name of the
   cited reporter volume, the court which issued the decision; and
(4) the prior or subsequent history, if any, of the case.

Here's an example of a citation to a federal case:

Jackson v. Metropolitan Edison Co., 348 F. Supp. 954
(M.D. Pa. 1972), aff'd, 483 F.2d 754 (3d Cir. 1973),
aff'd, 419 U.S. 345 (1974).

If you've read Chapter 1 of this book ("Sources of the Law"), you already know what some of the abbreviations in this citation mean. For example, as explained in Chapter 1, "F. Supp." refers to Federal Supplement, the case reporter which includes United States District Court decisions. (The Blue Book contains a comprehensive collection of abbreviations of all case reporters at the federal and state levels.)

The numbers in the citation also have meaning. Using "348 F. Supp. 954" from the example, the first number refers to the volume in the series, and the second number refers to the page in that volume where the report of the decision begins. Here, you would find a decision in the case of Jackson v. Metropolitan Edison Company in volume 348 of the Federal Supplement series, beginning at page 954 in that volume.

Finally, "v." stands for "versus" (that is, "against"), as in "Jackson versus (or against) Metropolitan Edison Company."

Now, here's what the example tells the reader:

A decision in the case of Jackson v. Metropolitan Edison Company is reported in volume 348 of the Federal Supplement, beginning at page 954 of that volume. This decision was issued by the United States District Court for the Middle District of Pennsylvania [M.D. Pa.] in 1972. The District Court's decision was affirmed [aff'd] on review by the United States Court of Appeals for the Third Circuit [3d Cir.], with the Third Circuit's decision issued in 1973 and published in volume 483 of the Federal Reporter, Second Series [F.2d], beginning at page 754 in that volume. The Third Circuit's decision was reviewed and affirmed [aff'd] by the United States Supreme Court, whose decision was issued in 1974 and published in volume 419 of United States Reports [U.S.], beginning at page 345 in that volume.

Note that the parenthetical information after the citation to "419 U.S. 345" does not include the name of the court issuing the decision, i.e., the United States Supreme Court, because that is the only court whose decisions are published in the series called *United States Reports.* By contrast, the citations to "348 F. Supp. 954" and "483 F.2d 754" do identify the courts issuing the decisions—the United States District Court for the Middle District of Pennsylvania and the United States Court of Appeals for the Third Circuit, respectively—because the series *Federal Supplement and Federal Reporter, Second Series* each contain the published decisions of more than one court.

As the example of *Jackson v. Metropolitan Edison Company* demonstrates, citations compress a lot of information into a small space.

There are two final points about case citations that you should also note. First, you will sometimes come across citations that seem to have extra numbers in them. For instance, a particular reference to the District Court decision in *Jackson v. Metropolitan Edison Company* may look like this: 348 F. Supp. 954, 955. As you now know, the first number after "F. Supp." is the page on which the decision begins. The second and any subsequent numbers (as in 348 F. Supp. 954, 955, 957-58) refer to particular pages the writer of the citation wants you to examine in the decision. If a writer wants someone to look at a whole case in general, the citation would be the basic one with only the first page of the opinion included—for example, 348 F. Supp. 954. But if a writer wants to direct someone's attention to a particular part of the opinion, the citation would include the specific pages along with the first page of the opinion—for example, 348 F. Supp. 954, 956. Therefore, in doing legal research, if you encounter a case citation referring you to a specific page in a decision, be sure to check that page.

The remaining point to note about case citations is that many opinions (especially those from state courts) are reprinted in more than one source. Citations to these other sources are known as *parallel citations*; they direct the researcher to other verbatim reprints of the *same* decision, not to different decisions rendered at other stages of the proceeding (*not*, for example, to a subsequent decision affirming or reversing the original decision).

An example of a parallel citation is:

> *State v. Yoder,* 49 Wis. 2d 430, 182 N.W.2d 539 (1971).

This example shows that *State v. Yoder* is reprinted at 49 Wis. 2d 430 ("Wis. 2d" stands for *Wisconsin Reports, 2d Series*). The example also shows that *Yoder* is reprinted *verbatim* at 182 N.W.2d 539, which is the parallel citation ("N.W.2d" stands for *North Western Reports, 2d Series*). The *Blue Book* specifies for each case reporter when a parallel citation should be provided as part of a standard citation.

Signals

Citations are frequently introduced by words called "signals." These words indicate how the writer wants you to view the cited authority in connection with the principle that the citation relates to, such as whether the cited authority supports or contradicts the principle. In other words, the signal provides a concise shorthand *context* for the citation.

The ability of signals to provide an instant frame of reference makes them useful tools for communicating with the reader, as shown by the examples in Figure N (p. 28). For guidance on additional signals and rules for their use, consult the *Blue Book*.

Putting it all in perspective

If all these citation rules seem confusing, remember that for legal research purposes, function prevails over form. A citation serves to help you locate a legal authority or reference work. So long as you can extract the minimum information necessary to find that source—for example, the name of the reporter and the volume and page numbers where the case you need appears in the reporter—the citation serves its principal purpose, even if not in correct form.

When you write up your research results, however, you will need to pay close attention to proper citation form. A case or other authority, even one directly supporting the position you advocate, will have no value to you if you can't tell someone else where to find it. By using correct citation form in your legal writing, you present information in a vocabulary understood throughout the legal community. Your use of this standardized vocabulary substantially increases the likelihood that someone who reads your written work will be able to locate the material you cite.

In addition, conforming to proper citation form will give your work a more professional appearance, which may enhance your persuasiveness. Proper citation form subconsciously creates in many people, including judges, the impression that a legal writer who meticulously follows citation rules probably also conducts thorough legal research and engages in careful and thoughtful legal analysis.

In the end, therefore, following citation rules in your legal writing can have important practical benefits that can only enhance your research efforts.

Signal*	Explanation	Example
See generally	This signal indicates that the cited authority provides useful background information about a given point.	See generally Dresser, Ulysses and the Psychiatrists: A Legal and Policy Analysis of the Voluntary Commitment Contract, 16 Harv. C.R.-C.L. L. Rev. 777 (1982).
See, e.g.,	This signal indicates that the cited authority directly supports a proposition. It further indicates that other authorities also could have been cited for the same proposition, but that no purpose would be served by citing them all because their citation would be merely duplicative.	See, e.g., Bishop Processing Co. v. Davis, 213 Md. 465, 132 A.2d 445 (1957).
Cf.	This signal indicates that the cited authority states a proposition different from that stated by the person citing to the authority, but that the cited authority's proposition is sufficiently analogous to lend support.	Cf. 20 Am. Jur. 2d Courts § 92 (1965).
Contra	This signal indicates that the cited authority contradicts a given point.	Contra W. Prosser, Law of Torts § 34, at 180 (4th ed. 1971).

*For additional types of signals, see Rule 2.2 in A Uniform System of Citation (13th ed. 1981).

Figure N. Selected Examples of Signals in Citations

CHAPTER 3

Gathering and Analyzing Your Facts, and Identifying and Organizing the Legal Issues

Legal research does not occur in a factual vacuum: the purpose of researching the law is to ascertain the legal consequences of a specific set of actual or potential facts. *It is always the facts of any given situation that suggest—indeed, dictate—the issues of law that need to be researched.*

This chapter outlines the critical fact-related steps that must precede research in law books. These steps are:

(1) gathering the facts;
(2) analyzing the facts;
(3) identifying the legal issues raised by the facts; and
(4) arranging the legal issues in a logical order for research.

The first step—gathering the facts—may not be immediately relevant for someone in law school. In law school, fact patterns are frequently ready-made, as in exams or legal research seminar exercises, and do not require any additional searching. Nonetheless, reading the following section on "Gathering Your Facts" may provide students with a "feel" for the role facts play in actual lawyering.

The second, third, and fourth steps—analyzing the facts, and identifying and organizing the legal issues involved—*will* be crucially relevant for both law students and those doing legal research outside an academic setting. The sections titled "Analyzing the Facts," "Fact Analysis Exercise," "Identifying the Legal Issues," and "Organizing the Legal Issues" explain how to take the facts that you have gathered (or that are presented to you) and organize them in a way that facilitates identifying and researching the legal issues the facts raise. In doing so, these sections will also underscore the importance of thorough fact gathering.

Gathering your facts

In real life, the facts of a case typically do not present themselves neatly assembled. You must work to uncover them. In gathering facts outside a classroom setting, you should begin by ascertaining the likely sources of pertinent information. These sources will include:

People. It will often be possible to gather information from other people, such as clients, witnesses to an event that is central to the problem, victims, and perhaps any people to whom the witnesses or victims have spoken about the case. For example, in an assault and battery case, you may learn from oral accounts of witnesses that the victim said or did something to the attacker that provoked the assault, which would suggest an important potential legal defense for the accused attacker. Or, in a contract dispute, you may learn that the contracting party being sued is a six-year-old; that fact would suggest a legal defense (*i.e.*, lack of capacity to enter into a valid contract) that would excuse the six-year-old from upholding his or her end of the agreement.

Tangible evidence. Depending on the nature of the particular case, there may be physical evidence that will be significant. In a dispute about responsibilities under a written contract, for instance, the contract document itself will be central. Similarly, in a murder case, the actual weapon allegedly used will be important: one fact question might be whether the weapon has a size or force that could have caused the fatal injury.

Books, periodicals, and reports. Frequently, you can find crucial facts in books, periodicals, and reports containing scientific, geographic, meteorological, statistical, demographic, business, or other miscellaneous information. For example, a case may hinge on a witness' emphatic claim that he could "see everything" concerning a late-night automobile accident on an unlit country road because the full moon cast such a bright light. A local weather bureau's records may show, however, that throughout the night a heavy cloud cover completely blocked out all moonlight. Such evidence would, obviously, discredit the witness' story.

Similarly, in a case in which a person is suing to recover money for personal injuries suffered because of another person's wrongful conduct, hospital records would show the extent of the injuries, along with the attending physician's evaluation of the likelihood of rehabilitation and, perhaps, the physician's opinion as to how the injuries were caused.

There are probably infinite such opportunities to use facts drawn from these and other written sources. Some of the many written sources useful in gathering facts preliminary to conducting legal research are the following:

- Census publications
- Maps
- Statistical abstracts
- Local, state, and federal government agency reports
- Police reports
- Business records
- Publications of local and national special-interest organizations
- Newspapers and magazines

Expert witnesses. Many cases involve highly technical areas in which experts (or books and articles written by them) may be helpful. For example, suppose a building under construction suddenly collapses. No one's hurt, but the person paying to have the building constructed wants to know who is to blame for the loss of the building. Experts in such areas as structural engineering, metallurgy, or architectural design could be hired to ascertain the cause of the collapse.

"5W and H". As you gather your facts from the various sources in a particular case, you may find it helpful to use the "5W and H" technique used by fact-gathering journalists—that is, ask yourself about the *who, what, when, where, why,* and *how* of your case. What was done? Who did it, and to whom? When was it done? Where was it done? Why was it done? And how was it done? This approach ensures that all the pertinent questions will be asked, making it possible to identify all the significant facts.[11]

---

[11]As you dig out these elements in a complicated case, you may even find it useful to cross-file the "5W and H" information to help you see the relationships among the facts you have gathered. For example, set up a "who" file for each person (such as parties or witnesses) figuring in your case. Within each "who" file, you would include the basic information about that person and the relationship the person has to your problem. Each "who" file would also contain information about the what, when, where, why, and how for that person—*i.e.,* what that person did, when that person did it, and so on.

Similarly, you could set up a "when" file for each important date or time. Within each "when" file, you would include information about who did something at that time, what happened on that date, where the things occurred on that date, and so forth. You could also set up a "where" file that arranges information geographically.

For a description of how one lawyer effectively used such a cross-referencing system, see J. BRESLIN, HOW THE GOOD GUYS FINALLY WON 105-06 (Ballantine ed. 1975).

You may find other equally effective ways to handle the information you gather. But whatever organizing method you use, the important thing is to *have a workable system for collecting and organizing your facts.*

Analyzing the facts

Once you have all your facts assembled, you're ready to analyze them to determine the legal issues you need to research. This analysis involves thinking of words that describe the various aspects or characteristics of your problem. Here, you'll succeed most quickly if you use West Publishing Company's or Lawyers' Cooperative Publishing Company's suggested systems for categorizing the elements common to all legal problems. Figure O shows these publishers' categories.

In each of these categories, think of as many specific words and their synonyms as possible relating to your problem. If you simply can't think of any synonym, try an antonym; sometimes, if you can't describe something directly, you can get at a description indirectly by describing what it isn't. Similarly, if you can't think of specific terms (or, if you later find that the specific words you have selected don't lead your research anywhere), think of more generalized words fitting within the categories listed in Figure O. For instance, within the category of "things" or "objects," instead of the specific word "apartment," you might try the more generalized words "building," "real estate," or "property." Usually, though, more specific words yield quicker results than generalized ones. With a little practice, you'll soon become adept at thinking of appropriate descriptive words.

To see how analyzing facts around the West or Lawyers' Coopera-

West Publishing Company	Lawyers' Cooperative Publishing Company
1) PARTIES involved in the case	1) THINGS involved in the case
2) PLACES where the facts arose, and OBJECTS and THINGS involved	2) ACTS involved in the case
3) BASIS of the case or ISSUE involved	3) PERSONS involved in the case
4) DEFENSE to the action or issue	4) PLACES where the facts arose
5) RELIEF SOUGHT	

Figure O. Elements Around Which to Analyze Legal Problems

tive categories can suggest legal issues, it helps to consider an example, such as that in the following exercise.

Fact analysis exercise

FACTS. Tom Tenant signed a one-year contract to rent an apartment from Laurie Landlord. Shortly after moving in, Tom discovered that the apartment was overrun with cockroaches, making living there intolerable. What legal issues are raised by these facts?

Parties or persons. Fact analysis under this category involves identifying the status (*i.e.*, membership in a particular class or group, such as minors, aliens, or mental incompetents) of parties, and their relationships to one another (*e.g.*, parent-child, buyer-seller, doctor-patient). In our illustration, the parties or persons involved are landlord (or "lessor") and tenant (or "lessee"). Consequently, legal authorities (that is, cases, statutes, and so forth) involving persons in this relationship should be researched.

Objects and things involved. Here, the example involves a certain insect that makes the apartment unpleasant to live in. Therefore, your legal research should focus on authorities dealing with fact patterns involving cockroaches. That classification will likely turn out to be so narrow, however, that you can't locate sufficient relevant authorities and you will probably want to move to more generalized words, such as "insects," "vermin," "pests," or "animals."

If you still can't find any useful law using these words, you would then go back to the drawing board and re-analyze the facts of your problem. In the illustrative example, you were originally concerned simply with the fact of cockroaches in the apartment. Now you would reconsider *why* you had that concern: it was not the cockroaches themselves, but their effect on the habitability of the apartment, that bothered Tom Tenant. The significant factual inquiry is really into conditions that affect habitability. Therefore, you would start thinking of words describing other conditions besides cockroach infestation that can make dwelling places uninhabitable. Thus, you might consider "noise," "heat," "sanitation," "light," and anything else the presence or absence of which would affect habitability.

In short, you can analyze facts not only by moving from specific to generalized words within a classification; you can also use analogy to move from one word to other words representing different objects or things that may have similar legal consequences.

Places involved. "Place" may signify the specific location at which an event occurred. For example, "place" can relate to a type of building or structure, such as "apartment building," "condominium," "stadium," or "ice rink." Or, "place" may relate to the character of a location, such as "public" or "private," "rural" or "urban." In our illustration, for example, it might make a difference whether the apartment building is located in an urban or rural setting: cockroach infestation is frequently a widespread problem in urban areas and because of the difficulty of eradicating such infestation in many large cities, an urban landlord might have an obligation different from a rural landlord's in this respect.

"Place" also refers to the geographic location (or "jurisdiction")[12] where an event occurs. Because the place where something occurs usually determines which law will apply to the problem, you need to know what the relevant geographical jurisdiction is—that is, in what country, state, county, or municipality the event occurred.

Keep in mind that under the federal system of American government (see Chapter 1), both the federal government and state governments have certain regulatory powers they can exercise. Sometimes only the federal government can regulate on a given subject; sometimes only the states can lawfully regulate a subject; sometimes both the federal government *and* the states can simultaneously regulate a single subject. Where both the federal government and a state government have chosen to exercise their power over a given matter, they may do so in differing ways or degrees. Because there are no easy rules for determining when a legal research problem will involve federal or state (including county or municipal) law, or both, you should always check both federal *and* state law. As you become more familiar with the extent of the authority of each of the levels of government, you will develop a "feel" for which law is likely to apply. But until you do, the best and safest rule is to examine both federal and state law.

Returning to our illustration, because it involves a matter of habitability, state (and local, *e.g.*, municipal) law, rather than federal law, would normally govern. If the apartment building were located in, let's say, California, you would check California's state law; the particular county or city in which the building is located may also have housing or health codes that apply. It's possible, however, that federal law could apply, too: for example, if the landlord for the apartment building receives federal subsidies for renting to low-income tenants, federal law

---

[12]The term "jurisdiction" has two different meanings. As used in this discussion, "jurisdiction" refers to a geographical territory, *e.g.*, a state or a nation, in which a particular body of law applies. (In its other meaning, which you will encounter in other circumstances but which is not relevant here, "jurisdiction" means the authority of a court or other tribunal to take cognizance of a case and render a binding decision.)

may set maintenance and habitability standards with which the landlord must comply.

Basis of the case. This category concerns the legal theory on which the plaintiff's case is based. In our illustration, since there is a contract between Tom Tenant and Laurie Landlord, one legal basis would be that by not providing a habitable apartment, Laurie breached the contract. Therefore, the word "contract" or the phrase "breach of contract" would be appropriate.

Defense to the action. This category addresses matters the person being sued may be able to raise on his or her behalf to defeat the plaintiff's claim. In the case of Laurie Landlord, neighborhood conditions beyond her control—such as a town garbage dump being maintained next door—may make it impossible to eliminate cockroaches from the apartment building. The word "impossibility" or the phrase "impossibility of performance" would summarize this defense. Or perhaps Tom caused the roach problem in his apartment by his own actions, such as by leaving food remains around or by failing to keep the apartment reasonably clean. In that event, Laurie could claim that Tom's conduct precludes him from successfully suing her. The word "estoppel" would summarize this defense.

Relief sought. This category covers what the plaintiff is seeking. The relief sought will often depend on the preferences of the individual who is suing, as well as on the type of injury suffered. (In some situations, the law may also specify or limit the type of relief a person may seek.) In Tom Tenant's case, he may want to have Laurie Landlord forced to undertake a program of insect extermination. He may also want the legal right to withhold some or all of his rent payments until the problem is corrected. Or, Tom may want to get out of the year-long rental agreement altogether, without being liable for the rest of the year's rent, so he can move to a different dwelling. Finally, if it turns out that Tom's infestation problem has been so severe that he has had to seek temporary lodging in a motel, Tom may also want Laurie Landlord to reimburse him for his motel expenses. Some words that would describe these types of relief are "injunction"; "abatement" or "abatement of rent"; "rescission," "release," "discharge," or "cancellation"; and "damages."

Note. Until you become familiar with legal rules, standards, and terminology, you probably won't know until you are already fairly well into your research what words to identify under the categories of "basis of the case," "defense," and "relief sought." Consequently, you will probably want to concentrate at first on thinking of words under the categories relating to "persons," "things," and "places," and should not worry if you cannot initially identify words under the other categories. Nonetheless, it's helpful to be aware of all the categories, because they encompass all the elements of any given research problem.

Also, you may have noted that there is a degree of analytical overlap among some of the categories discussed above. Despite this, examining facts in light of the West and Lawyers Cooperative systems of fact categorization can be extremely productive because it helps in identifying the legal issues that need researching, as the following section demonstrates.

Identifying the legal issues

Analyzing the facts of a given research problem by using descriptive words within the categories discussed above—parties or persons; objects and things; places; basis of the case; defense; and relief sought—will suggest the legal issues requiring research. For example, the fact analysis exercise in the preceding section revealed several legal issues to research:

- Does a tenant in the state or municipality where Tom Tenant lives have a contractual right to enjoy (and does a landlord have the obligation to provide) a habitable rental unit?

- If so, does an infestation of cockroaches breach that requirement of habitability?

- If there has been such a breach, can the tenant require the landlord to correct the problem? Can the tenant withhold rent payments, cancel the contract, or hold the landlord liable for extra expenses he incurred because of the infestation?

As the landlord-tenant example shows, gathering your facts and then categorizing them for analysis will always suggest legal issues. These issues are the questions that the legal research process will attempt to answer. New issues will often become apparent once the research is underway. In addition, as your legal research familiarizes you with various fact patterns that may arise in the areas of law relevant to your problem, you may also find yourself re-assessing the relative significance of facts you have already gathered and, perhaps, determining that you need to gather additional facts.

Nonetheless, you will always need to conduct a preliminary fact analysis and issue identification in order to provide direction for starting the legal research itself. The more carefully you think through a problem before commencing your research, the more fruitful your research is apt to be.

Organizing the legal issues

When you have finished your preliminary evaluation of the facts and issues, there's still one short—but important—step you should attempt to take before actually opening the books to do your legal research. You need to consider whether the legal issues you've identified can be arranged in a logical order that will increase the efficiency and effectiveness of your research.

Occasionally, you may have a research project involving only a single, narrow issue. Frequently, however, research problems involve a variety of issues. Take, for example, the case of a person who decides to sue a newspaper he claims libeled him in an article published eight years earlier about his conduct in office when he served as city mayor. A few of the issues might include these:

1. The fact that the allegedly libelous article was published so long ago suggests one issue: because the law generally disapproves of bringing stale claims into court, the researcher should check to see if the time within which a libel action must be commenced has already expired.

2. Can the challenged article even be considered defamatory at all—or is the plaintiff simply over-reacting? In other words, might a court conclude that no one who read the article could reasonably think any less of the mayor because of what was published? (If so, the mayor has no basis for suing.)

3. Assuming the article could be considered damaging, does the newspaper have a defense, such as the truth of the article's assertions or the constitutional right to engage in public debate about government officials?

4. An issue may arise about the type of remedy the mayor may seek if he wins the lawsuit. For example, does the law limit him to demanding only enough money to compensate for the actual damage to his reputation, or may he also seek an additional amount to punish the newspaper?

A multi-issue problem like this requires an orderly research approach. Therefore, you should first analyze all the issues you have identified, to see how they relate to one another. In doing this analysis, pay particular attention to whether any of the issues could dispose of the problem fairly mechanically, at a threshold level. For example, in the libel action illustration above, if the law required the plaintiff to sue sooner than eight years after the publication occurred, that relatively simple issue would dispose of the entire matter, even if the plaintiff had been the object of the most scurrilous libel. When you find a dispositive threshold issue like this, place it at the top of your list of issues.

Usually you will find it most effective to research the issues in their logical order (where such an order is apparent to you). For instance, in our libel illustration, the order in which we have placed the issues in the list above represents a natural progression from considering whether the plaintiff can commence and maintain a suit; to whether (if so) the defendant has a successful defense; and, finally, to the remedy the plaintiff may ultimately seek if he prevails against the defendant.

In addition, you should note that by researching any potentially dispositive threshold question (such as whether a suit was commenced in time) first and working through it completely from start to finish before moving on to any other issue, you may quickly find a result that will dictate the answer to the problem. In most instances, however, you should not assume that your analysis that the threshold issue is dispositive in your favor will necessarily prevail: if it does not and you have not researched the remaining issues, you will have nothing upon which to fall back.

Now, for legal research . . .

Having gathered and analyzed your facts, done a preliminary identification of at least some of your legal issues, and (if possible) arranged your legal issues in a logical order, you're now ready to begin researching the law. Doing legal research is discussed in Part II.

PART II

Doing Legal Research

Part II explains the three essential steps in doing legal research:

• step one: finding the law (Chapter 4)

• step two: reading the law (Chapter 5)

• step three: updating the law (Chapter 6)

In addition, Chapter 7 offers helpful pointers about taking notes during research, and Chapter 8 suggests guidelines for determining when your research is completed.

CHAPTER 4

Step One:
Finding the Law

Introduction. In finding the law, you must initially distinguish *primary* sources (also referred to as "authorities") from *secondary* sources or authorities. Primary sources consist of *the law itself,* as expressed in constitutions, statutes, court decisions, and administrative regulations and decisions. (These primary sources, their institutional origins, and their relationships to one another were discussed in Chapter 1, "Sources of the Law.") Secondary authorities are everything else— essentially, writings or commentaries *about* the law found in primary sources. Secondary authorities include such publications as legal treatises and law review articles.

In working with primary authorities, you also need to make an additional distinction between *mandatory* authorities and *persuasive* authorities. Mandatory authorities are those, such as statutes or decisions of the highest court of a given jurisdiction, which must be followed by all courts within that jurisdiction. Persuasive authorities, on the other hand, offer guidance but need not be followed: for example, a decision of the New Mexico Supreme Court might be regarded as persuasive by the Idaho Supreme Court when it considers a similar kind of issue or case in its own jurisdiction, but it would not bind the Idaho court.

Figure P shows when and where primary authorities are mandatory or persuasive.

In finding the law, your ultimate goal is to locate mandatory primary authorities bearing on your legal problem. If these are either scarce or nonexistent, your next priority should be to find any relevant persuasive primary authorities. Finally, if all else fails, you might rely on relevant secondary authorities.

In addition, you should keep in mind an important point about court decisions as primary authority. Where a panel of judges decides a case,

41

Type of Primary Authority	When and Where Mandatory	When and Where Persuasive
U.S. Constitution	Always mandatory on all federal and state courts	N/A
U.S. Supreme Court decision interpreting and applying federal law	Always mandatory on all federal and state courts	N/A
Federal statute*	Always mandatory on all federal and state courts	N/A
Federal administrative regulation**	Always mandatory on all federal and state courts	N/A
U.S. Court of Appeals decision interpreting and applying federal law	Always mandatory on federal courts within the jurisdictional boundaries of the Court of Appeals issuing the decision	May be regarded as persuasive by federal and state courts that do not need to treat the decision as mandatory
U.S. District Court decision interpreting and applying federal law	Always mandatory on specialized lower federal courts, if any, within the jurisdictional boundaries of the District Court issuing the decision and over which the District Court has appellate jurisdiction	May be regarded as persuasive by federal and state courts that do not need to treat the decision as mandatory
State constitution***	Always mandatory on all state courts within the given state	N/A

(continues below)

Decision of a state's highest court interpreting and applying that state's law***	Always mandatory on all lower state courts within the given state	May be regarded as persuasive by federal and state courts that do not need to treat the decision as mandatory
Decision of a state's intermediate appellate court interpreting and applying that state's law***	Always mandatory on all lower state courts within the jurisdictional boundaries of the intermediate appellate court issuing the decision; in some states, may also be mandatory on lower state courts outside those jurisdictional boundaries	May be regarded as persuasive by federal and state courts that do not need to treat the decision as mandatory
State statute†	Always mandatory on all state courts within the given state	N/A
State administrative regulation††	Always mandatory on all state courts within the given state	N/A

(continues on p. 44)

The additional comments in the following footnotes bear only on the validity of the authority, *not* on its mandatory or persuasive character:

*   Assuming there is no conflict with the U.S. Constitution
** Assuming there is no conflict with the U.S. Constitution or a federal statute
*** Assuming there is no conflict with the U.S. Constitution, a federal statute, or federal administrative law
†   Assuming there is no conflict with the U.S. Constitution, a federal statute, federal administrative law, or that state's constitution
†† Assuming there is no conflict with the U.S. Constitution, a federal statute, federal administrative law, that state's constitution, or any of that state's statutes

Figure P. Primary Authorities: When and Where Mandatory or Persuasive

(continued from p. 43)

Note. Figure P summarizes when specific kinds of primary authorities are considered mandatory or only persuasive in judicial decision-making. Two scenarios, however, need some further elaboration.

• First, *the law of a state may at times be mandatory on federal courts.* Frequently, a federal court has to interpret, apply, or enforce the law of a particular state. On those occasions, the federal court must accept, as the starting point for its analysis, the state's interpretation of its own law. The federal court always remains free, however, to determine whether the state's interpretation violates federal law in any respect. In other words, the question of what a state's interpretation of its law is and the question of whether that interpretation is itself consistent with federal law are separate and distinct issues.

For instance, suppose a federal court is called upon to prohibit a state from enforcing one of its statutes because someone claims it violates his or her rights under the U.S. Constitution. Suppose also that the meaning of the state statute is not immediately clear from its language. Before the federal court can evaluate the statute's constitutional validity, it will need to know how the state has actually interpreted and applied the statute. For that information, the federal court will generally look to—and consider as mandatory—decisions from that state's appellate courts that have explained what the statute means. The federal court will then review that interpretation to determine whether the statute *as interpreted by the state courts* is constitutional.

• As a second point regarding when primary authorities are mandatory or persuasive, note that *the U.S. Supreme Court is the only federal court whose decisions on points of federal law are mandatory on state courts.* As far as state courts are concerned, interpretations of federal law made by U.S. Courts of Appeals or U.S. District Courts operate only as persuasive authority. Thus, for example, an Illinois state court would not have to follow the federal law interpretations issued by a federal court located in Illinois, though the Illinois state court would have to follow U.S. Supreme Court decisions interpreting federal law. See, *e.g., United States ex rel. Meyer v. Weil,* 458 F.2d 1068, 1070 (7th Cir. 1972); *United States ex rel. Lawrence v. Woods,* 432 F.2d 1072, 1075–76 (7th Cir. 1970), *cert. denied,* 402 U.S. 983 (1971); *Owsley v. Peyton,* 352 F.2d 804 (4th Cir. 1965); *Seatec International, Ltd. v. Secretary of the Treasury,* 525 F. Supp. 980, 982 (D.P.R. 1981); *Woodall v. Keller,* 337 F. Supp. 595, 600 (D. Md. 1972).

As a practical matter, however, a state court will frequently follow lower federal court decisions on issues of federal law, such as how a particular federal statute should be interpreted. In general, a state court is most apt to adhere to lower federal court decisions on matters of federal law when the decisions have been rendered either by a U.S. District Court located within the state's geographic boundaries or by a U.S. Court of Appeals whose judicial circuit encompasses the state. (Recall that Chapter 1, "Sources of the Law," describes the geographical organization of the federal court system. See pp. 7–10.)

Figure P. Primary Authorities: When and Where Mandatory or Persuasive (continued)

the report of the case may contain concurring or dissenting opinions in addition to the opinion of the court (that is, the majority opinion). Only the opinion of the court is mandatory authority. Any concurring or dissenting opinions do not constitute binding statements of the law, although they may be useful as persuasive authority in some circumstances. See the definitions for "concurring opinion" and "dissent" in the glossary in Appendix L.

Finally, you should be aware that court opinions frequently contain statements and commentary that are not essential to the court's resolution of the precise issues presented for decision. For example, a court might suggest a result it would reach on a hypothetical set of facts. These gratuitous or incidental remarks are referred to as "dicta" or "dictum," and are not binding authority.

Law-finding techniques. Three generally accepted approaches prevail for finding the law:

(a) *Descriptive word or fact word*
(b) *Known authority*
(c) *Known topic*

Each approach has certain advantages, and each is appropriate for researching state or federal case law, statutory law, administrative law, or constitutional law.[13] This chapter explains these three approaches, as well as a few other useful ones that supplement the main three.

---

[13]In our discussion of finding the law, finding constitutional law will not be treated separately. Although constitutions and statutes are separate types of law (with the constitution of a given level of government taking precedence over that governmental unit's statutes), constitutions are, with respect to the steps for finding the law, simply a special form of statute. That is, you find constitutions and statutes in generally the same way: constitutions are normally included in federal and state statutory compilations, and constitutional provisions reprinted in sets of annotated statutes will usually have accompanying annotations of cases interpreting and applying them, just as statutes do. Therefore, all references in this chapter to procedures for finding statutory law are also intended to encompass the techniques for finding relevant constitutional provisions.

The one significant difference between researching constitutional provisions and researching statutes is that with respect to constitutions you can also find case interpretations of constitutional provisions in federal and state case digests (digests, remember, were discussed in Chapter 1) under the topic heading "Constitutional Law." The cases summarized in the digests under the topic "Constitutional Law," along with the cases whose annotations accompany constitutional provisions reprinted in statutory compilations, comprise the principal sources for researching constitutional law at both the federal and state levels.

Because constitutions deal with governmental and societal issues on a broad scale, they generally do not directly affect legal problems as frequently as other kinds of law (*i.e.*, cases, statutes, and administrative regulations and decisions), which deal with more specific matters. Nonetheless, although most of your legal research problems likely will not involve constitutional issues, you still need to be aware of the possibility that a constitutional provision may well apply.

Approach A:
Descriptive word or fact word

The descriptive word or fact word approach is the most commonly used method for finding the law. *You should use this method first unless you already know the citation of a case, statute, constitutional provision, or administrative rule relevant to your problem.* The descriptive word method has the advantage of allowing you to begin your legal research even if you know little or nothing about legal rules or theories.

If you have followed the process of gathering, organizing, and analyzing your facts outlined in Chapter 3, the descriptive word approach should follow naturally. The idea here is to use the "5W and H" technique to gather all the significant facts of your problem, and then to build on those facts by thinking of words (called "descriptive words" or "fact words") that describe the important factual aspects of your research problem and that can be organized under categories of characteristics common to all research problems. The categories are the same ones discussed in Chapter 3 under the section on "Analyzing the Facts":

1) PARTIES involved in the case *OR*	1) THINGS involved in the case
2) PLACES where the facts arose, and OBJECTS and THINGS involved	2) ACTS involved in the case
	3) PERSONS involved in the case
	4) PLACES where the facts arose
3) BASIS of the case or ISSUE involved	
4) DEFENSE to the action or issue	
5) RELIEF SOUGHT	

With your descriptive words in hand, you're ready to begin your research. As your first research step, you have to decide whether to begin by researching in primary or secondary materials. Unless you commence with the "Generalized Approach" discussed later in this chapter, you will start with primary sources—court decisions, statutes, constitutional provisions, and administrative regulations.

Statutes and administrative regulations. Whenever your research focuses on primary sources, you should normally start with statutes, because they can control the other kinds of primary law (except constitutional provisions): administrative regulations exist only by virtue of a statute authorizing their promulgation, and court decisions can be—and often are—overturned or at least modified by statutes.

Therefore, begin your research under the descriptive word approach by examining the index to the relevant set of codified statutes, preferably an *annotated* set of statutes (such as *U.S. Code Annotated* or *U.S. Code Service*), which will contain brief summaries—*i.e.*, "annotations"—of cases that have interpreted and applied the statutes. Look for your descriptive words in the index. If your descriptive words are included there, the index entries under them will refer you to specific statutes relating to your words. (Of course, you won't always find your descriptive words in the statutory index: it may be that no statute deals with your problem, or that the descriptive or fact words you have chosen may not coincide with the publisher's, which means you will need to try some new words.)

If you find index entries under your descriptive words, read the statutes to see if they appear relevant or applicable to your research problem.[14] If they do, check the case annotations following the relevant statutory provisions to see if any seem to summarize cases construing or applying the statute in a way that bears on your problem. Because statutory language very often contains some ambiguity, many statutes need interpretation, which is provided by the courts.[15] Judicial interpretation of statutes, where it exists, becomes in effect a part of the statutes. Therefore, statutory research must include a search for interpretative case law, as well.

Figure Q is a sample page from a set of annotated statutes, showing a statute and accompanying case annotations.

If you find relevant-sounding case summaries, retrieve and read the actual cases. If the cases interpret or apply the statute in a way relevant to your problem, note and summarize them for future reference.[16]

In addition, as you examine the statutes, check for grants of rule-making authority—that is, statutory authorizations for administrative agencies to formulate, issue, and enforce regulations implementing statutory objectives. At the end of each statute appearing in an annotated set of statutes, cross references may be given, where appropriate, to *administrative rules and regulations* interpreting or implementing the statute.

If a statute does authorize an administrative agency to make rules and regulations, you should check the relevant federal or state administrative code or administrative register (depending on whether you are researching a federal or state statute). If you're not sure whether the

---

[14]Sometimes, cross-references to other, possibly related statutes will appear in a list following an individual annotated statute, and checking these may also help you determine whether you have located all the relevant statutory provisions.

[15]Reading and interpreting statutes will be covered in more detail in Chapter 5.

[16]Chapter 7 discusses "How to Take Effective Notes." Chapter 5 covers special points about taking notes on cases; see pp. 91–93, on "Briefing Cases."

§ 71–3–13.   Maximum and minimum recovery.

(1) Compensation for disability or in death cases shall not exceed forty dollars ($40.00) per week, nor shall it be less than ten dollars ($10.00) per week, except in partial disability cases and in partial dependency cases.

statute

(2) Maximum recovery. The total recovery of compensation hereunder, exclusive of medical payments under section 71–3–15, arising from the injury to an employee or the death of an employee, or any combination of such injury or death, shall not exceed seventeen thousand dollars ($17,000.00).

SOURCES: Codes, 1942, § 6998-07; Laws, 1948, ch. 354, § 6b; 1950, ch. 412, § 4; 1958, ch. 454, § 2; 1960, ch. 279; 1968, ch. 559, § 4, eff from and after passage (approved August 9, 1968).

Research and Practice References—
58 Am Jur (1st ed), Workmen's Compensation §§ 295, 320.
99 CJS, Workmen's Compensation §§ 301, 303, 321.

ALR Annotations—
Limit of compensation fixed by Workmen's Compensation Act as inclusive or exclusive of medical or hospitalization expense. 128 ALR 136.

JUDICIAL DECISIONS

1. In general.
2. Partial disability cases.
3. Partial dependency cases.

———

interpretative case summaries or "annotations" of the statute

1. In general

The interpretation to be placed on the language used in this section [Code 1942, § 6998-07] is that the total amount of weekly benefits to be paid by the employer in totally dependent cases, regardless of the number of dependents, shall not be less than $10 per week. Truck Trailer Sales & Service Co. v Moore, 244 M 317, 141 So 2d 541.

Where a claimant began work 4 weeks preceding the date of injury and had worked 3 days the 1st week, 2 days during the 2d week, and 3 days during each of the next 2 weeks and her total earnings amounted to $51.28, she should have been awarded compensation in the amount of $10 per week rather than an award based on an aver-

age weekly wage of $25. Pepper v Barrett, 225 M 30, 82 So 2d 580.

2. Partial disability cases

This section [Code 1942, § 6998-07] applies to an award for permanent partial disability. Wiygul Motor Co. v Pate, 237 M 325, 115 So 2d 51.

Order of attorney-referee and the commission finding that claimant's loss of wage earning capacity was $6 per week, and awarding claimant compensation for permanent partial disability at rate of $4 per week, was reversed and judgment entered in supreme court amending the findings so as to show the claimant's loss of earning capacity at $17.50 per week, and awarding compensation to the claimant for permanent partial disability at the rate of 66 and ⅔ per cent of that amount. Hale v General Box Mfg. Co. 235 M 301, 108 So 2d 844.

3. Partial dependency cases

The 1950 amendment to this section [Code 1942, § 6998-07] providing for a

Figure Q. Sample Page: Annotated Statute

statute authorizes rule-making, play it safe and check the index to the appropriate set of federal or state administrative regulations. As with the procedure for researching statutes, start by looking for your descriptive words in the index to the code or register, which will lead you to any pertinent regulations.[17]

With administrative regulations, however, you generally won't find accompanying case annotations in the administrative code or register; you will only be able to locate interpretative cases through the following techniques:

- by using the annotations to the authorizing statute;

- by checking a looseleaf service in the area of law covered by the regulation (see Chapter 6 and Appendix B);

- by Shepardizing the regulation (see Chapter 6);[18]

- by searching the data base of a computer-assisted law retrieval system (if your library has one) for references to the regulation;[19] or

- by inquiring at the administrative agency that issued the regulation and which interprets and enforces it.

Cases. After you have finished your search for relevant statutes and administrative regulations, do a descriptive word search for court decisions next. Start by finding the appropriate federal, state, or regional *case digest* set, such as *Federal Practice Digest 2d, California Digest,* or *North Western Digest 2d.*[20] Second, look for your descriptive words in the index to the digest. When you find your words there, you will be referred to titles of digest topics and sub-topic numbers dealing with your words. Next, move from the index to those topics and sub-topics in the digest itself. There you will find single-paragraph case summaries of pertinent court decisions.

Figure R shows a sample page of case summaries from a West digest.

---

[17] At the federal level, the *Code of Federal Regulations* has a separate index volume that is revised semi-annually to reflect the codification of regulations as of January 1 and July 1 each year. The index to the *Federal Register* is published monthly, on a cumulative basis; the index for December acts as the cumulative index for the entire year of the *Register.* To locate items published in the *Register,* you need to check the most recent monthly index, plus the contents of each subsequently published daily issue of the *Register.* At the state level, indexing procedures vary.

[18] This can only be done at the federal level, *i.e.,* with the *Code of Federal Regulations.* State administrative regulations cannot be Shepardized.

[19] Computerized research is discussed in Appendix A.

[20] Recall that digests were described in Chapter 1, "Sources of the Law."

two years, or both, does not deny equal protection or due process, or violate any constitutional provision. 18 U.S.C.A.App. § 1202(a)(1); U.S.C. A.Const. Amends. 5, 14.—U. S. v. Kozerski, 518 F.Supp. 1082.

D.C.N.J. 1979. Statute prohibiting unlawful receipt of firearms shipped or transported in interstate commerce by person under indictment for offense punishable by imprisonment exceeding one year did not deny equal protection as applied to person under indictment for nonviolent offenses. 18 U.S.C.A. § 922(h)(1).—U. S. v. Weingartner, 485 F.Supp. 1167, appeal dismissed 642 F.2d 445.

Statute prohibiting receipt of firearms shipped or transported in interstate commerce by person under indictment for offense punishable by imprisonment exceeding one year did not create unconstitutional irrebuttable presumption that any person under indictment for specified offenses had propensity for violence. 18 U.S.C.A. § 922(h)(1).—Id.

D.C.N.Y. 1982. Provisions of New York Penal Law raising criminal possession of a weapon in the third degree from a misdemeanor to a felony on the basis of a prior conviction and calling for second felony offender treatment because of the same prior felony conviction do not violate due process or double jeopardy. N.Y. McKinney's Penal Law §§ 70.15, 265.01, 265.02(1, 4).—Cassesse v. People of State of New York, 530 F.Supp. 694.

D.C.N.Y. 1981. State statute providing that pistol license may be revoked and cancelled at any time in city of New York by licensing officer is not unconstitutionally vague. N.Y.Penal Law § 400.00, subd. 11.—Brescia v. McGuire, 509 F.Supp. 243.

D.C.Pa. 1977. Ordinary standard of administrative review does not apply to decisions of Bureau of Alcohol, Tobacco and Firearms revoking license to sell firearms and ammunition; since statute provides for introduction of evidence beyond that contained in administrative record, district court's review is "de novo." 18 U.S.C.A. § 923(f)(3).—Shyda v. Director, Bureau of Alcohol, Tobacco and Firearms, U. S. Dept. of Treasury, 448 F.Supp. 409.

On de novo review of decision of Bureau of Alcohol, Tobacco and Firearms revoking dealer's license to sell firearms and ammunition, court would treat Bureau's motion for summary judgment as any other motion for summary judgment by examining matter afresh, using entire record to determine whether there was material issue of fact necessitating further proceedings. 18 U.S. C.A. §§ 921 et seq., 923(f)(3); Fed.Rules Civ.Proc. rule 56, 28 U.S.C.A.—Id.

In order to prove "willful" violation of recordkeeping requirements of Gun Control Act sufficient to support revocation of license to sell firearms and ammunition, Bureau of Alcohol, Tobacco and Firearms must prove that licensee knew of his legal obligation and purposefully disregarded or was plainly indifferent to recordkeeping requirements; there is no requirement of bad purpose as might be imposed with respect to determination of willfulness in criminal prosecution. 18 U.S.C.A. § 923(g).—Id.

Where licensee admitted on stand under oath that he was aware of specific legal obligations under Gun Control Act to record dispositions of firearms within seven days and to maintain dispositional records for ammunition, and where there was no substantial controversy as to proof that extremely serious breaches of recordkeeping practices occurred in that licensee sold or delivered more than 1,600 firearms without recording their disposition and in that ammunition-disposition records were not maintained in a bound book or in chronological order, licensee was

guilty of "willful" violation of such recordkeeping requirements. 18 U.S.C.A. § 923(g).—Id.

⊆⇒4. Manufacture, sale, gift, loan, possession, or use.

U.S.Pa. 1980. Statute authorizing imposition of enhanced penalties on a defendant who uses or carries a firearm while committing a federal felony may not be applied to a defendant who uses a firearm in the course of a felony that is proscribed by a statute which itself authorizes enhancement if a dangerous weapon is used; sentence received by such a defendant may be enhanced only under enhancement provision in statute defining felony he has committed. 18 U.S.C.A. § 924(c).—Busic v. U. S., 100 S.Ct. 1747, 446 U.S. 398, 64 L.Ed.2d 381, on remand 639 F.2d 940, certiorari denied 101 S.Ct. 3055, 452 U.S. 918, 69 L.Ed.2d 422.

Where, through combination of aiding and abetting statute and statute making it unlawful to assault a federal officer, defendant was found guilty as a principal of using a firearm to assault undercover agents, codefendant's gun became defendant's gun as a matter of law for purposes of assault statute, which provided for enhanced punishment when the assaulter "uses" a deadly weapon, and thus statute authorizing imposition of enhanced penalties on a defendant who "uses" or "carries" a firearm while committing a federal felony could not be applied against defendant on theory that defendant was merely "carrying," as opposed to "using," his gun. 18 U.S.C.A. §§ 2, 111, 924(c), (c)(1, 2).—Id.

U.S.Va. 1980. Federal firearms statute prohibits felon from possessing a firearm despite the fact that the predicate felony may be subject to collateral attack on constitutional grounds. 18 U.S.C.A. App. § 1202(a)(1).—Lewis v. U. S., 100 S.Ct. 915, 445 U.S. 55, 63 L.Ed.2d 198.

C.A.Ala. 1981. Government must prove both willingness to deal and more than occasional sale in order to prove status of accused as one engaged in business of dealing in firearms. 18 U.S.C.A. § 922(a)(1), 924(a).—U. S. v. Berry, 644 F.2d 1034.

C.A.Ala. 1981. Under statute prohibiting a convicted felon from receiving, possessing, or transporting any firearm that has moved in interstate commerce, separate prosecution units can arise either from showing of separate receipts or separate possessions; separate receipts can be established by showing that the weapons were acquired at different times or places, and separate possessions can be established by showing either that the weapons were stored in different places or that the weapons were acquired at different times or places. 18 U.S.C.A.App. § 1202(a)(1).—U. S. v. McCrary, 643 F.2d 323.

C.A.Ala. 1979. In proceedings to accept guilty plea to charge of receiving firearms transported in interstate commerce, Government was not required to demonstrate that defendant was aware of interstate character of weapon. 18 U.S.C.A. § 922(h); Fed.Rules Crim.Proc. rule 11, 18 U.S.C. A.—Lambert v. U. S., 600 F.2d 476.

C.A.Ala. 1979. Defendant had constructive possession of weapons if he had intent and power to exercise dominion and control over weapons. 18 U.S.C.A. App. § 1202(a).—U. S. v. Smith, 591 F.2d 1105.

C.A.Ala. 1977. U. S. v. Woods, 560 F.2d 660, certiorari denied 98 S.Ct. 1452, 435 U.S. 906, 55 L.Ed.2d 497.

C.A.Ariz. 1981. As used in statute which prohibits the receipt by a convicted felon of a firearm that has been shipped in interstate commerce, the term "receipt" includes any knowing acceptance or taking of possession of a weapon. 18 U.S.C.A. § 922(h).—U. S. v. Lipps, 659 F.2d 960.

Source: West Publishing Company © 1982

Figure R.   Sample Page: Case Digest Summaries (See also Figure I, p. 14)

When you find one-paragraph digest summaries that seem to apply to your research problem, note the case citations contained in them. When you finish searching through the summaries, retrieve the cases you've noted and read them. If any of them apply to your problem, summarize them for future reference.

If you have access to a computerized legal research system, you can search its data base for your descriptive words, instead of (or in addition to) searching for those words in a digest index. The computer will locate all cases containing your descriptive words. Appendix A presents an introduction to computerized legal research.

Summary. Figure S summarizes in graphic form the technique for finding the law using the descriptive word or fact word approach.

The following checklist also highlights points to keep in mind when using the descriptive or fact word approach:

- Select as many descriptive or fact words as possible. Normally, use specific rather than general words—but not too specific. For example, "cockroach" is better than "animal," but probably not as good as "insect" or "vermin."
- Start your research with annotated statutes accompanied by one-paragraph case summaries.
- Check relevant statutes for administrative rulemaking authority.
- After checking for statutes and administrative regulations, move on to a descriptive or fact word search for cases.

Approach B:
Known authority

Occasionally, you may start your research already knowing the citation of at least one legal authority—*i.e.*, case, statute, or administrative regulation—that may apply to your problem. Perhaps you got the citation from someone else, or you may have discovered it in your preliminary background reading (see "A Generalized Approach," discussed later in this chapter). If you have such a citation (referred to here as a "known case," "known statute," or "known regulation"), *you've got a ready-made shortcut in your research*: start by simply reading the case, statute, or regulation.

Known statute or administrative regulation. If you're working with a known statute, you'll next need to discover how courts have dealt with it. There are several ways to find those cases. First, check the case

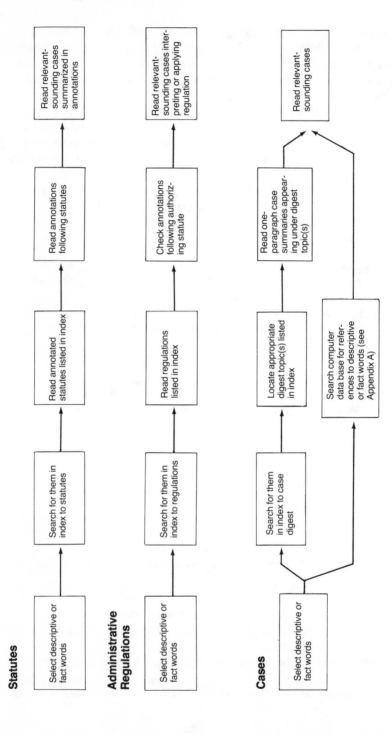

Statutes

Select descriptive or fact words → Search for them in index to statutes → Read annotated statutes listed in index → Read annotations following statutes → Read relevant-sounding cases summarized in annotations

Administrative Regulations

Select descriptive or fact words → Search for them in index to regulations → Read regulations listed in index → Check annotations following authorizing statute → Read relevant-sounding cases interpreting or applying regulation

Cases

Select descriptive or fact words → Search for them in index to case digest → Locate appropriate digest topic(s) listed in index → Read one-paragraph case summaries appearing under digest topic(s) → Read relevant-sounding cases

Search computer data base for references to descriptive or fact words (see Appendix A) → Read relevant-sounding cases

Figure S. How to Find the Law Using the Descriptive or Fact Word Approach

annotations (if any) listed after the known statute in the annotated set of statutes. If any cases applying or interpreting the known statute appear relevant to your problem, you should read them.

Second, you can locate cases interpreting your known statute by Shepardizing the statute in the appropriate set of *Shepard's Citations.* (Shepardizing is explained in Chapter 6.)

Finally, if you have access to a computerized legal data base, you can also locate cases referring to your known statute by typing in the statutory citation and instructing the computer to search for references to it. (See Appendix A for more about computerized legal research.)

If you have a known administrative regulation, you will also need to locate cases that have interpreted and applied the regulation. The techniques for doing this are listed earlier, on page 49.

Figure T graphically depicts the research techniques for finding interpretative cases dealing with known statutes and regulations.

Of course, just because you know one statute or administrative regulation that applies does *not* mean you know *all* the statutes or regulations that apply. To ensure thoroughness in your research, you should also follow up with a "descriptive word" type of search in the relevant annotated statutes and administrative code or register indexes for any other pertinent statutes or regulations. (See "Approach A: Descriptive Word or Fact Word," discussed in the preceding section.)

Known case. As with statutes and regulations, knowing the citation of one case does not mean you have found all the relevant cases, and you should follow up with a "descriptive word" search here, too, using the index to the relevant digest. But you can also start by moving with ease directly from your known case to other cases *without* going through a "descriptive word" search. To locate *subsequent* cases in this way that may have interpreted your known case in a significant manner, Shepardize your known case (see Chapter 6) or search a computerized legal research service's data base for references to it (see Appendix A).

With a known case, you can also locate other cases (whether decided before *or* after the known case) that deal with the same legal issue or issues that interest you in your known case. Here's how to do it:

1) Retrieve the volume containing your known case, and open to the first page of the case.

   For illustrative purposes, we've reprinted as Figure U the first page from the *Supreme Court Reporter* version of *Lewis v. United States,* which would be the "known case."

2) Review the headnotes (the numbered one-paragraph sum-

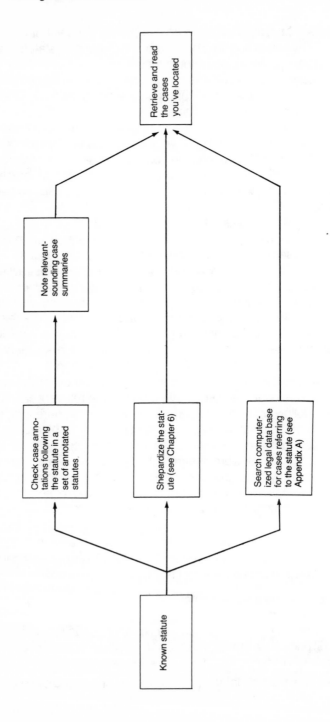

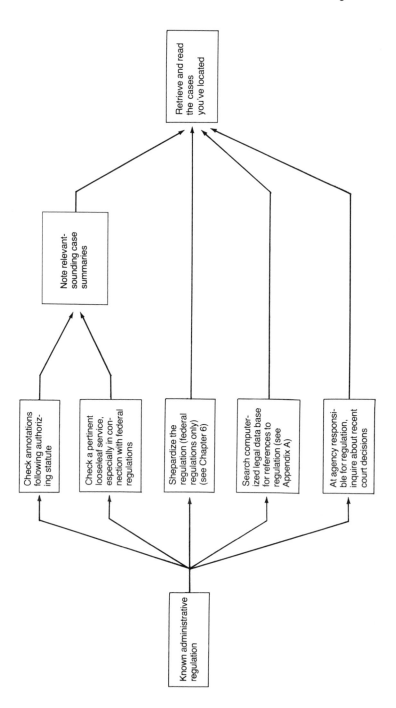

Figure T. How to Find Cases Interpreting Known Statutes and Administrative Regulations

maries of the points of law decided in the case) appearing at the outset of the case. Appendix D reprints Figure U with an explanation of the elements of a headnote.

3) Pick the headnotes that seem pertinent to your research problem. Note their digest topic titles and "Key" or section numbers. In the second headnote in Figure U, for example, "Criminal Law" is the topic title and "641.1" is the Key number. (Recall that Chapter 1, "Sources of the Law," explains the relationship between case reporters and digests, with the digests acting in effect as grand indexes to the reporters.)

4) Retrieve the digest volume that contains the same topic and the same "Key" or section numbers found in the known case headnotes you think are pertinent.

Note. Some jurisdictions have more than one digest, each published by a different company. Because each digest publisher has its own digesting system, *it is essential that the publisher of the case reporter and the digest be the same* when using the "known case" approach to find other cases. The headnote topics and "Key" or section numbers of one publisher's case reporters will not correspond to the topics and "Key" or section numbers of another publisher's digests.

5) In the digest volume you've retrieved, turn to the topic and "Key" or section numbers you selected from the headnotes of your known case. There, in the digest, you'll find all the other published cases in the jurisdiction covered by the digest that have dealt with your chosen points of law.

The digest you use in this "known case" approach will determine how many cases you find, and from what jurisdiction or court they come. The *Supreme Court Digest*, for example, will lead you only to other U.S. Supreme Court cases on point; *Federal Practice Digest 2d*, on the other hand, will yield *all* federal cases digested under that topic. A state digest will give you only decisions arising out of cases commenced in the state and federal courts located in that state, while the *Decennial Digests* or current *General Digest* will turn up all federal *and* state cases digested under the particular topic and "Key Number" in West's National Reporter System during a given period.

Caveat. It isn't necessary, in connection with using the "known case" approach, to know whether a particular known case itself actually applies to your research problem. Even if your known case happens to be utterly useless in other respects, so long as its headnotes indicate that it deals with a point of law relevant to your problem, the headnote

445 U.S. 55

LEWIS v. UNITED STATES

Cite as 100 S.Ct. 915 (1980)

915

445 U.S. 55, 63 L.Ed.2d 198

George Calvin LEWIS, Jr., Petitioner,

v.

UNITED STATES.

No. 78–1595.

Argued Jan. 7, 1980.

Decided Feb. 27, 1980.

Defendant was convicted in the United States District Court for the Eastern District of Virginia, Robert R. Merhige, Jr., J., as a convicted felon with unlawful possession of a firearm. On appeal, the United States Court of Appeals for the Fourth Circuit, Donald Russell, Circuit Judge, 591 F.2d 978, affirmed. On certiorari, the Supreme Court, Mr. Justice Blackmun, held that: (1) federal firearms statute prohibits a felon from possessing a firearm despite fact that predicate felony may be subject to collateral attack on constitutional grounds, and (2) federal firearm statute which prohibits felon from possessing a firearm even if predicate felony may be subject of collateral attack on constitutional grounds does not violate due process clause of Fifth Amendment.

Affirmed.

Mr. Justice Brennan dissented and filed opinion in which Mr. Justice Marshall and Mr. Justice Powell joined.

1. Weapons �4

Federal firearms statute prohibits felon from possessing a firearm despite the fact that the predicate felony may be subject to collateral attack on constitutional grounds. 18 U.S.C.A. App. § 1202(a)(1).

2. Criminal Law ⚑641.1

Under Sixth Amendment, an uncounseled felony conviction cannot be used for certain purposes; however, that uncounseled conviction is not invalid for all purposes. U.S.C.A.Const. Amend. 6.

3. Constitutional Law ⚑258(3)

Weapons ⚑3

Federal firearm statute which prohibits a felon from possessing a firearm even if predicate felony may be subject to collateral attack on constitutional grounds did not violate due process clause of Fifth Amendment. 18 U.S.C.A. App. § 1202(a)(1); U.S. C.A.Const. Amend. 5.

4. Weapons ⚑17

Prosecution for unlawful possession of a firearm by a felon does not open the predicate felony conviction to a new form of collateral attack. 18 U.S.C.A. App. § 1202(a)(1).

Syllabus *

Held: Even though petitioner's extant prior state-court felony conviction may be subject to collateral attack under *Gideon v. Wainwright*, 372 U.S. 335, 83 S.Ct. 792, 9 L.Ed.2d 799, it could properly be used as a predicate for his subsequent conviction for possession of a firearm in violation of § 1202(a)(1) of Title VII of the Omnibus Crime Control and Safe Streets Act of 1968. Pp. 918–922.

(a) The plain meaning of § 1202(a)(1)'s sweeping language proscribing the possession of firearms by any person who "has been convicted by a court of the United States or of a State . . . of a felony," is that the fact of a felony conviction imposes firearm disability until the conviction is vacated or the felon is relieved of his disability by some affirmative action. Other provisions of the statute demonstrate and reinforce its broad sweep, and there is nothing in § 1202(a)(1)'s legislative history to suggest that Congress was willing to allow a defendant to question the validity of his prior conviction as a defense to a charge under § 1202(a)(1). Moreover, the fact that there are remedies available to a convicted felon—removal of the firearm disability by

* The syllabus constitutes no part of the opinion of the Court but has been prepared by the Reporter of Decisions for the convenience of the reader. See *United States v. Detroit Lumber Co.*, 200 U.S. 321, 337, 26 S.Ct. 282, 287, 50 L.Ed. 499.

Figure U. First Page of a Case Report: Using Headnotes in the Known Case Approach for Finding the Law

See Appendix D for an explanation of this page.

information in your known case will still lead you to the appropriate place in a digest, where you may find summaries of cases that are more pertinent to your problem than your original known case was.

At some point, however, you will need to decide whether to rely on your known case in stating your legal position. In making this determination, it is always essential to actually *read the case itself*; do not rely solely on the summaries contained in the headnotes. First, the headnotes may fail to catch important nuance. Second, even if the headnotes do accurately summarize the points of law contained in the case, the precise factual context of a case may bear significantly on the legal application of the points of law: if your facts differ substantially from those in the reported case, the point of law may apply differently or not at all to your own problem. You can't know whether any of these difficulties exist without reading the case. Therefore, always read the case.

Summary. Figure V depicts the techniques for finding case law from a single known case.

A variation: the partially known authority. Sometimes, you may know of a particular case or statute that is potentially applicable to your research problem, but you don't have enough of the citation to locate the authority. For example, someone may suggest you look at the "Steelworkers Trilogy" of cases or the federal "Equal Credit Opportunity Act," but may not be able to tell you the exact citation. Even without that information, you can still find the authority—and use the "known case" or "known statute" research approach discussed immediately above— if you first take one of the following steps:

Cases

- If you know the name of one of the principal plaintiffs or defendants in the case, you can locate the case through either the Table of Cases or the Defendant-Plaintiff Table found in federal and state case digests. The Table of Cases lists alphabetically, by the principal plaintiffs' names, the titles of all the cases summarized in the particular digest. (The Defendant-Plaintiff Table does the same thing, except that it lists the defendants' names first.) After a case title, the table provides the title, volume, and page number of the case reporters where the case is reprinted. (In addition, the entry in the Table of Cases will also indicate the digest topics under which the case has been digested.)

  If you know in which state the case was decided, you would check the party tables in that state's digest. Similarly, if the case is a federal one, check the tables in the appropriate

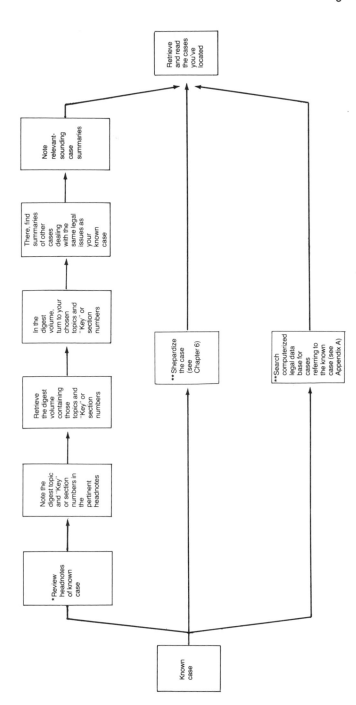

*Using the headnotes will lead you to both prior *and* subsequent cases dealing with point(s) of law in your known case.
**This technique will locate *subsequent* cases interpreting your known case.

Figure V. How to Find Case Law from a Single Known Case

federal digest (*e.g., U.S. Supreme Court Digest* or *Federal Practice Digest 3d*). If you're not sure in which jurisdiction the case was decided, check the Tables of Cases in the various *Decennial Digests* and *General Digests.*

● Sometimes a case will be referred to by a popular name, such as the "Legal Tender Case" or "The 'Flopper' Case," instead of its official name. If you know only the popular name of a case, you can find the case's citation in a volume titled *Shepard's Acts and Cases By Popular Names,* which provides comprehensive coverage of both federal and state cases. You can also use the cumulative Popular Names Table in the sixth series of the *Decennial Digests* (for federal and state cases) or the Popular Names Table in West's *U.S. Supreme Court Digest* (for Supreme Court cases only).

Statutes

● Occasionally a statute will be referred to by a popular name, such as the "Unfair Frozen Dessert Sales Law" or the "Federal Firearms Act," rather than by its statutory citation. There are several ways you can find the citation: look up the statute's popular name in the Shepard's volume titled *Acts and Cases By Popular Names,* which covers both federal and state statutes; check the "Table of Acts By Popular Names or Short Titles" found in each individual set of federal and state *Shepard's Citations*; or check the "Popular Names" tables found in most annotated sets of state and federal statutes.

Approach C: Known topic

Cases. If you feel confident you know what area of law your problem involves (*e.g.,* sales, wills, taxation, civil rights), you can skip the case digest index. Instead, go directly to the appropriate case digest topic and peruse the table of contents until you find a sub-topic that relates to your research problem. (The digest system, remember, was explained in Chapter 1.)

For illustration, a sample page showing the first page of the digest topic "Civil Rights" from a West Publishing Company case digest is reprinted in Figure W.

Although experienced legal researchers frequently use the "known topic" approach, it is generally not an effective technique for the beginning researcher until he or she gains at least some familiarity with the body of American law and the scope of the various digest topics. Legal topic ———————————→ **CIVIL RIGHTS**

SUBJECTS INCLUDED

General rights of personal nature; more particularly those rights protected by civil rights statutes

Prohibitions against discrimination because of race, color, sex, or other reasons

Federal and state remedies for violations of such rights or prohibitions

SUBJECTS EXCLUDED AND COVERED BY OTHER TOPICS

explanation of this topic's scope of coverage

Conspiracies to violate civil rights, see CONSPIRACY

Constitutional rights, see CONSTITUTIONAL LAW

Criminal prosecutions, restrictions on procedure, see CRIMINAL LAW

Federal courts, jurisdiction and venue, see FEDERAL COURTS

Interstate commerce, establishments and operations affecting, see COMMERCE

Jury, right of trial by, see JURY

Privacy, invasion of, see TORTS

School desegregation, see SCHOOLS

Voting rights, see ELECTIONS

For detailed references to other topics, see Descriptive-Word Index

---

Analysis

summary outline of sub-topics covered

I. RIGHTS PROTECTED AND DISCRIMINATION PROHIBITED, ⊄1–12.2.

II. REMEDIES FOR VIOLATION, ⊄12.3–75.

  (A) FEDERAL REMEDIES, ⊄12.3–60.

    1. IN GENERAL, ⊄12.3–30.

    2. EQUAL EMPLOYMENT OPPORTUNITIES, ⊄31–60.

  (B) STATE REMEDIES, ⊄61–75.

I. RIGHTS PROTECTED AND DISCRIMINATION PROHIBITED.

sub-topics

⊄1. Rights protected by civil rights laws in general.

2. Statutory provisions.

2.1. —— Power to enact and validity.

3. Discrimination prohibited in general.

4. Public accommodations.

5. —— Inns and restaurants; bars and taverns.

6. —— Theaters and places of exhibition or entertainment.

7. —— Public conveyances.

8. —— Places of business or public resort.

8.1. —— Private clubs.

8.2. Public facilities.

9. Public education.

Source: West Publishing Company © 1980

Figure W.   First Page of a Sample Case Digest Topic

publishers have digested the law under hundreds of topics that can be tremendously useful, but beginners at legal research typically are aware of only a few broad topics, such as "contracts" or "property." As a result, beginning researchers using the "known topic" approach will almost certainly overlook numerous pertinent digest topics. For example, if a research problem involves a contract, the digest topic "Contracts" will probably occur to a researcher, but other contract-related topics (such as "Bonds," "Guaranty," "Sales," or "Vendor and Purchaser") may actually be more relevant to the research problem.

For researchers who decide to use the "known topic" approach, each digest publisher provides a complete listing of its digest's individual topics. This listing normally appears in at least the first volume in the digest set. If you decide to use this approach, check the publishers' lists for pertinent topics that may not have already occurred to you. Lists of the digest topics used by West Publishing Company are included in Appendices G and H in Part III of this book.

Statutes and administrative regulations. While experienced researchers may use the "known topic" approach with statutes or regulations, beginning researchers will normally not find it helpful. Statutory and administrative codes organize statutes and regulations by grouping them together topically according to common subject matter, but these topical groupings are not arranged alphabetically within the codes. Thus, they are unlike case digests, which arrange case law topics in alphabetical order. For the "known topic" approach, this difference is significant: for example, in a case digest, a topic such as "patents" will always be found somewhere between topics beginning with "o" (such as "obscenity") and "q" (such as "quieting title"), whereas statutes dealing with patent law will be grouped together, but that grouping will be located somewhat arbitrarily within the larger set of statutes. Consequently, using the topical method to locate a statutory or administrative code provision can be a time-consuming chore for the beginner.

Nonetheless, numerous areas of the law are governed by statutes or regulations that comprehensively treat a particular topic. Examples include the law affecting insurance, corporations, motor vehicles, taxation, and consumer credit. If you feel confident that your research problem is governed by statutory or administrative law, and you know from experience where the relevant statutes or regulations are located within a code, you can go directly to the appropriate statute or regulation without consulting the code's index. This procedure thus effectively bypasses the "descriptive word" approach discussed earlier, and is largely similar to the previously described "known statute" or "known regulation" approach.

A practical recommendation. Experienced researchers often find the "known topic" approach very useful. Beginning researchers, because of their lack of familiarity with legal topics, are generally better off using the "descriptive word" approach instead, or (where appropriate) the "known authority" approach.

A Specialized Approach: Words and Phrases

If your research problem involves or turns on a legal definition of a term, you can go straight to a publication called *Words and Phrases*. This resource is a multi-volume "dictionary" of words and phrases that courts have defined for legal purposes in the context of particular decisions. *Words and Phrases* lists the terms alphabetically, along with citations to federal and state cases that have construed or interpreted them.

Figure X shows a sample page from West's *Words and Phrases*.

Example. Suppose your research problem involves zoning regulations that prohibit constructing a jail in a residential neighborhood. Suppose also that a government agency wants to build a half-way house for parolees and to place it in a residential neighborhood. Finally, suppose that no pertinent statute or administrative regulation has defined either the word "jail" or "half-way house."

The legal issue for research is whether the half-way house would be a jail (because if so, its presence in the neighborhood would violate the zoning regulations). In your research, you will want to determine precisely what the characteristics of a jail are, as opposed to those of a half-way house. By using *Words and Phrases*, you may be able to make significant headway in your research by simply looking up the judicial definitions listed under "jail" or "half-way house."

Not every research problem lends itself to an approach relying on *Words and Phrases*, and not every word or phrase you may need defined will appear in *Words and Phrases*. But when a precise judicial definition is needed, you should not overlook *Words and Phrases* as an important research tool.

In addition to the *Words and Phrases* series of volumes, *case digests* usually contain either a topic entry or a separate volume titled "Words and Phrases" that lists significant terms interpreted by courts in the jurisdiction covered by the particular digest. So, if you're interested in seeing whether a term has been defined in, say, South Carolina, check first in the "Words and Phrases" section of the *South Carolina Digest*. If you don't find your term there (or if you do, but you also want

JAIL

JACTUS

The word "jactus" is used in the maritime law to designate a portion of a cargo or vessel which is drawn overboard at time of peril for the purpose of preventing the loss of the vessel and cargo. It is also used to designate the act of throwing such goods overboard. Barnard v. Adams, 51 U.S. 270, 303, 10 How., 270, 303, 13 L.Ed. 417.

JADE

Cross References

Precious Stones

JAGGER

A "jagger" is a point of iron projecting from the end of an iron shaft and produced by the blow of a hammer on the end of the shaft. Persinger's Adm'x v. Alleghany Ore & Iron Co., 46 S.E. 325, 102 Va. 350.

JAI ALAI FRONTON

A "jai alai fronton" is a form of gambling. Rodriguez v. Jones, Fla., 64 So.2d 278, 280.

JAIL

In general—p. 3
City jail—p. 3
Dedication to public use—p. 4

Cross References

County Jail
House
Imprisonment Within Prison Walls of Any Jail
Inhabited Dwelling House
Prison
Prison or Jail
Public Building
Public House
Public Work
State Jail or Penitentiary
Structure
Sufficient Jail

In general

A jail is a house or building used for the purpose of a public prison, or where persons under arrest are kept. State v. Bryan, 89 N. C. 531, 534.

County "jail", whether for adults or juveniles, is a place for legal detention of all

In general—Cont'd

persons, who come within the provisions of laws which authorize law enforcement officers to detain them. McArthur v. Campbell, 280 S.W.2d 219, 220, 225 Ark. 172.

A "jail" is a prison appertaining to a county or municipality in which are confined, for punishment, persons convicted of misdemeanors committed in the county or municipality. Denham v. Com., 84 S.W. 538, 539, 119 Ky. 508.

A building used as a jail, and in which a prisoner is confined for a violation of law, is within the protection of a statute punishing jail deliveries, though it is not situated in an incorporated town, and is not the property of the county. Irvington v. State, 78 S.W. 928, 929, 45 Tex.Cr.R. 559.

While the primary function of a "jail" is a place of detention for persons committed thereto, under sentence of a court, it is also the proper and usual place where persons under arrest or awaiting trial are kept until they appear in court and the charge disposed of. Grab v. Lucas, 146 N.W. 504, 505, 156 Wis. 504.

Where admission of arrested accused to hospital was engineered by arresting officer and accused was under police surveillance during the 19 days of his stay there, even though there was no prison ward in hospital, hospital was a "prison" or "jail" within statute to effect that an accused is entitled to have calculated as part of term of sentence any time spent in prison or jail prior to his conviction and before sentence. People ex rel. Broderick v. Noble, 207 N.Y.S.2d 467, 468, 26 Misc.2d 903.

The statute providing that the word "jail" shall be taken to include workhouse, and "workhouse" shall be taken to include jail "whenever the context so requires or will permit," does not mean that the words "jail" and "workhouse" are used interchangeably, but only that the proper word will be deemed substituted where one word has been erroneously used in a statute for the other and the context affords means of construction; and the distinction between "jail" and "workhouse" is to be preserved. State ex rel. Hurst v. Sullivan County, 120 S.W.2d 32, 33, 173 Tenn. 414.

A newspaper's sub-headlines concerning plaintiff and stating "man held in jail since

Figure X. Sample Page from *Words and Phrases*

definitions from other states), you can go on to the multi-volume *Words and Phrases*, where you may find the term defined by courts in other jurisdictions.

Finally, if you have access to a computerized legal data base, you can also type in your word or phrase to locate citations of cases in which it appears, including those cases that define the word or phrase. See Appendix A for a discussion of computerized legal research.

A Generalized Approach: encyclopedias, treatises, law reviews, and other secondary legal sources

The research approaches discussed so far are designed to lead you directly to primary [21] sources of law (court decisions, statutes, administrative regulations, and constitutional provisions). If you have little or no general knowledge of the areas of law involved in your research problem, however, you will be at a disadvantage in developing an informed research approach because you won't know what points of law to look for as you search through the primary legal authorities. Therefore, before you begin your search in primary sources, you may find it helpful to obtain some generalized background on the areas of law your problem involves. Several kinds of secondary legal sources exist to help you gain this initial overview.

You may also find it helpful later in your research to re-examine the generalized secondary sources more carefully to put the results of your primary-source research in a broader perspective. But for the researcher working in an unfamiliar area of the law, the greatest strength of generalized secondary sources is their ability to supply instant background information. The most frequently used generalized sources are discussed in the remainder of this section.

Legal encyclopedias. These publications present comprehensive summaries of hundreds of legal subjects. Encyclopedias do not critically analyze the law; instead, they only summarize legal rules developed by federal and state courts. Also, legal encyclopedias do not explain in detail how these rules operate in specific factual settings. Despite these drawbacks, however, encyclopedias generally offer good introductions to particular areas of law about which you know little or nothing.

Consequently, you will usually find it helpful to begin your research

---

[21]Primary and secondary sources were defined and distinguished at p. 41.

in any unfamiliar area of law by reading the appropriate topical article in an encyclopedia.

Two legal encyclopedias dominate American legal research: *Corpus Juris Secundum* (abbreviated *"C.J.S."*), published by West, and *American Jurisprudence 2d* (abbreviated *"Am. Jur. 2d"*), published by Lawyers Cooperative.[22] Both encyclopedias have substantial similarities:

- Each arranges its articles alphabetically into more than 400 subjects. Each encyclopedia provides a complete listing of all the topics in the set, either in each volume or in each index volume. Each set also has an extensive index.

- Each encyclopedia is written in narrative form.

- Each encyclopedia uses extensive footnotes to present citations of reported federal and state court decisions supporting particular points of law.

- Each encyclopedia emphasizes only the *prevailing* rule of law. Different states often have different legal rules for the same factual situation. The rule followed by a majority of the states is called the "majority" or "prevailing" rule, and that's the rule the encyclopedias would focus on. Even so, there would be some discussion of any minority rule followed by a significant number of states.

Some differences exist between the two sets of encyclopedias:

- *C.J.S.* footnotes seek to cite *all* reported federal and state cases relevant to a specific point of law decided since the publication of *Corpus Juris*, the predecessor of *C.J.S.* On the other hand, *Am. Jur. 2d* has footnotes to *selected* reported decisions.

- *C.J.S.* is cross-referenced to West Publishing Company's "Key Number" system. In other words, *C.J.S.* directs you to appropriate topics and "Key" numbers in West case digests, where you will find summaries of relevant court decisions. (See the glossary in Appendix L for a definition of "Key number.") *C.J.S.* also cites to annotation articles in *American Law Reports Annotated* (discussed later in this chapter).

---

[22] In addition to these two encyclopedias, which have national coverage, a number of states have their own encyclopedias covering only their own law. These local encyclopedias have the same general format and features as do *C.J.S.* and *Am. Jur. 2d,* and are used in the same way.

- *Am. Jur. 2d* cross-references to articles in *American Law Reports Annotated; to Restatements of the Law* (discussed later in this chapter); to other Lawyers Cooperative publications, such as *Am. Jur. Proof of Facts*; and to law reviews (also discussed later).

- *Am. Jur. 2d* has a Desk Book that functions as a legal almanac. The Desk Book contains numerous charts, tables, lists, and graphs, including such items as:

  (a) organization charts of the federal government agencies;
  (b) addresses and telephone numbers of federal government departments;
  (c) crime and prison statistics;
  (d) labor arbitration rules of the American Arbitration Association;
  (e) automobile speed formulae;
  (f) financial tables (simple interest, compound interest, and annuity tables);
  (g) abbreviations of legal reports and treatises;
  (h) tables of descent and distribution for inheritance purposes; and
  (i) historical documents (*e.g.*, Magna Carta, Mayflower Compact, Washington's Farewell Address, Monroe Doctrine)

You enter the encyclopedias by using either the "descriptive word" approach or the "known topic" approach. If you don't know the topic of law involved in your research problem, but you have some descriptive or fact words (see p. 46), look up those words in the general index to the encyclopedia. The index will point you to the relevant topics and sections in the encyclopedia. If you do already know the legal topics your problem involves (*e.g.*, burglary, patents, labor relations), simply go straight to the appropriate topic.

When you use legal encyclopedias, you should remember two important points. First, legal encyclopedias are secondary, *not* primary, legal authorities. Too many legal researchers view them—and cite them—as if they were primary sources rather than simply generalized summaries of the law.

Second, just because an encyclopedia cites a case in connection with a proposition relevant to your research problem does not mean that the cited case will actually apply to your problem. An encyclopedia description of a case usually will not catch the case's full legal significance or nuance. When you read a case, you may find that, contrary to your first impression of it from the encyclopedia, its facts are so distinguishable from those of your problem that the case does not have the effect you originally anticipated.

In summary, encyclopedias serve as a useful starting point in your research; they are not an ending point. Your research will be quite incomplete if you confine it solely to reading *C.J.S.* or *Am. Jur. 2d.*

Treatises and hornbooks. Treatises (also sometimes called "hornbooks," although this term is generally reserved for treatises written particularly for a student audience) present scholarly analyses of particular areas of law, such as constitutional law, torts, worker's compensation, or civil procedure. Depending on the depth of treatment, a treatise may run for several volumes.

A treatise is roughly analogous to a topical article in a legal encyclopedia. In addition, however, a treatise typically offers critical analysis, including extensive interpretation of significant cases and doctrines in the area of law. Further, treatise authors will frequently express strong opinions about the current state of the law and how the law ought to develop.

Like encyclopedias, treatises cite cases to support the authors' views of the law. Unlike encyclopedias, though, treatises also cite varied sources other than cases, such as other treatises, government reports, and even social science research. Because of the range of materials on which treatises rely and the scholarly analytical nature of their coverage, they often offer significant help in getting a fix on the history, current status, and probable or possible development of legal doctrines. In fact, some influential treatises have shaped the law's development because of their authors' expertise or insight. As you develop research experience, you'll discover—through the frequency of their citation by judges and other legal scholars—which treatises carry weight in their fields.

Because treatises deal with specific legal topics, to use them you need to categorize your research problem by the subject(s) it involves. You can then find relevant treatises by looking under the appropriate topic headings in your law library's card catalog. You can also find treatises by checking in a publication called *Law Books in Print.*

Once you select a treatise, review its table of contents carefully. The table of contents will normally provide a detailed outline of the subject covered by the treatise and should give you a good idea of how scholars analyze that topical area of law.

As with legal encyclopedias, treatises constitute a starting point for legal research, not an ending point. They offer overviews of specific areas of the law and provide ready sources of pertinent citations to cases, statutes, and other primary authorities, which you can use as "known authorities" for locating additional primary authority. (See "Known Authority" approach, above.) Further, because treatises offer in-depth analysis, they can help you significantly in doing the evaluation involved in the "reading" phase of your research. (This phase is discussed in Chapter 5, "Reading the Law.")

Restatements of the Law. *Restatements* are treatise-like publications produced by committees of distinguished judges, law professors, and practicing lawyers, all working under the auspices of the American Law Institute, a non-profit organization devoted to scholarly legal research and continuing education for lawyers. Although not formally adopted in whole by either legislatures or courts as primary authorities, *Restatements* have become so generally respected and cited by courts that they often seem in fact to have achieved the status of primary authority. Occasionally, courts will specifically adopt as part of a state's common law a particular principle set out in a *Restatement*.

There are several *Restatements*, each dealing with a specific legal subject, *e.g.*, torts, agency, contracts, trusts, property. The *Restatements* seek to summarize and "restate" general principles of American common law, much like legal encyclopedia articles do. The *Restatement* principles generally represent consensus views of specific rules of law prevailing among the fifty states. Unlike legal encyclopedias, however, *Restatements* also provide some analysis and sometimes even try to predict how the law will develop. In this respect, they resemble treatises. In addition, the *Restatements* set forth commentary on each restated principle, as well as examples of particular applications and variations of the principles.

Each *Restatement* has its own index. There is also a general index to the first editions of all the *Restatements*. If you know that a particular *Restatement* relates to your research problem, look up in its index the descriptive or fact words you've identified as useful for researching your legal problem. The index will direct you to the appropriate part of that *Restatement*. If you are uncertain whether a *Restatement* applies, or which one applies, start by looking for your descriptive or fact words in the general index to the first editions of all *Restatements;* this index will point you to both the correct *Restatement* and the appropriate section within that *Restatement*. (Note that some original *Restatements* have been superseded by second editions. If a second edition of a particular *Restatement* has appeared, you can use its index to find the relevant sections.)

Also, the second editions of the *Restatements* contain cross references to West Publishing Company's "Key Number" digest system and to Lawyers Cooperative's *American Law Reports Annotated* series. Consequently, you can move easily and quickly from the *Restatements* to the cases themselves.

Law reviews. Law reviews are periodical publications containing articles and commentaries written by law professors, lawyers, and law students, and edited by students (or, less frequently, by law professors) at various law schools. These articles analyze and critique noteworthy court decisions, statutes, and legal doctrines, and seek to place them in perspective.

Law reviews vary substantially in their editorial philosophies and goals, as well as in their quality. Law reviews from the well-known "national" law schools—e.g., Harvard, Yale, University of Michigan, Berkeley, Chicago—generally focus on matters of national legal significance. Further, they seek to deal with matters at the frontiers of legal doctrine and tend toward theory and abstraction. Other law reviews tend more frequently to focus on legal matters of interest to a particular state or geographic region. These reviews are generally oriented more toward practicing lawyers in the particular jurisdiction. The value of a particular kind of law review will vary depending on your research needs.

The standard way of finding law review articles is to look up the descriptive or fact words you've selected as relevant to your problem in a legal periodical index. The three major ones are:

- *Index to Legal Periodicals*
- *Current Law Index*
- *Legal Resource Index* (which is on microfilm)

In terms of the number of periodicals indexed, *Legal Resource Index* is the most comprehensive of the three indexes.

Each of the services indexes law review material according to author and legal subject matter. The indexes also have tables of cases which list alphabetically the names and citations of cases that have been the principal subjects of law review treatment; if you know a relevant case, you may quickly find law review analyses of it by checking the table of cases in the indexes. Similarly, the indexes have tables of statutes in which you may be able to locate articles commenting on a statute you have identified as relevant to your problem.

Law review articles can also be found in other ways:

- They are often cited by courts in their written decisions, so you are apt to come across relevant law review material as you read case law bearing on your research problem.

- In addition, the notes following annotated statutes may refer to law review articles relating to statutory subject matter.

- Similarly, some case digests will cite to law review articles.

• Some secondary sources, such as treatises and *Am. Jur. 2d*, also cite to law reviews.

• Finally, *Shepard's Citations*, an important research tool explained in Chapter 6, frequently directs researchers to relevant law review articles.

There is no hard and fast rule on when to consult a law review article. If you know little or nothing about the law applicable to your legal problem, you probably won't seek out law review articles until you've first examined legal encyclopedias, treatises, some cases, or perhaps an *American Law Reports* annotation. At that point, you may have a handle on the applicable legal doctrines, but still feel you don't have a firm grip on how everything fits together. A good law review article, if available, may then help synthesize and crystallize your research findings.

You may also want to look for law review articles in two other situations. First, if you know a bit, or even a great deal, about the applicable law, a good law review piece may bring you up to date on recent developments or help you determine what the next step is apt to be in the development of the relevant legal doctrines. Second, if all the primary legal authorities bearing on your research problem run against you, a law review article criticizing the current state of the law and advocating a change may help you in setting forth your position.

American Law Reports Annotated. This Lawyers Cooperative publication, commonly referred to as *"A.L.R.,"* reprints opinions of *selected* state and federal cases (*not* all published opinions), each of which is followed by a detailed analysis—that is, an annotation—of a specific point of law or fact situation raised in the case. The case reprinted in full is used as an illustration, a jumping-off point, for the annotation. The annotation, which is prepared by editors at Lawyers Cooperative, collects, arranges, and analyzes federal and state law on the legal point or fact pattern being annotated. In addition, *A.L.R.* provides similar annotations on selected federal statutes and administrative regulations; these annotations collect, arrange, and analyze cases interpreting the subject statute or regulation.

A.L.R. currently consists of five series: *A.L.R.1st* through *A.L.R.4th*, plus *A.L.R. Fed.* Federal authorities until 1969 are collected in *A.L.R.1st* through part of *A.L.R.3d*; since 1969, federal cases, statutes, and regulations have been collected and annotated in *A.L.R. Fed.*

In researching in *A.L.R.*, it's usually best to begin with the most recent series: nearly all the annotations in *A.L.R.1st* have been superseded by subsequent *A.L.R.* annotations, as have many annotations in

A.L.R.2d. (The process of updating *A.L.R.* is discussed in more detail in Chapter 6; see p. 117 n.43.)

A.L.R. has several methods for locating its material, depending on which *A.L.R.* series you are examining:

- *Quick Indexes.* As of this writing, each series of *A.L.R.* has a Quick Index. *A.L.R.1st* has its own index, as does *A.L.R.2d. A.L.R.3d* and *A.L.R.4th* share a combined index. *A.L.R. Fed.* has its own index, including a separate index volume containing a table of federal statutes and regulations annotated or cited in *A.L.R. Fed.*

    Using the descriptive or fact words you've identified as pertinent to your research problem, you look through the Quick Index as you would through any index. When you find the term you're looking for, you'll find a listing of *A.L.R.* annotations—*not* a listing of individual authorities—relating to that term. (You find the citations to the authorities in the annotation itself.)

- *Word Index. A.L.R.1st* and *A.L.R.2d* each has its own word index; the other series do not, because Lawyers Cooperative has determined that *A.L.R.* users generally prefer the Quick Indexes.

    Using your descriptive or fact words, you search for them in an *A.L.R.* Word Index in the manner you would use any index.

- *Digest. A.L.R.1st* and *A.L.R.2d* each has its own digest; *A.L.R.3d, A.L.R.4th*, and *A.L.R. Fed.* share a combined digest. These digests organize the law into hundreds of alphabetically arranged legal topics, and refer you to annotation articles in *A.L.R.* The digests also cross-reference you to corresponding topics in *Am. Jur. 2d,* Lawyers Cooperative's legal encyclopedia.

    A major drawback to the *A.L.R.* digests, however, is that they have no index. This omission requires you already to know which broad topical areas of the law (such as privacy or bankruptcy) your research problem involves.

- *Tables of Cases.* The combined Quick Index to *A.L.R.3d & 4th* and the digests for *A.L.R.1st* and *A.L.R.2d* contain tables of cases. These tables list those cases reported in full in *A.L.R.*, not those cases cited in the *A.L.R.* annotation articles. If you know the name and non-*A.L.R.* citation of a case bearing on your research problem, you can locate its treatment in

A.L.R. through the table of cases, if the case has been the subject of an *A.L.R.* annotation.

* *Table of Statutes and Regulations.* The Quick Index to *A.L.R. Fed.* has a separate volume that contains tables of federal statutes and regulations that are either annotated or cited in *A.L.R. Fed.* If you know the citation of a federal statute or regulation relevant to your research problem, simply look up the citation in the table, which will direct you to either a full annotation on the authority or some other, more limited reference to it.

* *A practical suggestion.* In the end, you may find that the easiest way to locate an *A.L.R.* annotation is by first researching your problem through Lawyers Cooperative's legal encyclopedia, *Am. Jur. 2d*, the index to which is more comprehensive (and often simpler to use) than the *A.L.R.* indexes and digests. The *Am. Jur. 2d* index will direct you to the appropriate topical articles in *Am. Jur. 2d*, where you will find footnoted cross-references to pertinent *A.L.R.* annotations.

In determining when to turn to *A.L.R.* in your research, you will probably find its use most helpful if you have already identified—through other research sources—a federal or state case, a federal statute or regulation, or a general point of law relevant to your problem and you want to locate cases from courts throughout the country also dealing with the same point or authority. For example, if you have already found a state case in your own jurisdiction dealing with a particular point of law, you may want to analyze national trends on that point or identify persuasive authorities more helpful to your position than your own jurisdiction's mandatory authority is. *A.L.R.* annotations are quite thorough in collecting in one place reported cases from various jurisdictions bearing on the point of law, fact pattern, or issue treated in the annotation. Therefore, despite the frequently confusing format and often inadequate indexing of the *A.L.R.* system, *A.L.R.* should not be overlooked as a potential legal resource.

Secondary sources: summary. Even though the secondary sources discussed above are helpful, you should always remember that unless explicitly adopted by law-making bodies, statements in secondary sources are *not* the law. They are only persuasive, not mandatory, authority. At best, secondary sources only summarize or offer analyses of the governing law made by courts, legislatures, and administrative agencies; at worst, they may mislead by not accurately reflecting the state of the law in *your* jurisdiction.

Therefore, you cannot safely rely exclusively on secondary sources, but must instead always look for and read for yourself the primary, mandatory authorities—*e.g.*, your jurisdiction's cases, statutes, administrative regulations, and constitutional provisions—bearing on your research problem. Only when your jurisdiction has no mandatory primary authority on your research issue (or when you want to suggest how a court in your jurisdiction might want to consider interpreting or modifying your jurisdiction's relevant mandatory primary authority) should you emphasize secondary sources in the final presentation of your legal arguments.

Finding the law through other legal research sources

The preceding sections of this chapter cover the primary and secondary sources in which the vast majority of legal research is done. As you do your own research, however, you will encounter references to a few other sources not mentioned in this chapter. The more significant of these additional sources are briefly described in Appendix B.

Finding the law through computerized research

Computers have recently entered the field of legal research, and their significance has grown steadily. Computer-based legal research uses the same approaches for finding the law as discussed in this chapter (although adapted, of course, to accommodate the unique characteristics of computers). The important point here is simply to recognize that computers have become an important law-finding tool. Appendix A provides an introduction to computer-based legal research.

Finding the law through updating

Updating the law, which analytically is the third and final step in legal research, involves making sure the legal authorities you've located in your "finding the law" phase still constitute valid statements of the law. As you update your authorities, however, you will also be finding more new authorities. Therefore, updating the law also functions as a technique for finding the law. Chapter 6 discusses how to update the law.

In general, you won't use every approach for each research problem. Also, the suggestions about when to rely on the various approaches are not intended as hard and fast rules about effective research strategies. What will work best will depend on the particular matter being researched, as well as on how much or how little you know about the subject you are researching. As you gain experience in doing legal research, you will become increasingly adept at working the available approaches into an overall strategy for solving legal problems.

- *A Generalized Approach* (pp. 65–74). If you have little or no general knowledge of the areas of law involved in your research problem, you will probably want to begin by reading one or more secondary sources. These include: legal encyclopedias (*Corpus Juris Secundum, American Jurisprudence 2d*); treatises and hornbooks; *Restatements of the Law*; law reviews; and *American Law Reports Annotated* (*A.L.R.*).

- *Known Authority Approach* (pp. 51, 53–60). If you start your research knowing the citation of a constitutional provision, case, statute, or administrative regulation relevant to your research problem, or if you find one through your preliminary reading of secondary sources, you will probably find it most helpful to start your primary-source research by reading the known constitutional provision, case, statute, or regulation.

  With known cases, statutes, and constitutional provisions, you can then use the case headnote information (*i.e.*, digest topic and Key or section number) and statutory annotations accompanying these authorities to locate additional primary authorities. With a known case, statute, or constitutional provision, you can also search a computerized legal data base (see Appendix A) or Shepardize (see Chapter 6) for cases dealing with it.

  When you have a known administrative regulation, you can find cases dealing with it by checking the annotations accompanying its authorizing statute; by checking a looseleaf service (useful primarily with federal regulations); by Shepardizing it (federal regulations only); by searching a computerized legal research data base for references to it; or by inquiring at the administrative agency responsible for promulgating the regulation.

To ensure thoroughness in your research, you should also supplement your "known authority" approach with a "descriptive word or fact word" search.

● *Descriptive Word or Fact Word Approach* (pp. 46–51, 52). You should generally use this as your first approach in your primary-source research unless you start out already knowing the citation of a relevant primary authority. Look up your descriptive or fact words (see pp. 32–36) in the index for the applicable case digests, set of annotated statutes, or administrative code. The index will direct you to appropriate primary authorities.

● *Known Topic Approach* (pp. 60–63). Use this approach only if you feel quite confident you know what area of law your problem involves. If you think you know the area, go straight to the appropriate case digest topic and search its table of contents for relevant subtopics. With statutes and administrative regulations, turn directly to the appropriate subject-matter grouping within the statutory or administrative code.

● *Words and Phrases Approach* (pp. 63–65). Use this specialized approach if your research problem involves or turns on a legal definition of a term. Refer to the multi-volume publication *Words and Phrases,* or to the "Words and Phrases" topic or volume in a particular case digest series. Or search a computerized legal data base (see Appendix A) for cases defining the word or phrase in which you are interested.

● *Finding the Law Through Computerized Legal Research.* Computer-based legal research uses the same techniques for finding the law as discussed in this chapter, although adapted for the computer. Appendix A provides an introduction to computerized legal research.

● *Finding the Law Through Updating.* When you update the legal authorities you have discovered in your "finding the law" phase, you will also be finding new authorities. Consequently, updating the law is also a law-finding technique. Chapter 6 explains updating.

CHAPTER 5

Step Two: Reading the Law

> "One does not progress far into legal life without learning that there is no single right and accurate way of reading one case, or of reading a bunch of cases."[23]

Having found the law, your next step is to read it. Although this may seem rather mechanical—after all, what's so mysterious about reading a book?—reading law consists of more than merely passing printed words in front of your eyes. You need to decide what significance to attach to what you read. All law is not created equal: some law will be better for you than other law, and the real trick here is to evaluate properly what the "right" law is and whether it helps or hurts your case. This evaluation lies at the heart of a lawyer's work, and is crucial to the development of any legal argument. If you rely on "bad" law, you may as well rely on no law at all.

Once you locate a case, statute, administrative regulation, or constitutional provision, you must evaluate its usefulness to you. This analysis involves two steps: *internal* evaluation and *external* evaluation.

Evaluating the law:
Internal evaluation

An internal evaluation involves reading the particular legal authority you have found and determining whether, on its own terms, it applies to the fact situation in your research problem. The process consists of two

---

[23]Llewellyn, *Remarks on the Theory of Appellate Decision and the Rules or Canons About How Statutes Are To Be Construed*, 3 VAND. L. REV. 395, 395 (1950).

overlapping elements: first, an analysis of the facts of the authority to determine how similar they are to the facts of the research problem; and second, a determination of the authority's intended legal significance and impact with respect to the research problem. At this point, it's irrelevant whether the authority helps or hurts your position: in legal research, you need to understand the support for your opponent's position as well as for your own.

Cases. The need for an internal evaluation of judicial decisions is tied to the doctrine of *stare decisis*. This court-created doctrine says, essentially, that when a court has applied a rule of law to a set of facts, that legal rule will apply whenever the same set of facts is again presented to the court. In effect, cases with facts identical to those of a case already decided will (presumably) yield the same result as the earlier case. Among other things, *stare decisis* seeks to promote the even-handed administration of justice, ensure certainty and establish guidelines for individuals planning future conduct, and control the volume of litigation by letting parties know in advance how particular legal disputes would be resolved if they were commenced. Theoretically, a dispute will not be taken to court if the antagonists already know how it will turn out.

Given these considerations, the more *similarities* you find between your problem's facts and those of a decided case, the more likely that the decided case will determine your problem's outcome. Conversely, the more factual distinctions, the less likely that the decided case will control.

Whether you feel the facts of a particular court decision are analogous to your problem's will often depend on the level of generalization at which you operate and the degree of insight and creativity you bring to your research and analysis of the holdings of decided cases. Returning for a moment to the hypothetical fact pattern presented in Chapter 3 (see p. 33) will illustrate this point.

Recall that in that hypothetical landlord-tenant dispute, Tom Tenant complained to Laurie Landlord that cockroaches had overrun his apartment, making the dwelling impossible to live in. The landlord disclaimed any responsibility in the matter, and the tenant wanted to sue. Now imagine that in the tenant's jurisdiction there exists only one court decision dealing with landlord-tenant relations. That decision addresses a tenant's complaint about a cold apartment, and its holding states in its entirety:

A landlord must provide heat during the winter months adequate to permit a person to live in reasonable comfort.

At one limited level of generalization, a researcher would conclude that the case does not apply to Tom and Laurie's dispute. After all, the decided case involves heat, whereas their situation concerns little creatures running around making life unpleasant in Tom's apartment. Therefore, Tom's out of luck, you might conclude.

On another, more expansive level of generalization, however, a legal researcher could view the court decision as establishing a principle of landlord responsibility to assure tenants habitable dwellings. Under this view, whether the problem involves a faulty furnace or voracious vermin, the landlord has an obligation to fix the defect that makes the premises uninhabitable. Hence, Tom could win.

This technique of using analogy to evaluate the applicability of existing court decisions to new sets of facts lies at the core of the analytical process involved in lawyering. It is a creative process that makes lawyering more an art than a science, and as with any art, it requires practice to achieve mastery. As you work with this technique, simply keep firmly in mind that your goal is to find as many analogies and distinctions as possible, on as many levels of generalization as possible, between your immediate research problem and the court decisions you feel may bear on its resolution.

Statutes.[24] It's also necessary to perform an internal evaluation of statutes you feel may be relevant to your research problem, in order to determine whether they actually do apply. Although the term *stare decisis* is not used to explain the need for internally evaluating statutes, the underlying rationale is analogous: when a court holds that a statute applies to a particular fact pattern, that statute should be applied similarly to other similar fact patterns.

In addition, the actual internal evaluation process itself with respect to statutes is much like that for cases, although some differences exist. As with cases, the first step involves a factual consideration: do the "facts" of the statute resemble those of your research problem? Here, however, the "facts" are really the statutorily specified factual elements that must exist before the statute will apply to a particular legal problem.

Take, for example, a criminal statute using the following language to outlaw theft:

> It shall be unlawful for any person to obtain or exercise unauthorized control over the property of another person with intent to deprive him thereof.

[24]Unless otherwise noted, the principles discussed in this section on internal evaluation of statutes also apply to internally evaluating constitutional provisions, administrative regulations, and local ordinances.

In this instance, for the statute to apply, the facts that would have to exist in the research problem are:

- unauthorized control
- property of another
- intent to deprive

Thus, for example, the factual elements of theft would not be present when the owner of a watch gives it to a jeweler for repair: although the jeweler would have control over the property of another, that control would not be unauthorized and (presumably) the jeweler would not intend to deprive the owner of the watch. Hence, the statute wouldn't apply. But if someone were to break into the jewelry shop and take the watch to pawn it, there would be unauthorized control over another's property, along with (presumably) intent to deprive, and the statute evidently would apply.

Along with this process of factual analysis and comparison, you will need to evaluate the legal significance of the precise words used in the statute. Here, the goal is to determine the *legislative intent* behind the statute, *i.e.*, what effect the legislature intended the statute to have. The reason for undertaking this search follows from the general principle that bodies legally charged with creating law are entitled to deference with respect to the meaning of the law they create, so long as they act within the scope of their authority. When questions arise over the meaning of law created by other bodies of government, however, courts have the final responsibility for resolving them. With respect to statutory law, a court is legally charged with interpreting and then applying a given statute to effectuate the legislative intent the statute expresses (assuming the court does not find the statute constitutionally invalid). All legal researchers examining statutes engage in a similar search for legislative intent, but where a dispute occurs over statutory meaning that cannot be resolved short of litigation, a court will be the final arbiter for resolving the ambiguity and determining the statute's intended meaning.[25]

Ideally, every statute would be unambiguous on its face, *i.e.*, its

---

[25]As with statutes, legal researchers and courts must also determine the intent behind constitutional provisions, administrative regulations, and local ordinances, and they do so by looking to the intent of the authors: for statutes, that means looking to the records of the legislature; for constitutional provisions, it often means looking to the records of a constitutional convention and other contemporaneous writings, such as *The Federalist*; for administrative regulations, it means looking to records of the originating agency; and for ordinances, it means looking to records of the local legislative body (*e.g.*, city council, town board) that enacted the ordinance. Except for this difference in sources of intent, the problems in and techniques for evaluating constitutional provisions, administrative regulations, and ordinances are essentially the same as those for statutes (discussed in the text).

words would never be subject to more than one reasonable reading. Words, however, are imprecise tools. So in reality, the problem of statutory ambiguity arises frequently. Justice Felix Frankfurter addressed this problem in an instructive article on the process of reading statutes:

> [L]aws are not abstract propositions. They are expressions of policy arising out of specific situations and addressed to the attainment of particular ends. The difficulty is that the legislative ideas which laws embody are both explicit and immanent. And so the bottom problem is: What is below the surface of the words and yet fairly a part of them? Words in statutes are not unlike words in a foreign language in that they too have "associations, echoes, and overtones." Judges must retain the associations, hear the echoes, and capture the overtones.[26]

Thus, although the "civics class" principle stated earlier—that legislatures make laws and courts interpret them—is a sound starting point, it vastly oversimplifies the matter. As Professor William Statsky puts it in his book *Legislative Analysis: How to Use Statutes and Regulations*:

> The very attempt to add clarity, precision and meaning to legislative words by the courts inevitably puts the courts in the role of adding dimensions to those words. These dimensions take on the characteristics of "new" laws. The theorist will argue that courts cannot make law because this is the responsibility of the legislature; the realist will counter that since the responsibility of construction is so broad (given the clumsiness of words), it is sometimes impossible to separate the functions of law creation and law interpretation.[27]

In short, a legal researcher whose problem involves a statute will frequently find it necessary to determine what the legislature intended to accomplish by enacting the statute. In general, your safest course is, simply, never to assume the words of a statute mean what they may at first blush appear to mean to you. Instead, you should always anticipate the possibility that the statute you're researching—even a seemingly clear one—contains the seeds of ambiguity. (Whether the statute is in fact ambiguous is ultimately for the court to say.)

Ambiguity may arise for two reasons:

- In enacting statutes, legislatures are always responding in some way to matters consciously before them at the time of enactment: the legislature seeks either to remedy a known problem or to achieve a known goal. In this situation, ambigu-

---

[26]Frankfurter, *Some Reflections on the Reading of Statutes*, 47 COLUM. L. REV. 527, 533 (1947) (citations omitted).
[27]W. STATSKY, LEGISLATIVE ANALYSIS 24 (1975).

ity may arise for the legal researcher because the precise facts of the research problem may not be explicitly mentioned in the statute. The issue here is whether the legislature nonetheless had a *conscious intent* to have the statute apply to those facts.

- As time passes after the statute's enactment, factual situations may arise that the legislature may not have, or perhaps could not have, consciously anticipated when it passed the statute. Suppose, for example, a 19th century legislature enacted a statute (still on the books) providing copyright protection for "written works." When the statute was passed, no legislator could have foreseen the advent of computers or written computer programs. Can a written computer program be copyrighted under the statute? Here, the legal researcher must *extrapolate* the legislature's intent to cover a situation it did not—indeed, could not—anticipate.

Whether seeking to determine either a legislature's *conscious intent* or its *extrapolated intent*, the legal researcher's task is to determine how narrowly or expansively, how literally or loosely, to read the statute.[28]

For example, does a statute prohibiting "pedestrians" from travelling on the shoulders of interstate highways prohibit a rider on horseback from trotting along those highways? Does a bribery statute prohibiting giving a public employee "anything of value in connection with the performance of his or her duties of office" prohibit lobbyists from giving expensive gifts to a government official at his retirement party, held during business hours of the official's last week of employment? Does a statute making it unlawful to threaten a person with a "dangerous weapon, including machine guns, rifles, pistols, knives, and switchblades" cover the brandishing of a broken, jagged glass bottle? (In other words, is the statute's list of dangerous weapons intended to be all-inclusive, making the statute inapplicable to threats made with broken glass used as the weapon? Or is the statutory list merely intended to be illustrative, so that it would embrace any sort of dangerous object used as a threatening weapon?)

In ascertaining what meaning a legislature intended a particular statute to have, a researcher has several tools available:

---

[28]As you may have noted, this task is the same one a researcher faces in doing an internal evaluation of a court decision to determine how narrowly or broadly to construe its legal holding. *See* pp. 80–81.

● The *language* itself of the statute serves as the starting point.

● The statute's *context* can reveal legislative intent. For example, in evaluating one sub-section of a statute, read the other sub-sections of the statute. In addition, look at a statute's placement in the statutory code: does the chapter in which the statute is contained reflect, as a whole, a particular purpose that may guide your understanding of the individual statutes within it?

Further, statutes often contain provisions defining their key words for the purpose of interpreting and applying the statutes. These definitions often provide important clues about what the legislature intended the statute to accomplish. Consequently, you should always look for such definitional provisions, which typically are found in either the specific statute itself, or in a special definitional statute within the chapter containing the statute you are evaluating. (Sometimes, you may also find definitions in a separate chapter containing definitions that apply to all statutes in the code. To find such a chapter, check in the statutory code index under "definitions," "construction of statutes," "words and phrases," or a similar heading.)

Finally, a special context-related point regarding administrative regulations (which in other respects are evaluated according to the same principles governing statutory evaluation): because an administrative regulation may not validly extend beyond the limits of the authorizing statute under which it is promulgated, the statute establishes the context for evaluating the regulation. Therefore, you should read the authorizing statute when evaluating an administrative regulation.

● A third guide in evaluating legislative intent behind a statute is the statute's *history*. For example, the addition or deletion of words in successive drafts of the statute before its enactment, as well as amendments made after its enactment, can be telling clues to the legislature's purpose in passing the statute.

With respect to both federal and state statutes, annotated statutory compilations normally contain historical notes briefly summarizing the provisions of amendments made to the statutes. Moreover, these historical notes following annotated statutes list the session laws which have amended the statutes, allowing the researcher to retrace each statute's development.

At the federal level, you can more fully reconstruct legislative history through research in several sources: (1) the *Congressional Record*, a daily report of congressional activity, speeches, and debates, published by the U.S. Government Printing Office; (2) Congressional Information Service's reference works, which contain detailed indexes and abstracts summarizing legislation and related congressional documents; (3) the *Congressional Index*, a weekly looseleaf service published by Commerce Clearing House that indexes all legislation introduced in Congress; (4) the *U.S. Code Congressional and Administrative News*, a West publication that reprints enacted laws and some congressional committee reports relating to major pieces of legislation; and (5) congressional committee reports, transcripts of committee hearings, and other congressional documents. There are also miscellaneous legislative histories compiled for specific purposes by both the government and various private publishers.

At the state level, the written record of legislative history tends to be sparse. Normally it can be found only in bill files (that is, files in which notes and drafts pertaining to pieces of proposed legislation are collected), which are frequently stored in a central legislative reference or drafting bureau in the state capitol. In addition, legislative committees and their members may maintain separate notes and files on legislation they have considered.

Appendix K presents a detailed discussion of legislative history research, including explanations about legislative documents, the publications for identifying and finding those documents, and the research techniques involved.

Finally, as a practical matter, the need to trace the prior history of federal and state administrative regulations will not arise with great frequency. In general, though, reconstructing the history of federal administrative regulations will entail the following steps: researching in the *Code of Federal Regulations* and the *Federal Register*; tracing the legislative history of a particular regulation's authorizing statute; and in some instances, actually examining the relevant files at the agency involved. Of these techniques, researching legislative history behind statutes was discussed in the preceding paragraphs. For assistance in using the *Code of Federal Regulations* and the *Federal Register* to trace the histories of federal administrative regulations, consult *The Federal Register: What It Is And How To Use It,* a detailed and helpful publication of the Office of the Federal Register that is widely available in law libraries or from the Government Printing Office.[29]

As for state administrative regulations, compared to the system for promulgating, publishing, and indexing federal regulations, state systems seem primitive at best and are nonexistent at worst. If you need to research the history of a state administrative regulation, check with a law librarian to determine what materials may be available in your jurisdiction. You can also go directly to the government agency that promulgated the regulation and request assistance there.

In addition to a statute's language, context, and history as tools for ascertaining legislative intent, there are numerous formalized rules (often called *canons*) for construing statutes. Courts continue to pay deference to these well-known canons, so the legal researcher working with statutory law must be familiar with them. Nonetheless, these canons have a certain slippery quality to them, of which legal researchers also need to be aware. As Karl Llewellyn noted in his frequently cited *Vanderbilt Law Review* article on statutory construction:

> When it comes to presenting a proposed construction in court, there is an accepted conventional vocabulary. As in argument over points of case-law, the accepted convention still, unhappily requires discussion as if only one single correct meaning could exist. Hence there are two opposing canons on almost every point. . . .
>
> Plainly, to make any canon take hold in a particular instance, the construction contended for must be sold, essentially, by means other than the use of the canon: The good sense of the situation and a *simple* construction of the available language to achieve that sense, *by tenable means, out of the statutory language.*[30]

A sampling of Llewellyn's competing canons, which he gathered from reported court decisions and dubbed "thrust" and "parry," illustrates their slipperiness:[31]

---

[29]The address of the main Government Printing Office bookstore is 710 N. Capitol St., Washington, D.C. 20401. Branch bookstores are located in major cities throughout the country.

[30]Llewellyn, *supra* note 23, at 401 (emphasis in original).

[31]*Id.* at 401-05 (citations omitted).

Thrust	Parry
• "A statute cannot go beyond its text."	• "To effect its purpose a statute may be implemented beyond its text."
• "If language is plain and unambiguous it must be given effect."	• "Not when literal interpretation would lead to absurd or mischievous consequences or thwart manifest purpose."
• "Words and phrases which have received judicial construction before enactment are to be understood according to that construction."	• "Not if the statute clearly requires them to have a different meaning."
• "Every word and clause must be given effect."	• "If inadvertently inserted or if repugnant to the rest of the statute, they may be rejected as surplusage."
• "The same language used repeatedly in the same connection is presumed to bear the same meaning throughout the statute."	• "This presumption will be disregarded where it is necessary to assign different meanings to make the statute consistent."
• "Words are to be interpreted according to the proper grammatical effect of their arrangement within the statute."	• "Rules of grammar will be disregarded where strict adherence would defeat purpose."
• "Punctuation will govern when a statute is open to two constructions."	• "Punctuation marks will not control the plain and evident meaning of language."
• "Expression of one thing excludes another."	• "The language may fairly comprehend many different cases where some only are expressly mentioned by way of example."

Our discussion of how to interpret and construe statutes serves as an introduction to the fundamental principles and common pitfalls in reading statutory law. For a more in-depth treatment of the subject, the legal researcher can turn to several helpful sources. The Llewellyn and Frankfurter law review articles excerpted earlier in this chapter provide excellent scholarly perspectives on the subject of statutory construction. Professor F. Reed Dickerson's book titled *The Interpretation and Application of Statutes* is a longer, scholarly treatment of statutory construction. Professor William Statsky's *Legislative Analysis and Drafting* (2d ed. 1984) is a classroom-oriented introductory text on reading and analyzing statutes. Finally, Sutherland's multi-volume work titled *Statutory Construction* is a well-known and widely used reference tool that offers practical assistance in researching specific problems involving statutory construction.

Evaluating the law: External evaluation

If your internal evaluation (discussed in the preceding section) reveals that a legal authority your research has uncovered applies to your problem, you will then need to conduct an external evaluation of that authority. This evaluation requires you to determine the *current status* (*i.e.*, validity) of the authority.

For statutes and administrative regulations, this process includes determining whether the legislature or administrative agency has repealed or amended the statute or regulation, and whether court decisions have interpreted, limited, or invalidated the statute or regulation. In your research, you will occasionally come across court-invalidated statutes and regulations still in the books. This seeming anomaly occurs because a court declaration that a statute or regulation is unconstitutional does not automatically remove it physically from the books. Although an invalidated statute (or regulation) will be unenforceable to the extent of its invalidity, it will continue to appear in the written law until the legislature (or administrative agency) actually repeals it. Therefore, to avoid relying on invalid law, you must always conduct an external evaluation of statutes and regulations.

Similarly, you need to determine the current status of court decisions you think may be relevant to your research problem. Here, the external evaluation initially focuses on how subsequent court decisions have interpreted and applied your principal cases. Even well-settled cases of long standing may be overruled or limited by subsequent court decisions; case reporters are full of such modifications and reversals.

That's why, even when decided cases may appear (because of *stare decisis*) to dictate the result in your problem, you always need to do an external evaluation of the status of *all* your relevant cases.

Up to this point, the process described of external evaluation of statutes and court decisions overlaps substantially with the final step in legal research—updating the law—which is treated in the next chapter. That is, both external evaluation and updating overlap to the extent that each focuses on whether a particular legal authority is still technically valid law.

External evaluation (as we will be concerned with it in this chapter) also performs another important function, however: even if the particular authority has not been overruled, repealed, or otherwise invalidated, to be thorough you should nonetheless extend your external evaluation to include *setting the case or statute you've found in its broader legal context*. Here, your goal is to determine whether someone—you or your opponent—relying on that authority would be standing on solid or shaky legal ground. Some of the questions you would ask yourself as you examine cases and statutes are:

- Does a case represent simply one more routine application of a well-settled legal rule to a new set of facts? Or does it represent a new rule or an innovative twist on an old rule?

- Where a statute is involved, is it merely a legislative codification of a common law rule, or is it a departure? If a departure, how significant a departure is it?

- Does the case or statute reflect a novel policy or doctrine responding to emerging social conditions? Or does it reflect an archaic legal principle falling into increasing disfavor, perhaps because it no longer responds to changing social conditions?

Answering such questions will help you evaluate how strong or weak your (or your opponent's) position would be if based on the authorities you are evaluating. For example, the answers may suggest that the courts in your jurisdiction are considering departing from the precedents applicable to your research problem, and may be ready to modify or overrule an established legal principle.

In assessing how to answer the questions raised in this phase of your external evaluation, you should read recent court decisions interpreting or applying the primary authority you are evaluating, or which deal generally with the same issues. You can locate such court decisions through the updating techniques discussed in the next chapter.

You may also find it helpful, however, to turn to secondary

sources—*i.e.*, the legal literature that comments on primary sources.[32] Generally you'll find secondary sources most helpful when you research in a changing or unsettled area of the law. In addition to providing "instant" background at the outset of a research project (as discussed in Chapter 4), they often serve at later research stages to put primary sources in a broader legal context and help researchers see or develop connections between seemingly disparate legal principles and authorities. The secondary sources you will find most useful in this later stage are:

- treatises and hornbooks
- law reviews
- *Restatements of the Law*
- *A.L.R.* annotations

Secondary sources are discussed in more detail in Chapter 4 under "A Generalized Approach" (pp. 65–74).

Briefing cases

As you proceed with the reading phase of your legal research, you'll need to take notes. General pointers about note-taking are covered in Chapter 7. The art of taking notes on court decisions, however, has been refined over the years into a widely accepted technique, called "briefing," which serves both as an efficient means of recording notes and as an additional analytical tool. Briefing, as a specialized form of note-taking, is covered here.

Initially, summarizing cases may seem like a difficult, time-consuming, and perhaps unnecessary step, and you will probably find yourself tempted to avoid it altogether. Nonetheless, experience has shown briefing to be a valuable step in library research. Without some structured way of recording the cases you consider significant to your problem, you won't remember all the results of your research and will have to retrace your steps. Thus, the effort expended on briefing will ultimately save you work. Moreover, reading a case requires the researcher's close attention to extract all the implications of the court's decision, and briefing will assist you in focusing on the crucial aspects of a case and sorting out its helpful from its unhelpful points. Consequently, briefing is an especially useful analytical device for inexperienced researchers, for whom reading cases is normally a difficult and confusing process.

[32] Primary and secondary authorities were defined and distinguished at p. 41.

Briefing is a technique you can master with practice. As you do it, you'll develop your own unique briefing style that will best serve your purposes. Ultimately, your briefs will become shorter and more stream-lined, and include fewer elements. At the beginning, though, your briefs will probably seem (to you, anyway) like small books.

As a general guide, a brief should usually not run longer than a page. But no matter how short or long your brief, you should prepare it with an eye on certain elements in the case. A *comprehensive* brief would include:

• Name of the case

• Citation (including parallel citations, *i.e.*, citations to other re-porters reprinting the case)

• Date the decision was rendered

• Vote (*i.e.*, how many judges voted for and against the deci-sion)

• Author of the majority opinion

• Author(s) of concurring opinion(s), if any

• Author(s) of dissenting opinion(s), if any

• Procedural posture of the case

• Legal topic(s) covered by the case

• Summary of the facts

• Question(s) presented by the case (you should phrase each question so it can be answered with simply a "yes" or "no")

• Answer(s) to the question(s) presented

• Summary of the court's reasoning in reaching the answer(s)

• Summary of significant concurring opinion(s), if any

• Summary of significant dissenting opinion(s), if any

• Significance of the case (both in general and as it applies to your particular problem)

Not all of these points need be included in every brief. As you gain experience in reading and analyzing cases, you will develop your own sense of what to include in or omit from a brief. For illustration, a case (*Brown v. Board of Education*) and a sample brief of *Brown* appear as Appendix E in Part III of this book. Reading *Brown* and the accompany-ing brief should assist you in understanding how the briefing technique works.

Finally, note that you will generally brief a case most effectively if you read the case all the way through at least once before you even start to prepare a brief. If you begin to brief before you finish a preliminary reading of the entire case, you are apt to find that you have briefed unnecessary, irrelevant, or even inaccurate points of law or interpretations.

Summary of reading the law

The following checklists summarize the key questions you should ask yourself as you read the law:

Internal evaluation. Do an internal evaluation first, to determine whether the authority applies to your research problem.

Cases

- How similar are the facts of the court decision to those of your research problem?
- If the decision's facts differ, but the decision's holding is helpful to your position, can you re-characterize the decision's facts at some level of generalization that increases their similarity to the facts of your problem? Alternatively, if the decision's facts are similar to your problem's but the decision's holding undermines your position, can you re-characterize (*i.e.*, distinguish) the facts of the decision in a way that emphasizes distinctions, so that the holding will seem less relevant?
- If you conclude that a decision's facts are sufficiently similar to those of your research problem to make the decided case relevant, is the decision's holding relevant to any legal issues present in your problem?

Statutes

- Do the factual elements that trigger the statute's application parallel the facts of your problem?
- If the statute appears factually relevant to your problem, what is the statute's legal significance for your problem, *i.e.*, did the legislature intend the statute to apply to your situation?
- If the words of the statute are ambiguous, leaving its legal significance unclear, what legislative intent can you glean from evaluating the statute's language in light of the statute's context and legislative history?

External evaluation. If your internal evaluation reveals that a case or statute applies to your problem, you will then need to conduct an external evaluation of the authority to determine its current status, *i.e.*, validity.

- Has the case been overruled or otherwise severely limited? Has the statute been legislatively repealed or judicially invalidated? Answering these inquiries involves using the updating techniques discussed in Chapter 6—that is, Shepardizing; checking pocket parts, supplements, and looseleaf services; and, if you have access to a computerized legal research service, searching its data base for more recent authorities.

- If the case or statute has not been explicitly overruled, repealed, or otherwise invalidated, what is its current stature in the law? Would someone relying on the authority be standing on solid or shaky ground? Answering these questions also involves using the updating techniques covered in Chapter 6 to find recent cases discussing the case or statute under consideration. In addition, you may also find it helpful to turn to secondary sources such as treatises and law reviews (which are discussed in Chapter 4 under "A Generalized Approach") for their commentary, if any, on the authority.

Conclusion

By keeping in mind the points covered in this chapter, you should find that the "reading the law" phase of your legal research will take on a purpose and direction that will place the results of your "finding the law" phase in perspective. Moreover, reading the law effectively will help you think of new avenues of research to carry your "finding the law" process forward, resulting in the most thorough research possible.

CHAPTER 6

Step Three: Updating the Law

Analytically, the final step in doing legal research is updating the law. This step involves making sure the legal rules you've determined apply to your problem are still valid law. One of the worst blunders you can commit is to draw your legal conclusions or present your legal argument or theory based on your research findings, then learn—too late— that you should have discovered a subtle but significant change in the applicable law that occurred a week earlier. Because outdated law is worse than no law at all, your legal research must include careful attention to updating the legal authorities that govern your problem.[33]

This chapter covers the ways in which legal authorities are kept up to date, including:

- Shepardizing
- pocket parts and supplements
- looseleaf reporter services
- computerized searches

Shepardizing a case

This section could be sub-titled, "What you don't know about Shepardizing could be hazardous to the health of your legal research." Shepardizing is the most widely used method of updating the law. It involves tracing the subsequent treatment of cases, statutes, and some other

---

[33]In addition to updating the authorities on which you plan to rely, you'll also find it a good practice to update the authorities on which your opponent relies. By doing so, you may discover that your opponent's position is actually predicated on outdated law.

legal authorities[34] by using reference works called *Shepard's Citations* (often referred to as "citators"). Although citators at first appear to be formidable and impenetrable, you'll feel comfortable using them after a little practice.

A portion of a page from a Shepard's citator is reprinted in Figure Y to show its appearance. (How to interpret it is explained below.)

How to use Shepard's. *Shepard's Citations* make it possible for legal researchers to ascertain a known authority's current status. To use a Shepard's citator, you must have already found a legal authority about whose status you are curious. For the purposes of Shepardizing, this known material—case, statute, or whatever—is called the *cited* authority. The entries appearing in Shepard's under the cited authority you're interested in (*i.e.*, that you are "Shepardizing") are called the *citing* authorities: that is, these authorities—such as cases, law review and *A.L.R.* articles, Attorney General Opinions—are citing to (*i.e.*, referring to) the item in whose treatment you're interested.

Shephardizing a case: illustration.[35] Suppose you've determined that the Wisconsin case of *State v. Yoder*, 49 Wis. 2d 430, 182 N.W.2d

---

[34]Legal materials that can be traced through *Shepard's Citations* include the following:
Federal
- U.S. Constitution
- Federal statutes (in both the *U.S. Code* and *Statutes at Large*)
- Reported federal cases
- Federal administrative regulations (in the *Code of Federal Regulations*)
- Federal court rules
- Selected federal administrative decisions (*e.g.*, Securities and Exchange Commission)
- Patents, trademarks, and copyright citations and decisions
- Federal labor law cases and administrative decisions
- Opinions of the U.S. Attorney General
- Treaties and other international agreements
State
- State constitutions
- State statutes (in both codes and session laws)
- Reported state cases
- State court rules
- Opinions of the state Attorneys General
- Municipal charters and ordinances
Miscellaneous
- *Restatements of the Law*
- Law reviews
- American Bar Association Standards of Criminal Justice

[35]We've chosen a court decision to illustrate the Shepardizing process. Shepardizing other kinds of legal authorities simply involves substituting those authorities as the starting point, and then using the same general steps—finding the correct citator set and volumes, and so forth—as those for Shepardizing cases. These steps are explained in our Shepardizing illustration.

$-193-$ (181NW527)	q83W^{4}642	69W^{6}655		59MqL115
55W^{10}220	q83W^{4}664	70W^{1}98	$-330-$ (182NW551)	$-415-$ (182NW441)
61W^{7}382	85W^{3}767	70W^{6}101	58W^{4}722	49W^{5}713
61W^{7}453	86W^{4}430	70W^{6}185	60W^{5}274	65W^{2}766
61W^{7}523	$-255-$ (181NW487)	70W^{7}289	84W^{5}607	2Æ155s
64W^{7}227		70W^{1}290	82Æ473s	
65W104	$-263-$ (182NW512)	70W^{6}309	$-350-$ (182NW497)	$-430-$ (182NW539)
75W^{10}641	j50W^{7}116	71W^{4}99	50W730	a406US205
60MqL222	50W^{6}400	73W^{7}408	52W^{4}707	a32LE15
32Æ661s	50W^{3}403	73W^{7}610	53W769	a92SC1526
$-209-$ (181NW369)	50W^{4}403	73W^{9}683	55W^{4}486	s402US994
		73W^{4}708		
		73W^{6}708		
		e74W^{3}104		

Source: Shepard's Inc. of Colorado Springs © 1979

Figure Y. Extract of a Shepard's Citator Page

539 (1971), applies to your research problem. You will need to find out how courts have interpreted and applied *Yoder* since it was originally decided. In this example, *Yoder* would be the "cited case"; the subsequent cases referring to *Yoder* would be the "citing" cases. To Shepardize *Yoder* (or any other case), you would follow the steps outlined below.

A preliminary word of warning is in order, however. With sufficient practice, Shepardizing becomes a simple process, but in the beginning it can seem somewhat overwhelming. Each step in Shepardizing is discussed in detail in the explanation that follows because it is essential for the legal researcher to understand the process thoroughly in order to avoid making mechanical errors in using the citator volumes, thus rendering the entire effort useless. Nonetheless, you should not feel that you must absorb all the details covered here on your first reading. Skim through this section as an introduction and then head to the library to try your hand at Shepardizing, using this book as a guide.

Step 1. Find the proper set of *Shepard's Citations*. There are numerous sets of *Shepard's Citations*, only one of which will work for any given authority you are Shepardizing.

Shepard's publishes separate citator sets for:

- U.S. Supreme Court decisions (this Shepard's set also treats the U.S. Constitution, federal statutes, and the *Code of Federal Regulations*)
- *Federal Reporter* (both F. and F.2d)
- *Federal Supplement* (this Shepard's set also treats *Federal Rules Decisions*)
- each state
- West's regional reporters

There are also separate Shepard's citators for other legal authorities (*e.g.*, law reviews), but the federal and state case and statute citators are the ones you are apt to use most frequently.

To determine if you've located the set of *Shepard's Citations* appropriate for your problem, check the cover of the hardbound citator volume, where the set's title will be stamped in gold on the binding and front cover. For the example of *State v. Yoder*, a Wisconsin case, you would need the citator set entitled *Shepard's Wisconsin Citations*.

Step 2. Make sure you have all the necessary volumes in the appropriate citator set. Many sets of *Shepard's Citations* contain more than one volume, not all of which may treat the material you are Shepardizing.

Shepard's sets often have separate volumes for cases and statutes. Consequently, if you are Shepardizing a case, you need to use the volumes for Shepardizing cases, *not* the volumes for Shepardizing statutes; conversely, of course, you use only the statute volumes when Shepardizing a statute.

Also note that each volume in a citator set covers a different period during which the authority you are Shepardizing has been mentioned in other (*i.e.*, "citing") authorities. For instance, the Shepard's citator set for a particular state may have two volumes—one (let's say) covering citing cases decided from 1848 through 1971, and the other covering citing cases decided from 1972 to the present. If you were Shepardizing a case decided in that state in 1968, you would need to use both Shepard's volumes in that set. On the other hand, if you were Shepardizing a case decided in 1975, you would need to use only the second volume (covering 1972 to the present) because a 1975 court decision obviously would not be mentioned in a case decided between 1848 and 1971.

In other words, to Shepardize a given case for the entire period since its issuance, you may need to check several volumes in a citator set. To ensure that you are using the right volumes, examine (in the order listed) the following citator features:

● Locate the most recent paperbound supplement to your citator set.[36] Check the box in the lower right-hand corner on its

---

[36]Unless your citator set has been re-published recently in a hardbound volume, your set will have one or more paperbound supplement volumes. Each supplement has its month of issuance printed on the cover. Most citators are supplemented at least every two months. If your most recent supplement is more than two months old, check inside the supplement for the frequency of supplementation. If this information shows that the set should include a more recent pamphlet and you cannot find it, check with the librarian to find out if the library has received the supplement. In any event, you will be aware that you haven't completed your Shepardizing until you've checked the missing supplements.

front cover. This box, labelled "What Your Library Should Contain," lists all the volumes in the set that you might need to Shepardize your type of cited authority. Figure Z shows this box on the cover of a paperbound supplement to *Shepard's Wisconsin Citations*. If the supplement illustrated in Figure Z were the most recent supplement to *Shepard's Wisconsin Citations* at the time you were Shepardizing *State v. Yoder*, you would collect *all* the volumes listed in the box as necessary for Shepardizing cases. Thus, as the information in the box indicates, you would retrieve the 1979 bound volume for cases and the supplements dated February and March 1986.

● For each of the volumes you have collected, check the scope information on the cover (and, for hardbound volumes, on the spine). If the authority you are Shepardizing falls within the scope of the authorities listed there, you will need that citator volume in doing your Shepardizing. The scope information in Figure Z shows that the illustrated citator volume would be used to Shepardize all Wisconsin cases. This citator volume would therefore treat our illustrative case of *State v. Yoder*.

In some citator sets, such as those for federal courts, the large number of reported cases requires Shepard's to issue more than one volume (not counting supplements) for Shepardizing cases. When that occurs, instead of indicating that a citator volume covers all cases, the scope information on the cover or spine would show the specific range of cited cases you could Shepardize in that citator volume. For example, in the citator set for United States Supreme Court decisions, the scope information might show that one citator volume permits Shepardizing cases reported in volumes 1 through 313 of *United States Reports*, while a second citator volume permits Shepardizing cases in volumes 314 through 347 of *United States Reports*.

Step 3. Once you have selected the right Shepard's citator set and have collected all the necessary volumes in that set, next make sure you are Shepardizing in the correct tables of citations in those volumes. (The tables are the columns of small type, as illustrated in Figures AA and BB on pages 102 and 103.) To locate the correct table, you may find it helpful to check each citator volume's "Table of Contents" for the starting page of the tables that treat the series of the case reporter containing the case you're Shepardizing.

| VOL. 78 | MARCH, 1986 | NO. 6 |

Shepard's
WISCONSIN
Citations

) title of
citator set

(USPS 656270)

ADVANCE SHEET EDITION
CASES AND STATUTES

} scope
information,
indicating
what
authorities
you can
Shepardize
in this
volume

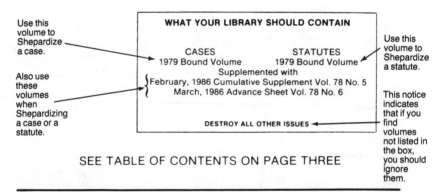

Use this
volume to
Shepardize
a case.

Also use
these
volumes
when
Shepardizing
a case or a
statute.

WHAT YOUR LIBRARY SHOULD CONTAIN

CASES   STATUTES
1979 Bound Volume   1979 Bound Volume
Supplemented with
} February, 1986 Cumulative Supplement Vol. 78 No. 5
March, 1986 Advance Sheet Vol. 78 No. 6

DESTROY ALL OTHER ISSUES

Use this
volume to
Shepardize
a statute.

This notice
indicates
that if you
find
volumes
not listed in
the box,
you should
ignore
them.

SEE TABLE OF CONTENTS ON PAGE THREE

SHEPARD'S/McGRAW-HILL
P. O. BOX 1235, COLORADO SPRINGS, COLO. 80901-1235

Figure Z. Front Cover of a Supplement to *Shepard's Wisconsin Citations*

Finding the correct citator tables is essential. Many case reporters are divided into consecutive *series,* and it's easy to Shepardize in the wrong series. For example, California Reports appears in three series: Cal., Cal. 2d, and Cal. 3d. If you were Shepardizing a case reported in Cal. 2d, you could easily turn by accident to the Shepard's table for cases reported in Cal. or Cal. 3d, when you should actually be using *only* the Cal. 2d tables.

The following warning signals may alert you that you are Shepardizing in the wrong tables:

• The case you are Shepardizing doesn't appear in the table.

• The volume number and page number of your case appear in the table, but the parenthetical parallel citation listed as the first entry under them differs from the one you know is the correct parallel citation for the case you are Shepardizing. (See steps 4 and 5, below, regarding how to locate volume and page numbers in Shepard's tables.)

• When you read the cases listed in the Shepard's volume as having mentioned the case you are Shepardizing, you don't find any reference to your case.

If you encounter any of these situations, go back and make sure you were Shepardizing in the correct table. If you were Shepardizing correctly according to the citation you have, then re-check the accuracy of your citation.

In finding the correct citator table, *parallel citations* present another "kink." (In the example of *State v. Yoder,* "182 N.W.2d 539" would be the parallel citation to "49 Wis. 2d 430.") Just as Shepard's citators have separate tables for each series *(e.g.,* Wis., Wis. 2d) of a given reporter system, the citators have separate tables for the different reporters *(e.g.,* the system of Wisconsin reporters, the system of North Western reporters) in which a case appears. Although you might think that the citations found in the table for the parallel reference would simply duplicate the ones found in the table for the primary reference, that isn't always a safe assumption.

For example, suppose a judge in Oregon referred to our illustrative case of *State v. Yoder* in his or her decision. The judge probably read *State v. Yoder* in its N.W.2d version rather than its Wis. 2d version. (It's much less expensive for libraries to purchase regional reporters than to purchase individual reporters for other states.) If the Oregon judge chose to cite *State v. Yoder* to only its N.W.2d version, the Oregon case would only refer to "182 N.W.2d 539" and would appear in the Wisconsin case edition of *Shepard's Citations* only in the tables for N.W.2d, *not*

Vol. 49   WISCONSIN REPORTS, 2d SERIES

85Æ1111s	– 246 –	60W⁶129	84W⁶324	49W⁴734	66AG139	65W⁶720	64Æ1297n
33Æ317s	(181NW490)	61W⁹24	84W⁶338	49W⁸734		f66W⁵109	
	50W²78	61W³295	j85W⁴588	50W⁷68	– 488 –	f66W⁶109	– 625 –
– 180 –	50W²729	61W⁹296	86W⁴432	53W³802	(182NW229)	67W⁶527	(183NW1)
(181NW346)	51W²269	61W¹542	86W⁴464	53W⁸802		f69W⁵548	
65W¹48	51W³269	61W⁷542	570F2d⁷1135	64W²579	– 491 –	f74W⁴110	– 638 –
	53W⁴89	62W⁶219	56MqL75	58MqL640	(182NW245)	76W³26	(183NW29)
– 185 –	53W³786	j62W⁴16	59MqL135	43Æ299n	52W³789	76W⁶326	US reh den
(181NW364)	55W⁵6	62W⁵33			70W⁸302	80W⁵143	in405US981
49W¹387	e55W²309	63W⁶130	– 299 –	– 392 –	d70W⁶572	j80W⁶179	s404US1063
[49W¹734	55W²480	63W¹310	(182NW481)	(182NW238)	81W²452	61AG142	s30LÆ751
[49W²734	55W³481	64W⁷421	54W⁵57	(70Æ3625)	59MqL52	1Æ1291s	s92SC735
51W²248	56W³695	f64W⁴496	63W⁵93	62W¹697	25Æ833s	33Æ17s	cc496F2d441
53W¹775	57W²506	64W⁴552	f65W²561	74W¹5			cc354FS805
53W²775	59W²³131	65W¹50	65W³567	476F2d⁴119	– 501 –	– 551 –	51W⁴673
53W¹802	60W²536	65W³82	f65W¹⁰570	506F2d⁴1150	(182NW459)	(182NW267)	51W³692
55W³191	62W²05	65W⁴664	65W⁶647	336FS²468	51W¹85	54W⁴452	51W⁴705
56W⁵716	63W⁴399	65W⁷728	67W⁷168	402FS³782	51W⁶06	55W²76	51W⁴711
57W³29	63W²481	65W⁸728	67W⁴406	37Æ7s	f65W⁶652	55W⁴77	51W³712
70W⁵185	63W²776	66W⁵29	70W⁵409	69Æ169n	73W³463	61W³08	56W⁴33
75W⁵69	64W²43	66W⁴117	72W⁶18	69Æ371n	81W⁸580	58MqL632	61W³362
82W²341	64W²53	66W³117	78W⁷271		60AG451		61W⁴364
58MqL640	64W²388	66W³252	83W⁴56	– 398 –	61AG147	– 565 –	413US⁴56
96Æ768s	68W⁸242	66W⁴252	85W³460	(42Æ1341)	63AG26	(182NW466)	37LÆ⁴456
33Æ335s	68W⁴646	67W⁸543	60AG246	f50W³168	66AG42	US cert den	93SC⁴2634
43Æ299n	71W⁷617	69W³265	60AG252	507F2d²545		in404US838	326FS1318
43Æ307n	76W²55	69W⁴78	63AG308	61AG377	– 513 –	58W¹683	
	83W²02	69W⁴512	63AG353	59MqL115	(182NW232)	60W⁷20	– 647 –
– 193 –	q83W⁴642	69W⁴655			54W⁴103	68W⁴235	(183NW93)
(181NW527)	q83W⁴664	70W¹98	– 330 –	– 415 –	54W⁸471	68W⁶235	f83W³616
55W¹⁰220	85W³767	70W⁴101	(182NW551)	(182NW441)	f54W⁶87	68W³250	408US¹686
61W⁷382	86W⁴430	70W⁴185	58W⁴722	49W⁸713	55W⁸406	70W⁸725	e408US²704
61W⁷453		70W⁷289	60W⁵274	65W²766	56W⁵393	71W⁵80	33LÆ¹642
61W⁷523	– 255 –	70W¹290	84W⁵607	2Æ155s	59W⁷125	73W⁸499	e33LÆ²652
64W⁷227	(181NW487)	70W⁴309	82Æ473s		59W³127	74W²62	92SC²2659
65W¹04		71W⁴99		– 430 –	f59W⁹211	74W⁶655	e92SC³2668
75W¹⁰641	– 263 –	73W⁷408	– 350 –	(182NW226)	64W⁸603	76W⁴505	332FS¹941
60MqL222	(182NW512)	73W⁷610	(182NW497)	a406US205	64W¹608	84W⁴23	58MqL550
32Æ661s	j50W⁷116	73W⁷683	50W⁷30	a32LÆ15	65W⁹768	84W¹51	71WLR951
	50W⁸400	73W⁴708	52W⁴707	a92SC1526	70W³733	85W⁶189	71WLR1120
– 209 –	50W³403	73W⁴708	53W⁷69	s402US994	70W⁸12	85W⁴757	70McL230
(181NW369)	50W⁴403	e74W⁴104	55W⁴486	s29LÆ160	71W¹810	72McL733	52TxL880
50W¹¹100	50W⁸692	j74W⁹143	58W²4	s91SC2173	75W⁴457	71Æ449s	7Æ3591s
52W¹743	50W⁸694	74W⁸267	63W²687	55W⁴353	82W⁴771	45Æ965n	
53W⁵428	51W⁴89	75W⁶9	69W¹574	63W⁴137	85W¹630	45Æ974n	– 662 –
53W⁵468	f51W⁸658	75W⁴247	69W²574	j556F2d⁴325	85W²631	82Æ254n	(183NW101)
59W¹190	d52W⁷500	75W⁸518	j69W¹600	j556F2d³326	85W²631	82Æ277n	
59W⁸191	52W⁶699	75W⁴519	j84W⁴196	83Æ1032s	83Æ1032s		– 667 –
59W⁴192	53W⁴455	f75W⁶530	86W³33			– 591 –	(183NW47)
59W¹494	53W⁷456	f75W⁷530	91Æ1046s	– 523 –	– 591 –	(182NW448)	56W³853
59W³503	53W¹481	75W⁷642		(182NW231)	(182NW231)	52W⁹391	71W550
64W⁷128	53W⁴562	75W⁸643	– 361 –	– 526 –	– 526 –	f55W¹686	72W⁴08
74W⁵264	54W⁸248	76W⁵275	(182NW262)	(182NW502)	(182NW257)	70W⁶751	78W⁶578
83W²47	54W⁸248	76W¹281	49W¹382	49W¹382	51W⁷372	70W⁶1037	82W⁴74
86W¹63	54W²248	76W²281	50W⁶8	50W⁶8	55W³423	82W⁶113	82W²477
e329FS⁷19	54W²249	76W⁴282	52W¹655	53W²479	59W⁷440	83W⁹842	82W³477
	54W²249	f76W⁴310	52W⁵656	58W⁴560	18Æ497s	18Æ497s	82W⁵478
– 220 –	54W⁶249	76W¹364	52W⁶661	89Æ540s			324FS²360
(181NW481)	54W³368	76W⁴364	53W¹544		– 537 –	– 612 –	33Æ1164s
53W⁵96	54W⁷464	f76W³530	j57W⁷35	– 463 –	(182NW282)	(182NW251)	
58W³14	54W⁴480	f76W⁹530	70W¹385	(182NW226)	50W⁸427	d56W¹811	– 678 –
68W²545	54W⁴573	77W⁴56	70W³385	d54W³518	53W¹332	j60W⁹171	(183NW8)
	d54W⁹577	f77W⁴175	76CR1073	59MqL694	53W³490		62W⁶04
– 231 –	e54W²618	f77W⁴175	89Æ540s	60MqL272	53W⁷781	– 678 –	71W¹580
(181NW345)	e54W⁴619	77W⁴419			54W¹467	(183NW8)	96Æ1292s
	54W²757	78W¹212	– 372 –	– 469 –	f54W³762	f85W²117	
– 233 –	55W¹8	78W³370	(182NW242)	(182NW276)	56W⁹733	f85W³117	– 683 –
(181NW418)	55W⁴9	79W¹239	51W³535		f56W⁴734	85W⁶192	(183NW11)
59Cor402	55W⁷129	79W⁷239	52W³483	– 481 –	59W³281	9WTA397	d52W⁴705
	55W⁷761	80W⁶146	f54W³478	(182NW225)	62W590	82Æ254n	53W³557
– 237 –	f56W⁶550	81W⁹297	57W³510			82Æ271n	53W709
(181NW413)	56W716	81W⁴473	63W³95	– 484 –	– 623 –		e54W³689
76W⁶43	d56W⁷737	82W⁹73		(182NW289)	(182NW291)		54W³748
19Æ520s	57W¹775	82W⁴622	– 379 –	62W616	51W¹552		55W²463
	57W⁸775	84W⁴65	(182NW505)	76W³175	52W¹120		58MqL648
	59W³33	f84W⁶152	f49W³458	83W²875	54W¹465		*Continued*

Figure AA.   Sample Page of Shepard's Tables (Wis. 2d Tables)

Vol. 178   NORTHWESTERN REPORTER, 2d SERIES (Wisconsin Cases)

Column 1

294NW^{3}443
e297NW^{3}497
478FS^{2}844
- 35 -
284NW^{3}678
289NW303
309NW^{3}23
- 56 -
291NW^{2}594
- 67 -
d304NW^{1}147
e313NW^{4}792
Vol. 179
- 641 -
318NW^{3}785
318NW^{1}789
- 777 -
Case 2
284NW^{3}40
284NW^{4}40
325NW^{18}707
- 784 -
e275NW^{1}99
292NW^{1}625
j292NW628
- 786 -
286NW^{7}577
597F2d^{5}562
597F2d^{2}563
- 797 -
291NW837
- 800 -
f321NW^{2}312
321NW^{1}313
- 805 -
275NW726
275NW^{6}728
313NW^{1}862
313NW^{2}862
- 836 -
486FS^{7}629
- 846 -
277NW^{3}152
277NW^{6}153
278NW^{4}891
e278NW^{6}893
- 851 -
279NW^{9}725
f285NW^{4}742
325NW^{4}691
- 855 -
277NW^{11}141
288NW^{1}841
288NW^{3}841
299NW^{1}208
313NW^{1}72
- 864 -
304NW^{2}166
532FS^{2}1352

Column 2

- 872 -
f274NW^{4}690
278NW^{3}874
e278NW^{2}875
279NW^{5}178
f310NW599
f310NW^{4}600
321NW^{2}318
j445US910
j100SC1089
d597F2d^{4}599
c597F2d^{6}601
487FS^{4}1116
512FS^{4}1144
- 881 -
278NW896
278NW^{2}898
- 885 -
274NW^{6}686
275NW666
275NW^{7}667
280NW^{7}180
288NW^{6}110
294NW^{7}523
- 889 -
289NW^{2}575
- 921 -
292NW^{1}666
300NW^{2}880
309NW^{2}6
f311NW^{2}589
311NW^{1}634
- 924 -
275NW^{6}666
292NW^{6}635
Vol. 180
- 1 -
285NW^{4}611
295NW^{5}186
310NW611
- 513 -
j287NW728
287NW^{3}768
- 521 -
286NW^{1}576
291NW^{9}578
302NW^{7}420
474FS^{1}969
f504FS^{4}1213
- 525 -
284NW^{2}698
HHb Ex28
- 529 -
312NW867
- 538 -
297NW^{3}816
299NW303
- 546 -
f280NW^{1}162
290NW^{10}543

Column 3

- 556 -
f275NW^{3}639
f275NW^{4}640
- 562 -
277NW^{6}857
- 578 -
289NW^{5}301
289NW^{6}303
e319NW^{9}852
- 601 -
319NW^{2}852
- 605 -
278NW^{2}228
- 607 -
299NW^{5}275
- 627 -
284NW900
j284NW904
- 631 -
275NW^{1}117
- 697 -
291NW^{4}895
- 699 -
294NW^{6}527
- 707 -
299NW^{1}638
- 735 -
279NW^{13}197
283NW^{14}624
283NW^{13}625
- 743 -
275NW^{4}689
275NW^{6}689
278NW^{8}840
295NW186
j307NW672
Vol. 181
- 346 -
286NW^{1}594
- 351 -
f686F2d^{5}466
- 355 -
279NW725
283NW^{3}463
284NW^{6}664
293NW^{9}483
- 364 -
285NW^{2}734
286NW^{5}562
- 374 -
285NW^{1}736
291NW^{2}459
- 383 -
14MJ541

Column 4

- 388 -
278NW^{3}866
280NW^{4}191
e291NW837
- 393 -
280NW^{9}160
- 400 -
306NW62
- 403 -
288NW^{4}112
- 420 -
e288NW^{4}811
288NW^{5}814
- 490 -
284NW738
286NW^{8}3
286NW^{7}3
d302NW^{7}439
307NW283
j321NW122
- 495 -
290NW^{2}507
290NW^{1}508
d290NW^{6}509
- 503 -
312NW^{1}852
- 516 -
286NW^{6}865
296NW769
504FS676
- 523 -
f284NW927
e285NW^{3}871
Vol. 182
- 232 -
285NW^{8}909
- 238 -
f524FS^{1}864
f524FS^{2}864
f524FS^{3}865
- 245 -
279NW^{6}200
283NW^{6}467
307NW^{5}886
- 257 -
274NW^{7}623
f296NW^{6}745
f296NW^{7}745
304NW^{2}779
320NW^{3}532
f325NW^{4}355
- 282 -
275NW^{4}167
286NW^{2}609
- 441 -
e286NW^{4}13

Column 5

- 459 -
301NW^{10}236
- 466 -
284NW^{1}073
306NW^{1}687
311NW^{2}249
319NW^{16}509
- 497 -
285NW^{2}875
- 502 -
314NW^{2}903
- 505 -
e286NW^{3}562
e286NW^{4}562
300NW^{5}874
- 512 -
278NW^{7}234
284NW^{9}460
284NW^{12}678
285NW^{15}914
285NW^{16}914
286NW^{5}562
288NW^{10}868
291NW^{11}522
291NW^{2}522
291NW^{6}822
298NW^{10}243
298NW^{14}824
298NW^{15}824
302NW^{1}357
302NW^{1}859
302NW^{1}863
302NW^{1}682
j302NW824
304NW^{10}750
306NW^{1}520
307NW^{10}320
309NW^{1}230
309NW^{10}349
311NW^{7}241
e311NW^{12}631
312NW^{10}873
320NW^{10}184
j320NW194
321NW^{10}154
321NW^{10}217
321NW^{1}284
321NW^{18}362
324NW^{11}428
325NW^{10}344
- 530 -
447US§458
j447US458
65L圧§268
j65L圧281
100S⁶2288
j100SC2299
f462FS^{5}529
477FS^{6}1219
- 539 -
f275NW^{1}104
299NW^{1}898
Vol. 183
- 11 -
280NW^{10}355
284NW^{1}617

Column 6

291NW^{10}464
f310NW^{12}634
- 18 -
312NW^{2}44
- 28 -
291NW^{2}837
- 29 -
292NW^{1}811
- 47 -
276NW^{1}774
277NW^{1}805
- 56 -
276NW^{1}273
316NW^{2}399
j316NW402
- 64 -
500FS890
- 70 -
481FS^{3}926
- 84 -
317NW503
- 103 -
277NW^{14}814
- 116 -
289NW^{11}371
- 133 -
f274NW^{1}696
j302NW^{1}148
277NW^{2}148
277NW^{3}148
277NW^{12}151
- 139 -
274NW^{10}659
275NW^{10}699
280NW^{3}355
280NW^{10}744
e312NW^{10}495
315NW^{4}355
318NW^{4}117
318NW^{5}17
- 143 -
299NW^{4}276
- 148 -
276NW^{1}779
284NW^{1}634
284NW^{2}634
286NW^{3}142
- 155 -
314NW^{4}900
- 158 -
294NW^{1}48
294NW^{5}48
324NW^{1}684
- 161 -
297NW^{1}59
- 836 -
275NW^{6}685
279NW^{2}188
280NW^{7}755

Column 7

Vol. 184
- 65 -
d653F2d
[^{5}1133
f476FS^{4}255
- 81 -
277NW^{1}836
- 88 -
Case 2
280NW^{5}251
280NW^{4}253
284NW^{5}677
285NW^{5}726
- 97 -
284NW697
- 107 -
295NW^{2}25
- 113 -
274NW^{4}611
284NW^{4}40
284NW^{4}602
286NW^{5}351
292NW^{1}614
- 127 -
280NW^{5}160
- 141 -
286NW^{2}567
286NW^{3}567
- 156 -
280NW746
q288NW161
j293NW918
f294NW^{1}3
294NW^{2}11
- 168 -
q276NW^{6}340
299NW^{3}858
306NW43
- 176 -
274NW^{6}663
320NW^{8}18
- 183 -
307NW^{2}252
- 189 -
298NW537
312NW^{8}806
312NW^{9}807
312NW^{10}807
- 433 -
294NW^{10}527
- 817 -
325NW^{2}81
Vol. 185
- 300 -
289NW^{3}277
- 306 -
275NW177
284NW^{7}680
Continued

Column 8

280NW^{12}756
284NW597
f286NW^{5}358
f286NW^{6}358
f286NW^{7}358
f286NW^{8}358
291NW^{5}51
f291NW^{12}552
305NW^{9}173
f306NW^{6}684
f306NW^{7}684
f306NW^{8}684
306NW^{12}689
j306NW694
311NW218
311NW^{12}219
311NW^{6}247
321NW250
321NW^{6}251
480FS^{12}874
- 846 -
321NW^{2}121
- 848 -
588F2d^{5}771
- 865 -
276NW^{1}321
278NW242
- 871 -
275NW^{6}192
276NW^{8}758
286NW^{5}47
307NW^{1}222
- 876 -
274NW^{4}691
274NW^{9}691
278NW^{4}874
279NW^{8}179
487FS^{11}119
512FS^{4}1143
512FS^{5}1143
- 886 -
275NW^{3}118
284NW664
j291NW495
- 889 -
j321NW257
- 896 -
285NW^{2}922
302NW^{6}59
- 899 -
294NW^{4}553
315NW^{3}371
- 902 -
308NW^{4}411

Figure BB.   Sample Page of Shepard's Tables (N.W.2d Tables)

in the Wis. 2d tables. So, if you had Shepardized *State v. Yoder* only under the Wis. 2d tables, you would have missed the Oregon case citing *State v. Yoder.* Therefore, to be absolutely sure your Shepardizing of a case is as thorough as possible, you need to Shepardize in the tables for all parallel citations, as well as in the table for the principal citation.

Step 4. Once you have located the correct citator table, look in it for the volume number of the case you are Shepardizing.

Figures AA and BB show sample pages from, respectively, the Wis. 2d and N.W.2d tables of *Shepard's Citations* for Wisconsin cases. Note these standard citator features:

- The name and series of the case reporter treated by the tables on a given page are printed in the center of the top margin of the page.

- The number of the first case reporter volume treated by the tables on a given citator page appears in large boldface type in the upper left- or right-hand corner of the page. In Figure AA, the citator page begins with coverage of volume 49 of Wis. 2d; the citator page in Figure BB begins its coverage with volume 178 of N.W.2d.

- Figure BB also illustrates the situation of a citator page containing tables for more than one volume of a case reporter. In such a circumstance, the volume numbers of the case reporters appear in large boldface print throughout the citator page, wherever a new table begins. In Figure BB, the citator page begins with a table for volume 178 of N.W.2d, and continues through tables for volumes 179 to 185.

Step 5. After you have found the citator page(s) containing the volume number of the case reporter in which the case you are Shepardizing is published, find in the citator tables the number of the beginning page of your case. Then examine the citator entries listed under it.

As you look down the columns in Figures AA and BB, you'll see boldface numbers set off by dashes on each side. Each such number represents the beginning page of a cited case. In the example of *State v. Yoder*, 49 Wis. 2d 430, 182 N.W. 2d 539, you would look for a boldface "—430—" in Figure AA and a boldface "—539—" under "Vol. 182" in Figure BB, which are the beginning pages of *Yoder* in 49 Wis. 2d and 182 N.W.2d, respectively.

The letters and numbers appearing in the columns under each boldface page number are the citations of the legal authorities that have referred to the case being Shepardized. The basic information given for each authority (*i.e.*, "citing authority") that mentions the case being Shepardized consists of:

```
        - 430 -
     (182NW539)
     a406US205
     a32L℞15
     a92SC1526
     s402US994
     s29L℞160
     s91SC2173
       55W⁶353
       63W⁴137
     j556F2d⁴325
     j556F2d²326
     120PaL539
     3Æ1401s
```

Source: Shepard's Inc. of Colorado Springs © 1979

Figure CC. Shepard's Table for the Wis. 2d Version of *State v. Yoder*, 49 Wis. 2d 430, 182 N.W.2d 539

- The volume number of the citing authority. (This is the first number appearing in the citation.)
- The title of the citing authority, abbreviated according to a unique letter code established for Shepard's citators. (To interpret the abbreviation, refer to the table entitled "ABBREVIATIONS—REPORTS" at the front of the citator volume.)
- The page number in the citing authority on which you will find a reference to the case you are Shepardizing. (This number appears after the abbreviated title in the Shepard's citation.)

For example, in Figure CC (which shows the Shepard's table for the Wis. 2d version of *State v. Yoder*), "556F2d325" is the Shepard's citation of an authority that cites *Yoder.*

You will also encounter several other special features of the citations in the Shepard's tables:

- You may find one or more citations in parentheses at the top of a column of Shepard's citations. (In Figure CC, the parenthetical citation is 182 N.W.2d 539.) Such a parenthetical citation is a parallel citation of the case being Shepardized.
- Frequently, code letters will appear in front of citations in the Shepard's tables. (In Figure CC, an example of such a letter is the "s" in front of "91SC2173".) These letters indicate how the citing authority relates to the case being Shepardized. The code letters are explained at the outset of each Shepard's volume in a table entitled "ABBREVIATIONS—ANALYSIS." The abbreviations table for cases is reprinted in Figure DD.

History of Case

a (affirmed)	Same case affirmed on appeal.
cc (connected case)	Different case from case cited but arising out of same subject matter or intimately connected therewith.
D (dismissed)	Appeal from same case dismissed.
m (modified)	Same case modified on appeal.
r (reversed)	Same case reversed on appeal.
s (same case)	Same case as case cited.
S (superseded)	Substitution for former opinion.
v (vacated)	Same case vacated.
U S cert den	Certiorari denied by U. S. Supreme Court.
U S cert dis	Certiorari dismissed by U. S. Supreme Court.
U S reh den	Rehearing denied by U. S. Supreme Court.
U S reh dis	Rehearing dismissed by U. S. Supreme Court.

Treatment of Case

c (criticised)	Soundness of decision or reasoning in cited case criticised for reasons given.
d (distinguished)	Case at bar different either in law or fact from case cited for reasons given.
e (explained)	Statement of import of decision in cited case. Not merely a restatement of the facts.
f (followed)	Cited as controlling.
h (harmonized)	Apparent inconsistency explained and shown not to exist.
j (dissenting opinion)	Citation in dissenting opinion.
L (limited)	Refusal to extend decision of cited case beyond precise issues involved.
o (overruled)	Ruling in cited case expressly overruled.
p (parallel)	Citing case substantially alike or on all fours with cited case in its law or facts.
q (questioned)	Soundness of decision or reasoning in cited case questioned.

Source: Shepard's/McGraw-Hill © 1983 by McGraw-Hill, Inc.

Figure DD. Shepard's Analysis Codes for Cases

As Figure DD shows, the analysis abbreviations indicate one of two things: (1) how the case being Shepardized was handled as it worked its way through the legal system (the history of the case); or (2) how other courts have evaluated the case in the course of deciding later cases (the treatment of the case).

If no code letter appears in front of a Shepard's citation, then the authority mentioning the case being Shepardized has simply cited it for one of its legal propositions, but without any analytical discussion.

If the Shepard's table treating your case contains a lengthy list of citing authorities, pay particular attention to those preceded by an analysis abbreviation—especially "c", "d", "e", "h", "L", "o", "q", or "r". Such authorities will usually be the most important in helping you evaluate the case you are Shepardizing.

• A page number in a citation in the Shepard's tables refers to the page on which you will find a specific reference to the case you're Shepardizing—*not* to the first page of the author- ity that refers to your case. (In this respect, citations in She- pard's deviate from the usual citation format.) This character- istic of Shepard's citations allows you to go straight to the point in the citing authority where the case you are Shepardiz- ing is mentioned. You need not read the whole citing authority to find the reference to your principal case.[37]

Caveat. Although this convenient Shepard's feature saves time in locating specific references to authorities being She- pardized, you will almost always still need to read all or most of the citing authority in order fully to understand the signifi- cance of the reference.

- Often you will find a small raised number (*i.e.*, a superscript) immediately to the left of the page number in a Shepard's cita- tion. In Figure CC, an example is the small raised "4" in the citation "556F2d325". Superscript numbers in Shepard's ci- tations refer to the numbers of the headnote paragraphs in the case you're Shepardizing that deal with the specific points of law the *citing* case (*i.e.*, the case appearing in the She- pard's citator table) also deals with. In our example, the por- tion of the case you find at 556 F.2d 325 cites *State v. Yoder* for the point of law summarized in *Yoder*'s headnote number 4 in its Wis. 2d version. (Headnotes are defined in the glossary in Appendix L; see also Appendix D.)

  The superscript numbers in Shepard's can speed up your research significantly. Frequently you will need to update your research with respect to only one or two specific rules of law contained in the case you are Shepardizing. If these rules are summarized in the headnotes of your original case, make a note of the headnote numbers. Then, when you Shepardize, look for those same numbers appearing as superscripts in the citator table for the case you are Shepardizing. If you find those headnote numbers as superscripts in any citations in the Shepard's table, read those references first. They should deal with the same rules of law that were summarized in the num- bered headnotes in which you're interested in your principal

---

[37]Occasionally, you may find that you cannot locate your principal case in the text on the page to which Shepard's refers you. Before you conclude that you or Shepard's made a mis- take, carefully search any footnotes appearing on that page. Shepard's directs the re- searcher only to a specific page, without indicating whether the reference to the case being Shepardized appears in the text or in a footnote on that page.

case. In short, using the Shepard's superscript numbers can save you from reading cases citing your principal case for points of law that may be irrelevant to your research problem.

For instance, returning to Figure AA (p. 102), suppose you were Shepardizing the case reported at 49 Wis. 2d 263 and were interested in only the point of law summarized in headnote number 9 of that case. Looking at the Shepard's table for 49 Wis. 2d 263, you would discover (if you counted them) 122 references citing to that case. But only seven of those 122 references contain a superscript number 9. By using the superscript feature, you would quickly narrow your research from an unwieldy 122 authorities to a more manageable seven.

Caveat. In using the superscript feature you must remember, however, that different publishers of court decisions use different numerical headnote systems. For example, headnote 9 in the Wis. 2d version of a case (which is published by Callaghan & Company) will almost certainly deal with a different point of law than headnote 9, if there is one, in the N.W.2d version of that case (which is published by West).

Consequently, whenever you attempt to match a Shepard's superscript number with a case headnote number, you must make sure the headnote number you are using is from the case as published in the reporter identified in the top margin of the citator page on which the Shepard's table for your cited case appears. For example, you would match headnote numbers from cases reported in the Wis. 2d series with Shepard's superscript numbers appearing in the tables in Figure AA, *not* with the superscript numbers appearing in the tables in Figure BB. Headnote numbers from cases reported in the N.W.2d series would be matched with Shepard's superscript numbers appearing in the tables in Figure BB.

Summary: checklist for Shepardizing a case. The following checklist summarizes the steps described in the preceding paragraphs for Shepardizing a case:

● Find the proper set of *Shepard's Citations* (*e.g.,* the set for *Federal Supplement,* if you are Shepardizing a U.S. District Court case, or the set covering a particular state).

● Make sure you have collected all the necessary volumes in the appropriate citator set.

● Make sure you are Shepardizing in the correct tables of citations in the volumes you have collected.

• Once you have located the correct citator tables, look through them for the volume number of the case you are Shepardizing.

• Under the volume number of the case you are Shepardizing, find the beginning page number of your case.

• Examine the citator entries listed in the column(s) under that page number.

Sample Shepardizing exercises. To check whether you have understood the preceding explanation of how to Shepardize a case, you may want to try your hand at the following exercises. Answers to exercises 1 and 2 appear in Appendix F.

1. Find a United States District Court case that distinguished the point of law summarized in headnote 7 of the N.E.2d version of *Trustees of Tufts College v. Volpe Construction Co., Inc.*, 358 Mass. 331, 264 N.E.2d 676 (1970).

2. Find a Colorado state court case citing *Mabra v. Schmidt*, 356 F. Supp. 620 (W.D. Wis. 1973).

3. This exercise is open-ended: (a) Randomly select a volume from any federal, state, or regional case reporter series. A volume containing cases decided roughly five to ten years ago will probably work best. (b) From the volume, select any case. Try to pick a case with several headnotes, since such a case will probably have been cited more frequently than a case with only one or two headnotes. Make a note of the case's citation. (c) Then Shepardize the case.

   To determine whether you are Shepardizing the case correctly, choose one of the citations listed in the Shepard's table for the case you are Shepardizing. Locate the citing case you have chosen, and turn to the page indicated in its Shepard's citation. If you have Shepardized properly, you will find your original case mentioned somewhere on that page.

Some final points about Shepardizing cases. Although Shepardizing is an essential step in your legal research, don't be seduced into believing it will do more than it can. Shepard's citators offer only a *rough* guide to the treatment of a case; they can't convey nuance. For example, *Shepard's Citations* may indicate that a case has overruled the case you are Shepardizing, but Shepard's won't necessarily reflect whether the case was overruled on a point relevant to your particular research problem. Because a court decision usually deals with more than one legal principle, it can be overruled or limited with respect to one point of law without the precedential value of its other points being disturbed.

Similarly, the relevant citator tables may not list any citation with an "o" beside it. This would indicate that the case you are Shepardizing has not been explicitly overruled, either in whole or in part. (Remember, "o" is Shepard's code for "overruled.") Nonetheless, if you read the authorities which the citator lists as criticizing ("c"), distinguishing ("d"), explaining ("e"), harmonizing ("h"), limiting ("L"), or questioning ("q") the case you are Shepardizing, you may find that the case has been overruled for all practical purposes—*i.e.*, it has retained no real significance, is apt to be simply ignored by the courts as controlling precedent, and may soon be explicitly overruled.

So don't fool yourself. Although Shepard's citators are indispensable research tools, *you should not rely on them to the point of not actually retrieving and reading the authorities they cite.*

On the other hand, after you gain some experience in Shepardizing, you will discover that reading literally every authority cited (especially in a long table of citations) as referring to the case you're Shepardizing will often be needlessly time-consuming. Therefore, be alert for indications of how you can most efficiently adapt the Shepardizing process to your particular needs in connection with any given research problem.

For instance, if your initial research in encyclopedias, treatises, cases, or other substantive sources suggests that the point of law you are investigating is a fundamental one with ancient roots in the law, widely accepted policy underpinnings, and broad application to varied fact patterns, it is unlikely that the recent cases cited in Shepard's will have overruled or otherwise limited it.[38] In such a situation, it will normally suffice to read one or two of the most recently decided cases cited in Shepard's. Reading *all* the cases the citator indicates as mentioning the case you are Shepardizing will probably be merely repetitious and not yield significant insight into your research problem.

In connection with a different research problem, however, you may feel that the point of law in which you are interested stands on uncertain ground and that each case you can locate that mentions it will help you evaluate the current status of the point of law. Alternatively, you may feel you do not fully understand a point of law stated in the case you are Shepardizing, or that the application of the point of law may vary significantly depending on the factual context. In such situations, you will almost certainly benefit from reading as many as possible of the cases cited in Shepard's: as you read each new case, your understanding of the point of law should increase, and you should become aware of how different fact patterns operate to alter its application.

---

[38]In court decisions, indications that a point of law is solidly established include prefatory statements such as "In this jurisdiction, it is well-established that . . .", or "It has long been settled that . . .", or even "It is, of course, fundamental that . . . ." In addition, a point of law followed by a string citation of numerous cases in support of it may indicate that the stated legal principle is a fundamental one, unlikely to change. Finally, as you gain experience in particular substantive areas of the law, you will be able to recognize on your own many of the basic legal principles and themes that govern those fields.

Finally, whenever you decide it may be appropriate to screen Shepard's entries in lieu of reading them all, pay close attention to any superscript numbers that appear in the Shepard's citations. As discussed earlier (see pp. 107–08), these numbers will specifically direct you to legal authorities treating the particular points of law in which you are interested in the case you are Shepardizing. You can also screen large numbers of citations you find in Shepard's tables by concentrating on examining the most recent citing authorities: they will often summarize or clarify the intervening developments between the time your original case was decided and the present.

Shepardizing a statute[39]

As with cases, statutes (both federal and state) can be updated by Shepardizing. The steps used in Shepardizing statutes are roughly the same as for cases: you must select the correct set of *Shepard's Citations*; collect all the necessary volumes in that set; locate the correct tables in those volumes; and so forth. Although the general technique for Shepardizing statutes parallels that for cases, there are a few peculiarities you need to be aware of. These variations are explained in this section.

By Shepardizing a statute, you discover how it has subsequently been treated by courts and the legislature that enacted it—for example, whether it has been amended or repealed by the legislature, or has been interpreted by a court. In addition, Shepard's will indicate when the statute has been cited in other selected sources, such as law review articles, administrative decisions, and Attorney General Opinions.

As with cases, Shepard's uses unique coded abbreviations to convey information about legislative and judicial treatment of statutes. Figure EE reprints Shepard's treatment codes for statutes.

In addition to the different Shepard's codes for statutes, there are a few other points to remember about Shepardizing a statute:

- First, you should Shepardize the codified version of a statute (when available) rather than the session law version,[40] since

---

[39]Recall that for legal research purposes, ordinances and constitutional provisions are simply different forms of statutes. See pp. 5 n.3, 45 n.13. With respect to Shepardizing, too, they are handled in essentially the same manner as statutes. Therefore, the explanation of Shepardizing statutes also provides a general background that you can adapt to Shepardizing ordinances and constitutional provisions.

[40]Recall that, as pointed out in Chapter 1, session laws are a chronological compilation of statutory law, while statutory codes arrange these laws according to subject matter.

courts normally cite to statutory codes instead of session laws.

● Second, codified statutes are frequently renumbered; for example, a statute numbered § 299.01 might (for a variety of reasons) be renumbered as § 799.01 in a later statutory codification. To make sure you find all the authorities that have cited both the old and new number, you need to Shepardize the statute using both its current and former citations. Because more recent interpretations will usually be more useful, however, you should generally start by Shepardizing its current citation.

If you have a statutory citation that's several years old (a citation that you found, for example, in an older court decision), you should determine whether the citation is to the statute as it appears in the current statutory code. To do this, simply check in the latest edition of the code. If you don't find your statute there, it means either that the statute has been repealed or renumbered. If it has just been renumbered within the code, you can find its new number by looking in the current code's transfer table, which will cross-reference the old and new numbers. At that point, you'll have all the necessary information for thoroughly Shepardizing your statute.

● Third, when you Shepardize a statute, you must be sure you are using the Shepard's table corresponding to the edition of the code containing the statute in which you are interested. Because statutes change as a result of the passage of new session laws, statutory codes are recompiled periodically to reflect those changes. The recompilation process deletes statutes the legislature has repealed and adds other statutes and amendments to existing statutes enacted since the last recompilation. Consequently, a given statute in a code may differ from one recompilation to the next. To account for this characteristic of statutory codes, the Shepard's citators for statutes arrange their tables by the year of recompilation. For instance, if a statutory code is recompiled in every odd-numbered year, Shepard's will have a table of citations to the 1975 code, another to the 1977 code, yet another to the 1979 code, and so on.

It's critical to Shepardize in the table corresponding to the date of the statute you're seeking to update. Suppose, for example, you need to locate cases interpreting a statute as it appeared in 1977 because that was the year the pertinent facts of your research problem occurred. Shepardizing the statute as it existed in 1976 or 1978 or some other year would yield seriously misleading results if the 1977 version differed significantly from the other years' versions.

• Finally, if your research problem requires you to locate cases and other materials interpreting a specific sub-section of a statute, you can Shepardize just that particular sub-section. This technique is often speedier than finding case interpretations through the case annotations (the one-paragraph summaries) included in annotated statutes: the statutory annotations generally do not specify to which precise sub-sections, if any, they relate.

Operation of Statute
   Legislative

A	(amended)	Statute amended.
Ad	(added)	New section added.
E	(extended)	Provisions of an existing statute extended in their application to a later statute, or allowance of additional time for performance of duties required by a statute within a limited time.
L	(limited)	Provisions of an existing statute declared not to be extended in their application to a later statute.
R	(repealed)	Abrogation of an existing statute.
Re-en	(re-enacted)	Statute re-enacted.
Rn	(renumbered)	Renumbering of existing sections.
Rp	(repealed in part)	Abrogation of part of an existing statute.
Rs	(repealed and superseded)	Abrogation of an existing statute and substitution of new legislation therefor.
Rv	(revised)	Statute revised.
S	(superseded)	Substitution of new legislation for an existing statute not expressly abrogated.
Sd	(suspended)	Statute suspended.
Sdp	(suspended in part)	Statute suspended in part.
Sg	(supplementing)	New matter added to an existing statute.
Sp	(superseded in part)	Substitution of new legislation for part of an existing statute not expressly abrogated.
Va	(validated)	

   Judicial

C	Constitutional.		V	Void or invalid.
U	Unconstitutional.		Va	Valid.
Up	Unconstitutional in part.		Vp	Void or invalid in part.

Source: Shepard's/McGraw-Hill © 1983 by McGraw-Hill, Inc.

Figure EE. Shepard's Treatment Codes for Statutes

Updating administrative regulations

Like cases and statutes, administrative regulations also need to be updated.

Federal regulations. At the federal level, there are two ways to up-date regulations: (1) through *Shepard's Code of Federal Regulations Citations,* and (2) through the *Federal Register.*

Shepardizing a federal regulation in *Shepard's C.F.R. Citations* proceeds in much the same manner as Shepardizing a statute, de-scribed in the previous section of this chapter. When you use *Shepard's C.F.R. Citations,* you need to make sure you are in the correct table. The tables are arranged according to *C.F.R.* title number and section number. Once you locate the correct table, you will notice some unique features of the *C.F.R.* citator:

- The tables list only the court decisions (state and federal), law reviews, and *A.L.R.* annotations that have cited the regula-tion. Unlike Shepard's treatment of a statute (which will tell you, for example, whether the legislature has subsequently amended or repealed it), the Shepard's citator for *C.F.R.* will not indicate how an administrative agency itself has subse-quently handled one of its regulations. To check a regula-tion's history within an agency, you will need to refer to the *Federal Register,* which will be discussed shortly.

- Like statutes, federal regulations are changed frequently and recompiled periodically, making it necessary to be sure you are examining the Shepard's material corresponding to the specific version of the regulation in which you are interested.

    The *Code of Federal Regulations* (unlike most statutory codes) is not recompiled all at once, however; rather, various *C.F.R.* titles are recompiled at different times throughout the year. To accommodate this, the tables in *Shepard's C.F.R. Citations* are *not* arranged by year of recompilation. Instead, Shepard's indicates the year of recompilation (*if* it is men-tioned in the authority citing the regulation) as an element of the individual entries themselves in the Shepard's tables.

    If the citing authority indicates the year of the regulation, that year will be given in the Shepard's entry, preceded by an asterisk, like this:

    551 F2d 333 *1972

Where a citing authority does not mention the year of the regulation, the Shepard's entry will show a year preceded by a triangle, like this:

458 F2d 1117 △1972

This triangle means the year shown is simply the year of the citing authority, *not* the year of the regulation itself.

As noted earlier, Shepard's *C.F.R.* citator will not indicate how the administrative agency that promulgated a regulation has subsequently treated it (*e.g.*, renumbered, revised, or rescinded it). To discover the subsequent administrative history of a federal regulation, you need to consult the *Federal Register*, in which federal administrative agencies are required to publish their new or amended regulations and to indicate when regulations are rescinded. The *Federal Register* serves as a daily non-cumulative update that keeps *C.F.R.* current between its periodic recompilations.[41]

To use the *Federal Register* as an updating tool, you start with your citation of a regulation from the *C.F.R.* and then take the following steps:

• First, look up your regulation in the "List of C.F.R. Sections Affected," also known as "LSA." LSA is a separate pamphlet published monthly and contains cumulative tables showing where in the *Federal Register* you can find changes to particular regulations since their publication in the latest *C.F.R.* The LSA lists the affected *C.F.R.* sections by title number, chapter, part, and section, and indicates the changes involved.

• Next, because the LSA is only published monthly, you need to look up your regulation in the cumulative table titled "C.F.R. Parts Affected During [current month]" to locate any changes that have occurred since the latest LSA. This table, which appears at the end of each daily issue of the *Federal Register* in a section called "Reader Aids," tells you where in that month's issues of the *Federal Register* you can find changes made to particular regulations. Entries in the "C.F.R. Parts Affected" table list affected regulations according to *C.F.R.* title number and part number only; affected section numbers of regulations are not indicated.

---

[41]In effect, the *Federal Register* stands in essentially the same relationship to the *C.F.R.* as pocket parts or supplements stand to other kinds of legal authorities. Pocket parts and supplements are discussed later in this chapter.

To summarize the process of updating through the *Federal Register,* once you have located a regulation in *C.F.R.,* you update the regulation by consulting two tables. First, you check the *Federal Register*'s "List of C.F.R. Sections Affected," a cumulative monthly pamphlet that indicates the location in the *Register* of changes to regulations contained in the *C.F.R.* Second, you check the *Federal Register's* latest daily cumulative table titled "C.F.R. Parts Affected," in order to locate regulatory changes made since the most recent LSA.[42]

State regulations. You will generally find it difficult to update state administrative regulations. None of the editions of *Shepard's Citations* contains tables treating state regulations, and techniques for updating regulations vary from state to state. As a general matter, you should start by checking your state's administrative register (if there is one) for any changes that have been made to regulations published in the state's administrative code. In addition, you may want to contact the administrative agency that promulgated the regulation in which you're interested, to determine whether the agency has made any recent changes to the regulation.

Because there are few comprehensive ways to update state administrative regulations, you should also note that computers (which can be used to update all types of authorities) can be a helpful updating tool, where available. (See the section on "Updating Through Computers," later in this chapter.)

Updating by using pocket parts and supplements

Many legal resources are kept up-to-date through "pocket parts" and supplements. For legal resources (such as encyclopedias and treatises) that are not treated by Shepard's citators, pocket parts and supplements are the only non-computerized devices for updating. Even for cases and statutes, which are treated by Shepard's, the pocket parts and supplements for case digests and annotated statutes provide the starting point for updating.

Pocket parts are so named because the publisher leaves a slot (a "pocket") in the cover of the hardbound volume, into which subsequently issued paperbound updating pamphlets can be inserted. Legal publications using pocket parts include:

---

[42]For more about using the *C.F.R.* and the *Federal Register,* check your law library for a helpful publication called *The Federal Register: What It Is and How To Use It.* You can also obtain this publication directly from the U.S. Government Printing Office. *See* p. 87 n.29.

- case digests
- annotated statutes
- treatises
- legal encyclopedias
- *American Law Reports Annotated* ("A.L.R.")[43]
- *Words and Phrases*

Whenever you are researching in a hardbound publication kept current through pocket parts, it is *essential* that you examine the pocket parts. (It is generally best to do this at the same time you check the hardbound volume, or even immediately before checking the text of the hardbound volume; by doing so, you may avoid wasting a lot of time reading material that has been completely superseded.) Until you become familiar with which publications rely on pocket parts, a good practice is simply always to look inside the cover for a pocket part.

Pocket parts are usually published once every year for a given hardbound volume. They follow the same format as the hardbound volume to which they correspond, and report any relevant additions to or deletions from the main text that have occurred since the hardbound volume was published. For example, if you found that section 817.03 of a statutory code applied to your research problem, you would update it by looking under section 817.03 in the current pocket part inserted in the hardbound volume of the annotated statutes containing that section. The pocket part would reflect amendments to the statute, as well as annotations of cases that have interpreted and applied the statute since the publication of the hardbound volume.

Each new pocket part cumulates the previous pocket part plus in-

---

[43]*A.L.R.*'s updating format has gone through several changes over the years, resulting in a hybrid system that is unusual and sometimes unwieldy to use. *A.L.R.3d, A.L.R.4th,* and *A.L.R. Fed.* are all updated with cumulative pocket parts. *A.L.R.2d,* however, is updated with a separate set of books known as the *Later Case Service* (which is itself updated with pocket parts), and *A.L.R.1st* is updated by a separate set of books known as the *Blue Book of Supplemental Decisions* (every volume of which must be checked because they are not cumulative). In addition, by checking the "Annotations History Tables" found in the *A.L.R.* Quick Index volumes, you can determine whether a specific *A.L.R.* annotation has been supplemented (*i.e.,* updated) or superseded (*i.e.,* completely replaced) by a later *A.L.R.* annotation. The table in the combined Quick Index for *A.L.R.3d* and *A.L.R.4th* contains annotation histories for some *A.L.R.1st* annotations; for all annotations in *A.L.R.2d, A.L.R.3d,* and *A.L.R.4th*; and for some *A.L.R. Fed.* annotations. The *A.L.R. Fed.* Quick Index's Annotations History Table covers only annotations in *A.L.R. Fed.* Finally, the *A.L.R.1st Blue Book of Supplemental Decisions* also includes annotation histories for some *A.L.R.1st* annotations not treated in any of the other tables, so you should check it in addition to the Annotation History Table in the *A.L.R.3d & 4th* Quick Index.

As we said, *A.L.R.* has an unusual hybrid system for updating its material.

tervening developments, until the publisher issues a new hardbound re-
placement volume. Then the pocket part cycle begins again for the new
hardbound volume.

Because the law changes between pocket parts, publishers also
often issue paperbound books called *supplements*. The supplements
may appear on a monthly, bimonthly, or quarterly basis. Like pocket
parts, they follow the organization of the principal volumes to which they
relate. These supplements are usually cumulative, *i.e.*, they usually incorporate previous supplements while updating intervening developments as well. Finally, when new pocket parts are issued for the principal hardbound volumes to which the supplements relate, the new
pocket parts will include the material from the most recent pocket part
and the previous period's supplements, and a new cycle of supplements begins. This sequence of "pocket part-supplement-pocket part"
continues until the publisher decides to issue a new updated hardbound
volume.

Updating through
looseleaf reporter services

The term "looseleaf reporter services" is used in legal research to
describe a wide variety of publications roughly similar to newsletters.
These looseleaf reporters fill a gap in the reporting of primary legal authorities: because they are published monthly, weekly, or even daily
(depending on the particular looseleaf service), they generally contain
the most up-to-date information about court decisions, statutes, administrative regulations, and developing trends in the law. In most instances, their coverage will be more current than that of case reporters,
digests, annotated statutes, treatises, or any other primary or secondary source of legal authority—even taking into consideration these
sources' pocket parts and supplements (discussed in the preceding
section). In addition, looseleaf services usually contain more current information than can be obtained through Shepardizing (discussed in
earlier sections).

Consequently, to be absolutely sure your legal research is thorough, you may want to make your final research step a check of a looseleaf reporter service (if one exists in the relevant field) to determine
whether any last-minute development has significantly affected your
position.

Looseleaf services are topical reporters—that is, each particular
service reports cases or case summaries (sometimes including cases

that haven't been and won't be reported in any other source), statutes, editorial commentary, and miscellaneous items (*e.g.*, bibliographies and announcements of upcoming seminars) in specific, selected areas of the law, such as criminal law, environmental law, family law, and tax law. Within its specialized area of treatment, a looseleaf service's coverage generally is chronological, mirroring the actual development of the subject being reported. In short, looseleaf services are hybrid legal resources, providing both topical and chronological access to primary sources of law, much as if a case digest and case reporter were combined in one publication.

Each of the scores of commercially published looseleaf reporter services has its own idiosyncracies as to its internal organization, but all services have certain common characteristics:

- Each reporter service consists of a collection of periodically issued reports on a specific topical area of law.

- Each of these periodic issues covers a separate time period. In other words, their coverage is not cumulative, but reports only developments since the most recent issue.

- To accommodate its constant growth, each reporter service houses its issues in some sort of binder notebook.

- Each reporter service normally provides an extensive indexing system.

- Each service includes its own "how to use this reporter" feature, which explains how best to use the service.

Entering a looseleaf reporter service normally requires using both the topical and descriptive word techniques for finding the law.[44] First, you need to determine which broad legal topic (such as criminal law, bankruptcy law, etc.) your problem involves. Then, select a looseleaf reporter service (if there is one) treating that subject. Once you have your service, search its index for your descriptive words. If they are contained there, the index will direct you to the relevant parts of the service.

For an extensive bibliography of looseleaf reporter services, as well as a more detailed discussion of these services, consult *Reporter Services and Their Use*, an informative guide available directly from its publisher, Bureau of National Affairs ("BNA"),[45] or perhaps from your local law library.

---

[44]See Chapter 4 of this book for a discussion of these law-finding techniques.
[45]The address of BNA is 1231 25th Street, N.W., Washington, D.C. 20037.

Updating through computers

You can update *any* source—court decision, statute, administrative regulation, *Restatement of the Law,* treatise, etc.—by searching a computerized legal data base for references to it. By typing in the authority's title or citation, you can have the computer retrieve court cases (and some administrative agency decisions) that have referred to that authority. This computerized updating technique is especially helpful with respect to authorities, such as state administrative regulations or treatises, that cannot be Shepardized.

Appendix A contains a more detailed introduction to using computers in legal research.

Chart: summary of updating techniques

This chapter has explained updating as a process carried on with several tools: *Shepard's Citations*; pocket parts and supplements; administrative registers; looseleaf services; and computers. Figure FF correlates these updating tools with the type of legal publication being updated.

Closing thoughts on updating the law

For learning purposes, it is analytically useful to view updating as the final and separate phase of the three phases of legal research (the first and second being, respectively, finding the law and reading the law). Isolating the "updating the law" phase makes it less likely that you will forget or overlook it (with potentially disastrous consequences) in the course of what will often be extended legal research.

In addition, analytically isolating the updating phase provides a convenient vehicle for categorizing the assorted legal materials of Shepard's citators, pocket parts and supplements, and looseleaf reporter services into a single group based on their common prevailing function, *i.e.,* to bring the substantive law up to date. This framework helps the legal researcher understand the interaction of the multitude of reference works found in the average law library.

Nonetheless, it is also important to note that although updating is analytically the final step in legal research, in practice you will often find

	Shepard's Citations	Pocket Parts; Supplements	Looseleaf Services	Computers
Federal				
U.S. Constitution	•			•
U.S. Code Annotated versions of the United States Code	•	•	•	•
Statutes at Large	•		•	•
Court Decisions	•			•
Code of Federal Regulations	•	•†	•	•
Federal Register			•	•
Attorney General Opinions	•			•
State				
State Constitution	•			•
State Statutory Code State Statutory Code Annotated	•	•		•
State Session Laws	•			•
Court Decisions	•			•
State Administrative Code		•††		•
State Administrative Register				•
Attorney General Opinions	•			•
Secondary Sources				
Case Digests			•	•
Legal Encyclopedias			•	•
Treatises and Hornbooks			•	•
Law Reviews	•			•
American Law Reports *Annotated ("A.L.R.")*			•†††	•
Words and Phrases			•	•

†*Federal Register* functions in effect as a daily, non-cumulative "pocket part" or supplement to the *C.F.R.*

††State administrative registers function in effect as "pocket parts" or supplements to state administrative codes.

†††See note 43, *supra*, for a discussion of the peculiarities involved in updating *A.L.R.*

Figure FF. Summary of Updating Techniques

it best to update as you proceed through the phases of finding the law (see Chapter 4) and reading the law (see Chapter 5). Usually, you'll do some finding and reading, then some updating, then some more finding and reading, followed by more updating, and so on, until you decide you have reached the end of your research. Thus, updating is an intermediate step at times, too.

For example, if you update by Shepardizing a promising-sounding case immediately after finding and reading it, you can promptly identify (while your principal case is still fresh in your mind) subsequent cases that may explain, limit, or otherwise modify it. If you read the primary case together with the later cases analyzing it, the legal principles involved may come into sharp focus more quickly than if you wait to Shepardize until after you find and read all your primary cases in all the areas involved in your particular research problem, then Shepardize all of them, and then read all the cases you find through Shepardizing.

In short, as with everything complex, an analytical framework is essential. But theory should not inflexibly dictate practice. Once you understand the functions of the three major phases of legal research—finding, reading, and updating—you will then be in a position to fit them to your own changing needs.

Thus, you will discover that legal research does not always proceed in a linear fashion with all your "finding" preceding all your "reading," preceding all your "updating," and ending there. Rather, legal research often tends to look more like a wheel, which will continue to turn until *you* decide it should stop:

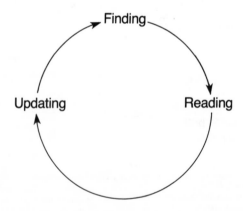

CHAPTER 7

How to Take
Effective Notes*

If you follow the methodology described in the preceding three chapters for finding, reading, and updating the law, you will do your legal research as quickly, efficiently, and thoroughly as possible. You will seriously undermine your efforts, however, if you lack a well-organized, concise technique for taking notes on your research findings.

While researching a given problem, you may examine dozens or scores of sources and spend a considerable amount of time. Even if you are lucky enough to complete your research without interruption, you cannot remember everything you read. Therefore, working without notes will almost always mean having to backtrack and duplicate your earlier, unrecorded efforts: you will read a source once initially to determine its significance, again if you come across its citation and can't remember whether you've already read it, and yet again when it comes time to prepare a court brief or other work based on your research.

Effective note-taking is the only way to avoid such duplication of effort. Moreover, even if you are not personally averse to duplicated effort, as a practical matter you will rarely have time for it. Consequently, although note-taking itself consumes some time, in the end it saves enormously more time than it requires—particularly if you use the note-taking techniques that experienced legal researchers have developed and refined over the years.

Beyond saving time, there are two other reasons for careful note-taking. First, the purpose of doing legal research is always to reach conclusions about the legal implications of particular sets of facts, so you

---

*One specialized form of note-taking—"briefing" cases—is discussed in Chapter 5, and won't be discussed here. This chapter focuses on broader points about note-taking in general.

can, for example, plan a course of conduct or frame a legal argument. If you do not create a clear record of your research findings, your conclusions will be based on a faulty foundation, *i.e.*, mere memory. Your research efforts will be largely wasted.

Second, taking notes helps ensure that you focus sharply on the particular case or other legal authority you are reading and that you think carefully about its meaning. In short, note-taking disciplines legal analysis, which is particularly critical for inexperienced researchers.

Because lawyers' livelihoods depend so heavily on doing research and doing it efficiently, they have refined the commonly used note-taking process into a tool specifically geared to the needs of legal researchers. The "tricks" are simple—and obvious, once pointed out— but many legal researchers discover them only after months or years of doing research. This chapter summarizes the note-taking tips effective legal researchers eventually discover. By reviewing these pointers, you can avoid learning them through trial and error.[46]

Plan before you start. Think through your research problem thoroughly before you even open a book. This step is crucial: otherwise, your research will consist of going through motions without having any idea of what you're looking for. As explained in detail in Chapter 3, you need to begin by identifying and organizing your legal issues, which will in turn provide the necessary starting point for your research.

Write down each legal issue involved in your problem, placing each one at the top of a separate sheet of paper. This simple organizational device for note-taking cannot be overemphasized, especially for beginning legal researchers. If you just record your notes one after another in chronological order as you uncover each legal principle, regardless of which issue the principle relates to, you will create a disorganized mass providing no framework for analyzing the overall meaning of your findings. You will be almost no farther ahead than if you had done no research at all: if you cannot locate your findings, they have no value. Proper organization is especially important if your problem is a complex one that you expect to research intermittently over an extended period.

By simply writing each issue as a heading at the top of a sheet of paper, one issue per sheet, you'll have an instant format for effective note-taking. Then, under each issue, list every principle and legal authority or secondary reference work you locate relating to the issue. In

---

[46]Of course, each researcher will develop a unique style of note-taking. But by incorporating some of the following time-tested fundamentals, each researcher won't have to reinvent the wheel.

other words, don't take notes according to the type of reference books you read, *i.e.*, all notes on all court decisions together or all notes on all statutes together. Rather, *organize by legal issue*.[47]

Also, if a particular principle or source looks like it may relate to more than one issue, list it separately under each appropriate heading. You will probably find it unnecessary to write out a full identification or discussion of the point or authority under each pertinent heading. Usually it will be enough to do that only once, but you should briefly cite to the point or authority in connection with each issue to which it corresponds.

As you proceed with your research, you may discover that your initial statement of an issue was too broad or too narrow. If that happens, simply revise your issue headings accordingly. For example, if you have viewed an issue too broadly, spin off one or more sub-issues, each of which then becomes a new heading.

Besides providing a format for note-taking, another important advantage of the "issue heading" approach will become apparent after you complete your research and turn to writing up the results. Legal research almost always leads to some kind of writing—a letter setting forth a legal position, a memorandum to a lawyer, a brief to a judge, or perhaps a proposal to a government committee.[48] The job of organizing your research results and conclusions for effective communication will be eased considerably and speeded up tremendously if your findings are recorded in separate categories, by issue. Notes about each issue will appear together, making their rewriting unnecessary in order to achieve a logical sequence. You can simply group notes about each given issue into a set, and then arrange the sets into the most suitable order. Within each set of notes, circle or underline the points you actually want to mention in your final written product. You may find it helpful

---

[47]The "issue heading" approach is the same for recording the results of statutory research as it is for case research—in both situations, you record your results by issue. But when dealing with research problems involving the operation of various sub-sections of a governing statute or an interpretation of the meaning of particular phrases of a statute, you may find the following variation helpful: include among your note-taking headings the precise statutory language under examination.

[48]For guidance on writing legal briefs, see BOARD OF STUDENT ADVISERS, HARVARD LAW SCHOOL, INTRODUCTION TO ADVOCACY (4th ed. 1985); and M. PITTONI, BRIEF WRITING AND ARGUMENTATION (3d ed. 1967). For additional assistance with legal writing generally, see G. BLOCK, EFFECTIVE LEGAL WRITING (2d ed. 1983); F. COOPER, WRITING IN LAW PRACTICE (1963); J. DERNBACH & R. SINGLETON, A PRACTICAL GUIDE TO LEGAL WRITING AND LEGAL METHOD (1981); R. GOLDFARB & J. RAYMOND, CLEAR UNDERSTANDINGS: A GUIDE TO LEGAL WRITING (1983); H. WEIHOFEN, LEGAL WRITING STYLE (2d ed. 1980); and R. WYDICK, PLAIN ENGLISH FOR LAWYERS (2d ed. 1985). Finally, two excellent texts for writers, legal or otherwise, who seek guidance on expressing themselves clearly are W. STRUNK & E. WHITE, THE ELEMENTS OF STYLE (3d ed. 1979) and W. ZINSSER, ON WRITING WELL (3d ed. 1985).

even to number these points to indicate the order in which you think they should be discussed. In this way, you can easily convert your notes into a working outline for your final written work.

Start taking notes as soon as you find a principle or authority that may be relevant to your research problem. You will often cover a large amount of material in the course of researching a problem, and it is therefore easy to forget a point if you don't record it immediately. If you wait, you may lose or forget it, and in the end you won't compile a complete record of all the points that bear on your problem. As a result, you will hobble yourself later when you attempt to sift through and weigh your findings.

Record your own opinions. It is also helpful to record any tentative conclusions you reach as you proceed through your research. As you find new principles and gain new insights into their meaning for your problem, your opinions are apt to change. By making notes of your opinions as you go, however, you can avoid returning to a view you once concluded was wrong, having forgotten that you ever reached that conclusion. You would probably realize the error eventually, but not before wasting more time and effort. Moreover, if your research is interrupted for a substantial amount of time, having a complete record of your earlier conclusions will refresh your memory and you won't have to re-think your research from scratch.

Finally, recording your tentative conclusions often makes it easier to subject them to fuller scrutiny, allowing you to detect errors in your thinking and to develop new avenues of research.

Use a simple but consistent "code" to indicate the status of your notations. As you read through various sources, you will come across references to other apparently promising sources and authorities that you will want to check. Normally, it will be inefficient to interrupt what you are reading and immediately locate and read each new cited authority. Rather, you will generally find it more efficient simply to make a note of the citations as you come across them (entering the notes under the appropriate issue headings), and then to examine these newly discovered authorities at a more convenient point in your research.

When you do turn to examining the citations you have listed, it is important to keep track of what you read. Otherwise, you won't know where you left off, and you may find yourself either re-reading or overlooking items on your list of authorities to be examined. Therefore, remember to place a check mark (or other such code) next to citations you have already looked at.

Other codes can also increase your research efficiency. For example, if you read an authority and it turns out merely to repeat information you've already found, you may want to just indicate that briefly in your notes, perhaps by placing a few parenthetical words—such as "(case restates the elements of a libel action)"—after the citation. Or, if the new authority turns out, after reading, to have no relevance at all to your problem, record an "X" or some such notation to indicate the citation's irrelevance. On the other hand, if an authority is particularly helpful, be sure to mark it with a prominent asterisk or other code so you won't over-look it in your notes. If the authority contains an especially quotable pas-sage you think you might want to use, note "good quote" along with the page on which it appears and a short description to help you re-locate it. There are few things more time-consuming or frustrating in legal re-search than knowing you came across a great case or quote some-where, and then not remembering where.

Finally, whenever you read an authority and find that it is central to the issue you are researching, you will need to Shepardize it. (See Chapter 6.) In order to keep track of which authorities you have Shep-ardized and those you have not, be sure to place an "S" or "Shep" or some similar notation next to those that have been Shepardized. If your research will continue over an extended period, during which time sup-plements to *Shepard's Citations* may become available, it is also a good idea to note next to each authority the date you Shepardized it. If you know when you previously Shepardized an authority, you will only need to check Shepard's supplements issued since that date in order to bring your Shepardizing current.

Record helpful case headnote numbers. As discussed in Chap-ter 6 (see pp. 107–08), the superscript numbers appearing in the case tables of *Shepard's Citations* can significantly speed up your Shepar-dizing. To take best advantage of Shepard's superscript feature, it is helpful to keep track of the numbers corresponding to any of a given case's headnote paragraphs that summarize legal principles you have determined bear on your research problem. Then, when you Shepar-dize the case, you can focus on those Shepard's entries with super-scripts corresponding to your selected headnote numbers, without hav-ing to re-check the case to identify the numbers.

Mark your notes with the date of research. It is a good practice to indicate on your overall set of notes the date on which the research was conducted. If your research is interrupted, a new pocket part or supple-ment to a reference book, for example, or an issue of a looseleaf re-porter service in the area of research, may come out before you resume your research. By checking the date on your notes, you will know how much updating will be necessary when you return to your research.

Summary

The following checklist summarizes the points covered in this chapter for effective note-taking:

- Plan before you start.
- Write down each legal issue on a separate sheet of paper as a heading for note-taking.
- Start taking notes as soon as you find a principle or authority that may be relevant to your research problem.
- Record your own opinions as you go.
- Use a simple but consistent "code" to indicate the status of your notations, including the dates of any Shepardizing.
- Record helpful case headnote numbers.
- Mark your notes to indicate the date of research.

As you gain experience in doing legal research, you will find that your note-taking becomes increasingly streamlined and that less note-taking will be necessary to do a thorough and efficient job of researching. Even then, however, the basic mechanics of note-taking outlined in this chapter will continue to be helpful. And while you are still moving toward that stage, these mechanics—by providing a clear, well-organized visual record of your findings—will go a long way toward ensuring that your research is complete, properly focused, and useful.

CHAPTER 8

When to Stop

By following the approach outlined in this book—*i.e.*, organizing your problem, and then finding, reading, and updating the law (recording the results as you go)—you will do your legal research with maximum efficiency and effectiveness. The techniques covered in this book will help you avoid false starts, unnecessarily duplicated efforts, and other time-consuming pitfalls.

While you should, naturally, seek speed and efficiency, it is also essential that you do your legal research thoroughly. The techniques explained in this book will help you achieve that goal, too, by organizing and directing your research in a logical, coherent, and comprehensive manner.

Eventually, though, even the most thorough researcher will come to ask, "Is it time to stop?" There is never an easy or automatic answer to this question. Keeping the following considerations in mind, however, can help you decide whether you have probably completed your research.

You cannot safely cut corners in legal research. You should explore each line of inquiry that appears relevant to your research problem, especially if you are a beginner. A good rule-of-thumb is to continue researching if you have any doubts about whether you would benefit from further research. The point will come, though, when you begin to sense that your continuing research efforts are turning up no new leads or authorities. You find yourself reading cases and articles that repeat the same principles and cite the same sources. Finally, you sense you are going in circles, with each new source you check referring you to statutes, cases, and other authorities that you have already examined.[49]

[49]Careful note-taking will help greatly here. Your notes will tell you at a glance whether you have already checked an authority. See Chapter 7.

At this point, you can probably safely conclude that you have found everything worthwhile that bears on your research problem. You will have a feeling of certainty, of confidence, that your research is complete (even if that research has not yielded a conclusive result).

There is an important practical reason for continuing your research until you reach this point of confidence, aside from the value of confidence as (often) being in itself a good indicator that your work is complete. The purpose of conducting legal research is to equip yourself to communicate a position effectively and persuasively to someone else. You are less likely to communicate effectively and persuasively if you have lingering doubts about your position. Of course, the position you communicate may not always have clear, well-settled legal precedent to support it. Often you will have to assert a forceful position in a murkily defined area of the law. But though the law may be uncertain, your views should not be. You should pursue your research to the point where it both tells you if gaps exist in the present law and, if they do, suggests to you sensible arguments as to how those gaps should be filled or how they are likely to be filled.

By following the methodology of finding, reading, and updating the law with these considerations in mind, you will do your research as quickly, efficiently, and thoroughly as possible, allowing you to put your results to work with confidence.

PART III

Appendices

APPENDIX A

Computerized Legal Research

This appendix provides a general introduction to computerized legal research. Because of frequent changes in the computer services available in this field, a specific discussion would go out of date almost as soon as it was written. In any event, a detailed discussion is unnecessary because vendors of the computer services provide comprehensive instruction manuals.

Computerized legal research services share a number of common characteristics, however, which this appendix introduces. As you familiarize yourself with using computers in legal research, keep in mind that computerized research requires an understanding of the same three-step process of finding, reading, and updating the law used in non-computerized research. The computer simply speeds up the process.

The two leading computerized legal research services are LEXIS (a service of Mead Data) and WESTLAW (a service of West Publishing Company). With each service, computerized research begins with a data base, generally consisting of the full text of whatever federal and state cases, statutes, administrative regulations and rulings, and other legal authorities the particular computer service has chosen to include. Each data base is sub-divided into "libraries." A "library" is made up of a discrete, related set of authorities. For example, in LEXIS, all federal cases and statutes are grouped together as the "general federal library." Similarly, the materials from a given state constitute a library. Libraries, in turn, are often further refined into "sub-libraries": the "general federal library" in LEXIS, for example, contains sub-libraries for U.S. Supreme Court decisions, U.S. Courts of Appeals decisions, and U.S. Claims Court decisions.

At the computer terminal, the user selects the library or sub-library he or she wants to search. Once in the correct library (analogous to being in the right case digest or set of statutes in non-computerized research), the researcher instructs the computer to search the library's data base for particular words or combinations of words. In instructing the computer, the researcher uses a technique analogous to the "descriptive or fact word" approach, the "known authority" approach, the "words and phrases" approach, or a combination of these. (See Chapter 4.) The researcher types the desired words, phrases, or citations on the computer terminal keyboard, often along with some other words that are generally called "logic connectors." These connectors tell the computer how the user intends the typed-in words to relate to one another during the search—for example, whether the computer should search for authorities containing all the typed-in words or for authorities containing just some of them. Once the computer has all the instructions the researcher wants it to have, the computer searches the designated library for the prescribed combination of words and then reports the results.

The computer programs allow the researcher to see on a video display screen as little as simply the citations, or as much as the full text of the authorities the computer finds containing the typed-in words in the required relationships to one another. If the search doesn't yield a helpful result, the researcher can refine the search by adding or deleting search words, modifying the logic connectors, or changing libraries and starting over.

For example, suppose you need to research a problem involving a state prison inmate who claims that prison officials are illegally refusing him access to reading materials. Suppose further that you have already discovered that the federal civil rights statute 42 U.S.C. § 1983 governs the research problem. You will want to locate any cases involving a similar fact pattern decided under that statute. You would certainly want to type the citation "42 U.S.C. § 1983" into the computer terminal. The computer, however, would inundate you with a listing of the thousands of cases that have cited that statute, and these cases would concern disputes about such diverse matters as religious discrimination and retaliatory job firings.

To focus your search somewhat, you could type an instruction to the computer to locate only cases that contain both the citation "42 U.S.C. § 1983" and either the word "prison" or "prisoner." This would limit the number of cases located, but you would still be flooded with cases of only marginal relevance to your own research problem, such as cases involving cell conditions, visitation rights, or probation revocations.

To find cases still closer to your own fact pattern, you could direct the computer to search only for cases containing the words "42 U.S.C. § 1983," "prison" or "prisoner," and "books." Finally, you could focus your search even further by typing in the additional word "censorship." As you define your search more carefully by giving the computer more precise words to search for, your search results should narrow in on cases of increasing similarity to your own fact pattern.

In effect, a computerized "descriptive word"-type search or a "words and phrases"-type search requires you to anticipate what words or combinations of words will appear in the text of legal authorities that may bear on your research problem. You must think from the perspective of a judge or legislator, and try to imagine what words they would use in a decision or statute dealing with a problem like yours.[50]

With respect to computerized "known authority"-type searches, typing in a primary authority's citation results in a search analogous to Shepardizing the known authority. (See Chapter 6.) The computer will search for and display the citations (or, if you choose, the full text) of all cases in which your known typed-in authority has been cited. You can also use this technique with any kind of secondary authority, such as a treatise or law review article: by typing in the name of the secondary authority, you can retrieve any cases that have cited it. Because the Shepard's citators used in non-computerized research don't treat most secondary authorities, this computer feature offers greater flexibility for updating a given secondary authority and for determining the influence it has had on judicial decision-making.

Finally, computerized research also allows highly specialized searches that would be nearly impossible—or at least tremendously tedious and time-consuming—to do without a computer. For example, if you wanted a list of all the opinions decided by a particular judge dealing with a specific legal issue, you could easily instruct the computer to assemble that list. Moreover, you could even limit that search to a specific period, e.g., from January 1, 1975 to the present.

For more detailed instructions on how to do computerized legal research, you should consult the user handbook supplied by the company providing whichever computer service you use.[51] Remember, however, that although computers can offer invaluable research assistance, they cannot make you any more effective as a researcher than you are when using conventional methods. You will still need to know and understand the essential steps involved in legal research.

In short, the computer can't make you smarter, just faster.

[50]Note that you also engage in a similar kind of anticipatory thinking process in non-computerized research. In that setting, however, you try to anticipate not the actual text of primary authorities, but the classifications and headings legal publishers would use to index them in such research sources as case digests, encyclopedias, and annotated statutes.

[51]If you want additional background information, you can also check Sprowl, *Legal Research and the Computer: Where the Two Paths Cross*, 15 CLEARINGHOUSE REV. 150 (1981).

APPENDIX B

Other Research Sources

Chapter 4, on "Finding the Law," discusses the primary and secondary sources in which the vast majority of legal research is done. In doing your legal research, you will come across references to a few sources not covered in Chapter 4. The most important of these are listed and briefly described below.

Administrative agency decisions. In addition to issuing regulations (see pp. 1, 3) administrative agencies also act in a quasi-judicial capacity by interpreting their regulations through administrative decisions and orders. These are subject to review by the courts, and their value as generally applicable legal precedent will vary from jurisdiction to jurisdiction and even from agency to agency within a jurisdiction. (Thus, unlike administrative regulations, which are legally binding throughout the jurisdiction in which the agency functions, administrative decisions may not necessarily constitute binding precedent.)

At the federal level, administrative decisions are reported both in official publications available through the U.S. Government Printing Office and in unofficial looseleaf reporter services (see Chapter 6 and p. 137) available from various commercial publishers, such as Bureau of National Affairs ("BNA"), Commerce Clearing House ("CCH") and Prentice-Hall ("P-H"). Because the official government publications are often poorly indexed and not published in a timely manner, the commercial looseleaf services are generally more helpful and are more frequently relied on by legal researchers. At the state level, publication practices for administrative decisions vary from state to state and from agency to agency; often, the best way of locating state administrative decisions is to contact the issuing agency directly.

With respect to updating administrative decisions, some federal administrative agencies' decisions can be updated through Shepardizing (see Chapter 6) in *Shepard's United States Administrative Law Cita-*

tions. For state administrative decisions, the best way of updating is to contact the agency for recent developments, since state administrative decisions are not treated in *Shepard's Citations.*

Attorney general opinions. The attorneys general of the United States and of individual states often issue written opinions interpreting statutes or providing other general legal advice and analysis to public officials. These opinions are usually only advisory, not binding. Nonetheless, attorney general opinions are frequently persuasive sources of legal analysis and may be taken into account by the courts in dealing with issues upon which attorney general opinions have been issued.

References to attorney general opinions can be found in the annotations contained in annotated federal and state statutory codes, and through Shepardizing (see Chapter 6). A local law library should have copies of the opinions of the attorney general of that state, and may also have copies of opinions of the U.S. Attorney General. If you have difficulty locating an attorney general opinion, contact the appropriate attorney general's office.

Ordinances. Ordinances are statutes passed by local governments, such as cities and counties, to regulate local matters, *e.g.*, traffic or zoning. Ordinances are sometimes compiled into codes; when they are not so codified, the best way to find individual ordinances is to contact the appropriate local government. Because ordinance codes rarely contain case annotations, the most useful aid for finding case law interpreting an ordinance is by Shepardizing the ordinance in the relevant state's *Shepard's Citations* (see Chapter 6) or by searching for references to the ordinance in the data base of a computerized legal research service (see Appendix A).

Looseleaf reporter services. These services, designed to be collected and stored in looseleaf or compression binders, encompass a wide variety of publications resembling periodically issued newsletters. There are numerous looseleaf services, each of which deals with a specific area of law. One of the distinguishing features of looseleaf services is that they often reprint court decisions (including decisions of lower state and local courts) and regulations and decisions of administrative agencies that are not published in any other source. Consequently, looseleaf reporter services can be essential law-finding tools, though mainly for researching highly specialized areas of the law (such as bankruptcy or securities) or for researching areas of the law where administrative decisions and regulations play an important role (such as tax law, where it is frequently necessary to locate rulings and announcements of the Internal Revenue Service that are not widely available outside of looseleaf reporters).

Because each looseleaf service issues periodic reports, often as frequently as weekly, they are usually more timely in their coverage than other primary sources, such as case reporters. This characteristic of looseleaf services also makes them useful tools for updating the law. Chapter 6 discusses the use of looseleaf services as updating tools, and a further description of these services is found there.

The three major publishers of looseleaf reporter services are Bureau of National Affairs ("BNA"), Commerce Clearing House ("CCH"), and Prentice-Hall ("P-H"). The services issued by these publishers cover such topical areas as: admiralty; antitrust and trade regulation; aviation; bankruptcy; banks and banking; consumer and commercial credit; copyright; criminal law; domestic relations; energy; environment; estate planning; fair employment; food, drugs, and cosmetics; health and safety; housing; insurance; labor relations; mass communications; patents; pensions; poverty; products liability; public utilities; securities regulations; social security; stocks and bonds; taxation; trademarks; trusts; unemployment compensation; wills; and worker's compensation.

Bar publications. Various bar organizations, such as the American Bar Association, the Association of Trial Lawyers of America, and state and local bar associations, sponsor and issue numerous publications dealing with a wide variety of legal subjects. These publications, especially at the state and local levels, tend to focus on matters of immediate concern to legal practitioners, and have a practical problem-solving rather than a scholarly emphasis. Articles in the periodical publications of many bar organizations can be found through the *Index to Legal Periodicals,* the *Current Law Index,* and the *Legal Resources Index.*

In addition, many of the bar organizations publish materials in connection with continuing legal education courses for lawyers. These publications may be available from the sponsoring organization or in your local law library.

Court rules. Each court system issues procedural rules governing how litigation will be handled as it moves through the courts. If you expect your legal problem to wind up in a court, you will need to know the court's rules of practice and procedure. These rules can be found in the federal and state statutes (for federal and state courts, respectively). Check in the relevant statutory code's index under "Civil Procedure," "Criminal Procedure," "Procedural Rules," or some similar heading. If you need additional assistance finding court rules, you can ask your law librarian, call your local bar association, or inquire at the court itself.

Also, several treatises exist on the subject of court procedure and rules, and they should be available at your local law library.

Practice and procedure books and form books. Practice and procedure books offer advice to legal practitioners about what steps they should follow to take a legal problem through a particular court system—what documents to file, when to file them, the elements of particular legal claims, practical suggestions for dealing with the court and opposing counsel, and so forth. Such books exist for the federal courts as well as for most state court systems.

Form books complement practice and procedure books by providing detailed examples of various documents, such as leases and wills, which practitioners can modify and adapt to their specific needs.

Practice and procedure books and form books are published by various commercial publishers and are generally available in law libraries.

Jury instructions. Books of standardized jury instructions contain summaries of federal or state law relevant to certain subjects on which courts frequently instruct juries. These pattern instructions also frequently contain historical or critical commentary as well as citations to specific legal authorities, making them useful supplementary research aids, where available. Check your law library.

APPENDIX C

Overview of Civil Procedure

The following summary introduction to how the legal system operates in the civil area is reprinted from LAW AND THE COURTS (1980), a pamphlet prepared by the American Bar Association's Standing Committee on Association Communications.

How a Lawsuit Begins. Court actions fall into two broad categories—civil and criminal. Civil cases are those in which an individual, business or agency of government seeks damages or relief from another individual, business or agency of government; these constitute the great bulk of cases in the courts. The most common example is the suit for damages arising from an automobile accident. A criminal action is one by the state or federal government against an individual charged with committing a crime.

This section deals with an average civil case. Civil actions generally are brought for breach of a contract (*ex contractu*), or for a wrong (*ex delicto*) or tort.

In the early days of the law, courts and lawyers were inclined to restrict the scope of legal actions. Thus, if a set of facts did not fit into an established legal "pigeon hole," the client was without remedy even though he had suffered a wrong to his person or property.

As a consequence, a new system–equity–evolved which provides a remedy that previously was not available. Equity covers such matters as preventing the continuance of a wrong (injunction), and compelling the performance of a contract to sell real estate or unique personal property (specific performance). Ordinarily neither a jury trial nor money damages can be obtained in proceedings in equity.

A person who believes that he has been injured or damaged by another person or business firm consults his lawyer and tells him the facts and circumstances which he believes constitute a cause of legal action. The attorney takes the client's statement, interviews possible witnesses, examines applicable statutes and court decisions, and tries to determine whether the client has a case.

If the attorney concludes the client does have a cause of action, he prepares and files a *complaint* or *petition* in the proper court. His client is the *plaintiff* and the person or firm against whom the case is filed is the *defendant.*

The petition states the facts of the plaintiff's action against the defendant and sets forth the damages, judgment or other relief sought. However, the mere filing of a suit is not proof that the plaintiff has a cause of action. Later events may demonstrate that his claim is invalid.

The attorney for the plaintiff also files with the clerk of the court a *praecipe for a summons.* This is a request for the court clerk to issue a *summons* or notice, and to direct the county sheriff to serve a copy of it on the defendant. In some states, a praecipe is not necessary and the summons is issued as a matter of course. In others, the summons may be served in advance of the filing of the petition or complaint. In still others, any person over 21 and not a party to the action may serve the summons.

After the sheriff has served the summons, he returns the original of the summons to the court, with a notation as to whether and, if so, how the defendant was served with the summons. Serving of the summons is the defendant's formal notification of suit. Filing a complaint and serving the summons commences the case.

After service, the defendant is entitled to a certain period of time within which to file his *pleading*, or answer, to the plaintiff's petition.

Jurisdiction and Venue. The attorney must select the proper county or district in which to file the case. A court has no authority to render a judgment in any case unless it has *jurisdiction* over the person or property involved. This means that the court must be able to exercise control over the defendant, or that the property involved must be located in the county or district under the court's control.

Certain actions are said to be *local*—that is, they may be brought only in the county where the subject matter of the litigation is located. An example of a local action would be an action for the foreclosure of a mortgage on real estate.

Other actions are said to be *transitory*—that is, they may be brought in any county in any state where the defendant may be found and served with summons. An action for personal injuries is an example of a transitory action.

Venue means the county or district where the action is to be tried. Venue may be changed to another county or district upon application or by agreement. Where wide prejudicial publicity has been given to a case before trial, a change of venue is sometimes sought in an effort to secure jurors who have not formed an opinion or to provide a neutral forum not charged with local bias. Venue also may be changed to serve the convenience of witnesses.

A *change of venue from the judge* usually is granted on an application, which claims that the judge has some relationship to the parties, attorneys or facts of the case, which prevents his being completely unbiased during the trial.

Preparation for Trial. The plaintiff and defendant, through their respective attorneys, attempt to marshal all of the pertinent facts bearing upon the case. The defendant may begin

his defense by filing certain pleadings, which may include one or more of the following:

Motion to Quash Service of Summons. Questions whether the defendant has been properly served with summons, as provided by law.

Motion to Strike. Asks the court to rule whether the plaintiff's petition contains irrelevant, prejudicial or other improper matter. If it does, the court may order such matter deleted.

Motion to Make More Definite and Certain. Asks the court to require the plaintiff to set out the facts of his complaint more specifically, or to describe his injury or damages in greater detail, so that the defendant can answer more precisely.

Motion to Dismiss. Asks the court to rule that the plaintiff's complaint does not state a legally sound cause of action against the defendant even if, for the purpose of the motion, the defendant admits that all the facts set out by the plaintiff are true. This was once called a *demurrer.*

Answer. This statement by the defendant denies the allegations in the plaintiff's petition, or admits some and denies others, or admits all and pleads an excuse.

Cross-petition or *Cross-complaint.* May be filed by the defendant either separately or as part of his answer. It asks for relief or damages on the part of the defendant against the original plaintiff, and perhaps others. When a cross-petition is filed, the plaintiff may then file any of the previously-mentioned motions to the cross-petition, except a motion to quash service of summons.

Reply. Either party in the case may file a reply, which constitutes an answer to any new allegations raised by the other party in prior pleadings.

Note: A *plea* or *pleading* refers to an answer or other formal document filed in the action. The words should not be used to describe an argument made in court by a lawyer.

Taking of Depositions. A *deposition* is an out-of-court statement of a witness under oath, intended for use in court or in preparation for trial. Under prevailing statutes and rules in most jurisdictions, either of the parties in a civil action may take the deposition of the other party, or of any witness.

Depositions frequently are necessary to preserve the testimony of important witnesses who cannot appear in court or who reside in another state or jurisdiction. This might be the testimony of a friendly witness—one whose evidence is considered helpful to the plaintiff or defendant, as the case may be. Or it might involve an adverse witness whose statements are taken, by one side or the other, to determine the nature of the evidence he would give if summoned as a witness in the trial.

The deposition may take the form of answers to written questions or of oral examination followed by cross-examination.

A deposition is not a public record, and not available to the press, until it is made so by court order.

A state may not compel the presence at a civil trial of a witness who is outside the state or who is in another county of the same state. When the testimony of such a witness is sought, the procedure is for the party seeking the testimony to apply to the court in which the case is pending for the issuance of a commission—commonly called *letters rogatory.* This is directed to an official or attorney in the jurisdiction where the witness is, empowering him to take the witness's deposition and forward it to the court.

In some states, it is not necessary to secure the issuance of a commission, but only to serve notice of the taking of the deposition upon opposing attorneys.

If a witness is absent from the jurisdiction or is unable to attend the trial in person, his deposition may be read in evidence. If a person who has given a deposition also appears as a witness at the trial, his deposition may be used to attack his credibility, if his oral testimony at the trial is inconsistent with that contained in the deposition.

Discovery. In addition to taking depositions in an attempt to ascertain the facts upon which another party relies, either party may submit written questions, called *interrogatories,* to the other party and require that such be answered under oath.

Other methods of discovery are: requiring adverse parties to produce books, records and documents for inspection, to submit to a physical examination, or to admit or deny the genuineness of documents.

Pre-Trial Conference. After all the pleadings of both parties have been filed and the case is *at issue,* many courts then set the case for a pre-trial hearing. At this hearing, the attorneys appear, generally without their clients and, in the presence of the judge, seek to agree on undisputed facts, called *stipulations.* These may include such matters as time and place in the case of an accident, the use of pictures, maps or sketches, and other matters, including points of law.

The objective of the pre-trial hearing is to shorten the actual trial time without infringing upon the rights of either party.

Pre-trial procedure, used extensively in the federal district courts, frequently results in the settlement of the case without trial. If it does not, the court assigns a specific trial date for the case, following the pre-trial hearing.

Source: American Bar Association © 1980

APPENDIX D

Case Headnotes and the Digesting System

Figure U from Chapter 4, which shows the first page of a court decision as published in West Publishing Company's *Supreme Court Reporter,* is reprinted here with an identification of the various parts of case headnotes.

As discussed on page 56, one helpful feature of case reporter headnotes in legal research is that their "Key" or section number information correlates with the organization of the same publisher's case digests, allowing easy movement between case reporters and case digests of a single publisher.

Note the "caveat" discussed at pages 56 and 58, however, that although headnotes are helpful research aids, they cannot substitute for actually reading for yourself the case material summarized in them.

445 U.S. 55   LEWIS v. UNITED STATES   **915**
                              Cite as 100 S.Ct. 915 (1980)

445 U.S. 55, 63 L.Ed.2d 198

George Calvin LEWIS, Jr., Petitioner,

v.

UNITED STATES.

No. 78–1595.

Argued Jan. 7, 1980.

Decided Feb. 27, 1980.

Defendant was convicted in the United States District Court for the Eastern District of Virginia, Robert R. Merhige, Jr., J., as a convicted felon with unlawful possession of a firearm. On appeal, the United States Court of Appeals for the Fourth Circuit, Donald Russell, Circuit Judge, 591 F.2d 978, affirmed. On certiorari, the Supreme Court, Mr. Justice Blackmun, held that: (1) federal firearms statute prohibits a felon from possessing a firearm despite fact that predicate felony may be subject to collateral attack on constitutional grounds, and (2) federal firearm statute which prohibits felon from possessing a firearm even if predicate felony may be subject of collateral attack on constitutional grounds does not violate due process clause of Fifth Amendment.

Affirmed.

Mr. Justice Brennan dissented and filed opinion in which Mr. Justice Marshall and Mr. Justice Powell joined.

1. Weapons ⊕4

headnote {
Federal firearms statute prohibits felon from possessing a firearm despite the fact that the predicate felony may be subject to collateral attack on constitutional grounds. 18 U.S.C.A. App. § 1202(a)(1).
}

2. Criminal Law ⊕641.1

headnote
number†   Under Sixth Amendment, an uncounseled felony conviction cannot be used for certain purposes; however, that uncounseled conviction is not invalid for all purposes. U.S.C.A.Const. Amend. 6.

* The syllabus constitutes no part of the opinion of the Court but has been prepared by the Reporter of Decisions for the convenience of

3. Constitutional Law ⊕258(3)   digest topic
                                                titles
Weapons ⊕3
      Federal firearm statute which prohibits a felon from possessing a firearm even if predicate felony may be subject to collateral attack on constitutional grounds did not violate due process clause of Fifth Amendment. 18 U.S.C.A. App. § 1202(a)(1); U.S. C.A.Const. Amend. 5.

4. Weapons ⊕17   key
                                 number of
      Prosecution for unlawful possession of   a sub-topic
a firearm by a felon does not open the   under a
predicate felony conviction to a new form   digest
of collateral attack. 18 U.S.C.A. App.   topic††
§ 1202(a)(1).

*Syllabus **

Held: Even though petitioner's extant prior state-court felony conviction may be subject to collateral attack under *Gideon v. Wainwright,* 372 U.S. 335, 83 S.Ct. 792, 9 L.Ed.2d 799, it could properly be used as a predicate for his subsequent conviction for possession of a firearm in violation of § 1202(a)(1) of Title VII of the Omnibus Crime Control and Safe Streets Act of 1968. Pp. 918–922.

(a) The plain meaning of § 1202(a)(1)'s sweeping language proscribing the possession of firearms by any person who "has been convicted by a court of the United States or of a State . . . of a felony," is that the fact of a felony conviction imposes firearm disability until the conviction is vacated or the felon is relieved of his disability by some affirmative action. Other provisions of the statute demonstrate and reinforce its broad sweep, and there is nothing in § 1202(a)(1)'s legislative history to suggest that Congress was willing to allow a defendant to question the validity of his prior conviction as a defense to a charge under § 1202(a)(1). Moreover, the fact that there are remedies available to a convicted felon—removal of the firearm disability by

the reader. See *United States v. Detroit Lumber Co.,* 200 U.S. 321, 337, 26 S.Ct. 282, 287, 50 L.Ed. 499.

Source: West Publishing Company © 1982

†See footnote on p. 145.
††See footnote on p. 145.

Footnotes for Appendix D

† The headnotes of each case are assigned consecutive numbers that act as an internal indexing system *for the contents of that case only.*
As you read through a case, you will generally find bracketed numbers at the beginning of various paragraphs in the text. Such a bracketed number indicates that the point of law discussed at that place in the decision is the same point of law summarized in the correspondingly numbered headnote.
For example, in the illustrative case of *Lewis v. United States,* if you were interested in finding the part of the decision discussing whether the Sixth Amendment prohibits the use of an uncounseled felony conviction, you would look for a "[2]" in the text of the decision. The part of the decision so labelled will elaborate on the point summarized in headnote 2.

†† The sample page in this appendix is from a West Publishing Company case reporter. It shows a "Key" number, which is a tradename West uses in its case reporter and digest system. West identifies thousands of narrow, separate points of law discussed in court decisions, designates those points as "sub-topics" under its broader digest topics (see Appendices G and H), and then assigns a permanent "Key" number to each sub-topic. These topics, sub-topics, and Key Numbers comprise the digesting system West uses for indexing its case reporters. Key numbers remain constant throughout all West digests and reporters, *i.e.,* all cases dealing with a given point of law will be summarized in West's digests under the same topic, sub-topic, and Key Number.
For example, in the sample page shown here, the point of law concerning whether prosecution for unlawful possession of a firearm by a felon opens the underlying felony conviction to a new form of collateral atack in the courts is digested by West under sub-topic Key number 17 of the digest topic "Weapons." If any other cases besides *Lewis v. United States* deal with the same point of law, West will also summarize those cases' treatment of the point and index the summaries under Key number 17 of the West digest topic "Weapons."
Publishers of non-West case reporters and digests use a similar indexing system, but in those publications the functional equivalent of a Key number is called a "section number," or occasionally a "paragraph number."

APPENDIX E

Briefing a Case:
Brown v. Board of Education and Sample Brief

As discussed in Chapter 5 ("Reading the Law"), briefing cases can serve as an important analytical tool, especially for beginning legal researchers. See pages 91–93. This appendix reprints the U.S. Supreme Court case of *Brown v. Board of Education,* 347 U.S. 483 (1954), which is followed by a sample brief we have prepared of it. There is no single correct way of briefing any case, but the suggested brief included here illustrates the general format a comprehensive brief would have.

BROWN *v.* BOARD OF EDUCATION.   483

Syllabus.

BROWN ET AL. *v.* BOARD OF EDUCATION OF TOPEKA ET AL.

NO. 1.   APPEAL FROM THE UNITED STATES DISTRICT COURT FOR THE DISTRICT OF KANSAS.*

Argued December 9, 1952.—Reargued December 8, 1953.— Decided May 17, 1954.

Segregation of white and Negro children in the public schools of a State solely on the basis of race, pursuant to state laws permitting or requiring such segregation, denies to Negro children the equal protection of the laws guaranteed by the Fourteenth Amendment— even though the physical facilities and other "tangible" factors of white and Negro schools may be equal. Pp. 486–496.

(a) The history of the Fourteenth Amendment is inconclusive as to its intended effect on public education. Pp. 489–490.

(b) The question presented in these cases must be determined, not on the basis of conditions existing when the Fourteenth Amendment was adopted, but in the light of the full development of public education and its present place in American life throughout the Nation. Pp. 492–493.

(c) Where a State has undertaken to provide an opportunity for an education in its public schools, such an opportunity is a right which must be made available to all on equal terms. P. 493.

(d) Segregation of children in public schools solely on the basis of race deprives children of the minority group of equal educational opportunities, even though the physical facilities and other "tangible" factors may be equal. Pp. 493–494.

(e) The "separate but equal" doctrine adopted in *Plessy* v. *Ferguson*, 163 U. S. 537, has no place in the field of public education. P. 495.

*Together with No. 2, *Briggs et al.* v. *Elliott et al.*, on appeal from the United States District Court for the Eastern District of South Carolina, argued December 9–10, 1952, reargued December 7–8, 1953; No. 4, *Davis et al.* v. *County School Board of Prince Edward County, Virginia, et al.*, on appeal from the United States District Court for the Eastern District of Virginia, argued December 10, 1952, reargued December 7–8, 1953; and No. 10, *Gebhart et al.* v. *Belton et al.*, on certiorari to the Supreme Court of Delaware, argued December 11, 1952, reargued December 9, 1953.

484   OCTOBER TERM, 1953.

(f) The cases are restored to the docket for further argument on specified questions relating to the forms of the decrees. Pp. 495–496.

Robert L. Carter argued the cause for appellants in No. 1 on the original argument and on the reargument. *Thurgood Marshall* argued the cause for appellants in No. 2 on the original argument and *Spottswood W. Robinson, III,* for appellants in No. 4 on the original argument, and both argued the causes for appellants in Nos. 2 and 4 on the reargument. *Louis L. Redding* and *Jack Greenberg* argued the cause for respondents in No. 10 on the original argument and *Jack Greenberg* and *Thurgood Marshall* on the reargument.

On the briefs were *Robert L. Carter, Thurgood Marshall, Spottswood W. Robinson, III, Louis L. Redding, Jack Greenberg, George E. C. Hayes, William R. Ming, Jr., Constance Baker Motley, James M. Nabrit, Jr., Charles S. Scott, Frank D. Reeves, Harold R. Boulware* and *Oliver W. Hill* for appellants in Nos. 1, 2 and 4 and respondents in No. 10; *George M. Johnson* for appellants in Nos. 1, 2 and 4; and *Loren Miller* for appellants in Nos. 2 and 4. *Arthur D. Shores* and *A. T. Walden* were on the Statement as to Jurisdiction and a brief opposing a Motion to Dismiss or Affirm in No. 2.

Paul E. Wilson, Assistant Attorney General of Kansas, argued the cause for appellees in No. 1 on the original argument and on the reargument. With him on the briefs was *Harold R. Fatzer,* Attorney General.

John W. Davis argued the cause for appellees in No. 2 on the original argument and for appellees in Nos. 2 and 4 on the reargument. With him on the briefs in No. 2 were *T. C. Callison,* Attorney General of South Carolina, *Robert McC. Figg, Jr., S. E. Rogers, William R. Meagher* and *Taggart Whipple.*

BROWN *v.* BOARD OF EDUCATION.   485

483   Counsel for Parties.

J. Lindsay Almond, Jr., Attorney General of Virginia, and *T. Justin Moore* argued the cause for appellees in No. 4 on the original argument and for appellees in Nos. 2 and 4 on the reargument. On the briefs in No. 4 were *J. Lindsay Almond, Jr.,* Attorney General, and *Henry T. Wickham,* Special Assistant Attorney General, for the State of Virginia, and *T. Justin Moore, Archibald G. Robertson, John W. Riely* and *T. Justin Moore, Jr.* for the Prince Edward County School Authorities, appellees.

H. Albert Young, Attorney General of Delaware, argued the cause for petitioners in No. 10 on the original argument and on the reargument. With him on the briefs was *Louis J. Finger,* Special Deputy Attorney General.

By special leave of Court, *Assistant Attorney General Rankin* argued the cause for the United States on the reargument, as *amicus curiae,* urging reversal in Nos. 1, 2 and 4 and affirmance in No. 10. With him on the brief were *Attorney General Brownell, Philip Elman, Leon Ulman, William J. Lamont* and *M. Magdelena Schoch. James P. McGranery,* then Attorney General, and *Philip Elman* filed a brief for the United States on the original argument, as *amicus curiae,* urging reversal in Nos. 1, 2 and 4 and affirmance in No. 10.

Briefs of *amici curiae* supporting appellants in No. 1 were filed by *Shad Polier, Will Maslow* and *Joseph B. Robison* for the American Jewish Congress; by *Edwin J. Lukas, Arnold Forster, Arthur Garfield Hays, Frank E. Karelsen, Leonard Haas, Saburo Kido* and *Theodore Leskes* for the American Civil Liberties Union et al.; and by *John Ligtenberg* and *Selma M. Borchardt* for the American Federation of Teachers. Briefs of *amici curiae* supporting appellants in No. 1 and respondents in No. 10 were filed by *Arthur J. Goldberg* and *Thomas E. Harris*

486   OCTOBER TERM, 1953.

Opinion of the Court.   347 U. S.

for the Congress of Industrial Organizations and by
Phineas Indritz for the American Veterans Committee,
Inc.

MR. CHIEF JUSTICE WARREN delivered the opinion of
the Court.

These cases come to us from the States of Kansas,
South Carolina, Virginia, and Delaware. They are pre-
mised on different facts and different local conditions,
but a common legal question justifies their consideration
together in this consolidated opinion.[1]

---

[1] In the Kansas case, *Brown* v. *Board of Education,* the plaintiffs
are Negro children of elementary school age residing in Topeka.
They brought this action in the United States District Court for the
District of Kansas to enjoin enforcement of a Kansas statute which
permits, but does not require, cities of more than 15,000 population
to maintain separate school facilities for Negro and white students.
Kan. Gen. Stat. § 72–1724 (1949). Pursuant to that authority, the
Topeka Board of Education elected to establish segregated elementary
schools. Other public schools in the community, however, are oper-
ated on a nonsegregated basis. The three-judge District Court, convened under 28 U. S. C. §§ 2281 and 2284, found that segregation
in public education has a detrimental effect upon Negro children,
but denied relief on the ground that the Negro and white schools
were substantially equal with respect to buildings, transportation,
curricula, and educational qualifications of teachers. 98 F. Supp. 797.
The case is here on direct appeal under 28 U. S. C. § 1253.

In the South Carolina case, *Briggs* v. *Elliott,* the plaintiffs are Negro
children of both elementary and high school age residing in Clarendon
County. They brought this action in the United States District
Court for the Eastern District of South Carolina to enjoin enforcement of provisions in the state constitution and statutory code which
require the segregation of Negroes and whites in public schools.
S. C. Const., Art. XI, § 7; S. C. Code § 5377 (1942). The three-
judge District Court, convened under 28 U. S. C. §§ 2281 and 2284,
denied the requested relief. The court found that the Negro schools
were inferior to the white schools and ordered the defendants to begin
immediately to equalize the facilities. But the court sustained the
validity of the contested provisions and denied the plaintiffs admis-

BROWN *v.* BOARD OF EDUCATION.   487

483   Opinion of the Court.

In each of the cases, minors of the Negro race, through their legal representatives, seek the aid of the courts in obtaining admission to the public schools of their community on a nonsegregated basis.   In each instance,

---

sion to the white schools during the equalization program.   98 F. Supp. 529.   This Court vacated the District Court's judgment and remanded the case for the purpose of obtaining the court's views on a report filed by the defendants concerning the progress made in the equalization program.   342 U. S. 350.   On remand, the District Court found that substantial equality had been achieved except for buildings and that the defendants were proceeding to rectify this inequality as well.   103 F. Supp. 920.   The case is again here on direct appeal under 28 U. S. C. § 1253.

In the Virginia case, *Davis* v. *County School Board*, the plaintiffs are Negro children of high school age residing in Prince Edward County.   They brought this action in the United States District Court for the Eastern District of Virginia to enjoin enforcement of provisions in the state constitution and statutory code which require the segregation of Negroes and whites in public schools.   Va'. Const., § 140; Va. Code § 22–221 (1950).   The three-judge District Court, convened under 28 U. S. C. §§ 2281 and 2284, denied the requested relief.   The court found the Negro school inferior in physical plant, curricula, and transportation, and ordered the defendants forthwith to provide substantially equal curricula and transportation and to "proceed with all reasonable diligence and dispatch to remove" the inequality in physical plant.   But, as in the South Carolina case, the court sustained the validity of the contested provisions and denied the plaintiffs admission to the white schools during the equalization program.   103 F. Supp. 337.   The case is here on direct appeal under 28 U. S. C. § 1253.

In the Delaware case, *Gebhart* v. *Belton*, the plaintiffs are Negro children of both elementary and high school age residing in New Castle County.   They brought this action in the Delaware Court of Chancery to enjoin enforcement of provisions in the state constitution and statutory code which require the segregation of Negroes and whites in public schools.   Del. Const., Art. X, § 2; Del. Rev. Code § 2631 (1935).   The Chancellor gave judgment for the plaintiffs and ordered their immediate admission to schools previously attended only by white children, on the ground that the Negro schools were inferior with respect to teacher training, pupil-teacher ratio, extracurricular activities, physical plant, and time and distance in-

488   OCTOBER TERM, 1953.

they had been denied admission to schools attended by
white children under laws requiring or permitting segregation according to race.   This segregation was alleged to
deprive the plaintiffs of the equal protection of the laws
under the Fourteenth Amendment.   In each of the cases
other than the Delaware case, a three-judge federal district court denied relief to the plaintiffs on the so-called
"separate but equal" doctrine announced by this Court
in *Plessy* v. *Ferguson,* 163 U. S. 537.   Under that doctrine,
equality of treatment is accorded when the races are
provided substantially equal facilities, even though these
facilities be separate.   In the Delaware case, the Supreme
Court of Delaware adhered to that doctrine, but ordered
that the plaintiffs be admitted to the white schools
because of their superiority to the Negro schools.

The plaintiffs contend that segregated public schools
are not "equal" and cannot be made "equal," and that
hence they are deprived of the equal protection of the
laws.   Because of the obvious importance of the question
presented, the Court took jurisdiction.[2]   Argument was
heard in the 1952 Term, and reargument was heard this
Term on certain questions propounded by the Court.[3]

---

volved in travel. 87 A. 2d 862. The Chancellor also found that segregation itself results in an inferior education for Negro children (see
note 10, *infra*), but did not rest his decision on that ground. *Id.,* at
865. The Chancellor's decree was affirmed by the Supreme Court of
Delaware, which intimated, however, that the defendants might be
able to obtain a modification of the decree after equalization of the
Negro and white schools had been accomplished. 91 A. 2d 137, 152.
The defendants, contending only that the Delaware courts had erred
in ordering the immediate admission of the Negro plaintiffs to the
white schools, applied to this Court for certiorari. The writ was
granted, 344 U. S. 891. The plaintiffs, who were successful below,
did not submit a cross-petition.

[2] 344 U. S. 1, 141, 891.

[3] 345 U. S. 972. The Attorney General of the United States par-
ticipated both Terms as *amicus curiae.*

BROWN *v.* BOARD OF EDUCATION.   489

483   Opinion of the Court.

Reargument was largely devoted to the circumstances surrounding the adoption of the Fourteenth Amendment in 1868. It covered exhaustively consideration of the Amendment in Congress, ratification by the states, then existing practices in racial segregation, and the views of proponents and opponents of the Amendment. This discussion and our own investigation convince us that, although these sources cast some light, it is not enough to resolve the problem with which we are faced. At best, they are inconclusive. The most avid proponents of the post-War Amendments undoubtedly intended them to remove all legal distinctions among "all persons born or naturalized in the United States." Their opponents, just as certainly, were antagonistic to both the letter and the spirit of the Amendments and wished them to have the most limited effect. What others in Congress and the state legislatures had in mind cannot be determined with any degree of certainty.

An additional reason for the inconclusive nature of the Amendment's history, with respect to segregated schools, is the status of public education at that time.[4] In the South, the movement toward free common schools, sup-

---

[4] For a general study of the development of public education prior to the Amendment, see Butts and Cremin, A History of Education in American Culture (1953), Pts. I, II; Cubberley, Public Education in the United States (1934 ed.), cc. II–XII. School practices current at the time of the adoption of the Fourteenth Amendment are described in Butts and Cremin, *supra,* at 269–275; Cubberley, *supra,* at 288–339, 408–431; Knight, Public Education in the South (1922), cc. VIII, IX. See also H. Ex. Doc. No. 315, 41st Cong., 2d Sess. (1871). Although the demand for free public schools followed substantially the same pattern in both the North and the South, the development in the South did not begin to gain momentum until about 1850, some twenty years after that in the North. The reasons for the somewhat slower development in the South (*e. g.,* the rural character of the South and the different regional attitudes toward state assistance) are well explained in Cubberley, *supra,* at 408–423. In the country as a whole, but particularly in the South, the War

490   OCTOBER TERM, 1953.

                Opinion of the Court.   347 U. S.

ported by general taxation, had not yet taken hold. Education of white children was largely in the hands of private groups. Education of Negroes was almost non-existent, and practically all of the race were illiterate. In fact, any education of Negroes was forbidden by law in some states. Today, in contrast, many Negroes have achieved outstanding success in the arts and sciences as well as in the business and professional world. It is true that public school education at the time of the Amendment had advanced further in the North, but the effect of the Amendment on Northern States was generally ignored in the congressional debates. Even in the North, the conditions of public education did not approximate those existing today. The curriculum was usually rudimentary; ungraded schools were common in rural areas; the school term was but three months a year in many states; and compulsory school attendance was virtually unknown. As a consequence, it is not surprising that there should be so little in the history of the Fourteenth Amendment relating to its intended effect on public education.

In the first cases in this Court construing the Fourteenth Amendment, decided shortly after its adoption, the Court interpreted it as proscribing all state-imposed discriminations against the Negro race.[5] The doctrine of

----

virtually stopped all progress in public education. *Id.*, at 427–428. The low status of Negro education in all sections of the country, both before and immediately after the War, is described in Beale, A History of Freedom of Teaching in American Schools (1941), 112–132, 175–195. Compulsory school attendance laws were not generally adopted until after the ratification of the Fourteenth Amendment, and it was not until 1918 that such laws were in force in all the states. Cubberley, *supra*, at 563–565.

[5] *Slaughter-House Cases,* 16 Wall. 36, 67–72 (1873); *Strauder* v. *West Virginia,* 100 U. S. 303, 307–308 (1880):

"It ordains that no State shall deprive any person of life, liberty, or property, without due process of law, or deny to any person within its jurisdiction the equal protection of the laws. What is this but

BROWN v. BOARD OF EDUCATION.   491

483   Opinion of the Court.

"separate but equal" did not make its appearance in this Court until 1896 in the case of *Plessy* v. *Ferguson, supra,* involving not education but transportation.[6] American courts have since labored with the doctrine for over half a century. In this Court, there have been six cases involving the "separate but equal" doctrine in the field of public education.[7] In *Cumming* v. *County Board of Education,* 175 U. S. 528, and *Gong Lum* v. *Rice,* 275 U. S. 78, the validity of the doctrine itself was not challenged.[8] In more recent cases, all on the graduate school

---

declaring that the law in the States shall be the same for the black as for the white; that all persons, whether colored or white, shall stand equal before the laws of the States, and, in regard to the colored race, for whose protection the amendment was primarily designed, that no discrimination shall be made against them by law because of their color? The words of the amendment, it is true, are prohibitory, but they contain a necessary implication of a positive immunity, or right, most valuable to the colored race,—the right to exemption from unfriendly legislation against them distinctively as colored,—exemption from legal discriminations, implying inferiority in civil society, lessening the security of their enjoyment of the rights which others enjoy, and discriminations which are steps towards reducing them to the condition of a subject race."
See also *Virginia* v. *Rives,* 100 U. S. 313, 318 (1880); *Ex parte Virginia,* 100 U. S. 339, 344-345 (1880).

[6] The doctrine apparently originated in *Roberts* v. *City of Boston,* 59 Mass. 198, 206 (1850), upholding school segregation against attack as being violative of a state constitutional guarantee of equality. Segregation in Boston public schools was eliminated in 1855. Mass. Acts 1855, c. 256. But elsewhere in the North segregation in public education has persisted in some communities until recent years. It is apparent that such segregation has long been a nationwide problem, not merely one of sectional concern.

[7] See also *Berea College* v. *Kentucky,* 211 U. S. 45 (1908).

[8] In the *Cumming* case, Negro taxpayers sought an injunction requiring the defendant school board to discontinue the operation of a high school for white children until the board resumed operation of a high school for Negro children. Similarly, in the *Gong Lum* case, the plaintiff, a child of Chinese descent, contended only that state authorities had misapplied the doctrine by classifying him with Negro children and requiring him to attend a Negro school.

492   OCTOBER TERM, 1953.

Opinion of the Court.   347 U. S.

level, inequality was found in that specific benefits en-
joyed by white students were denied to Negro students
of the same educational qualifications. *Missouri ex rel.
Gaines* v. *Canada,* 305 U. S. 337; *Sipuel* v. *Oklahoma,* 332
U. S. 631; *Sweatt* v. *Painter,* 339 U. S. 629; *McLaurin* v.
Oklahoma State Regents, 339 U. S. 637. In none of
these cases was it necessary to re-examine the doctrine to
grant relief to the Negro plaintiff. And in *Sweatt* v.
Painter, supra, the Court expressly reserved decision on
the question whether *Plessy* v. *Ferguson* should be held
inapplicable to public education.

In the instant cases, that question is directly presented.
Here, unlike *Sweatt* v. *Painter,* there are findings below
that the Negro and white schools involved have been
equalized, or are being equalized, with respect to buildings, curricula, qualifications and salaries of teachers, and
other "tangible" factors.[9]   Our decision, therefore, cannot turn on merely a comparison of these tangible factors
in the Negro and white schools involved in each of the
cases. We must look instead to the effect of segregation
itself on public education.

In approaching this problem, we cannot turn the clock
back to 1868 when the Amendment was adopted, or even
to 1896 when *Plessy* v. *Ferguson* was written. We must
consider public education in the light of its full development and its present place in American life throughout

---

[9] In the Kansas case, the court below found substantial equality
as to all such factors. 98 F. Supp. 797, 798. In the South Carolina
case, the court below found that the defendants were proceeding
"promptly and in good faith to comply with the court's decree."   103
F. Supp. 920, 921. In the Virginia case, the court below noted that
the equalization program was already "afoot and progressing" (103 F.
Supp. 337, 341); since then, we have been advised, in the Virginia
Attorney General's brief on reargument, that the program has now
been completed. In the Delaware case, the court below similarly
noted that the state's equalization program was well under way.   91
A. 2d 137, 149.

BROWN *v.* BOARD OF EDUCATION.   493

the Nation. Only in this way can it be determined if segregation in public schools deprives these plaintiffs of the equal protection of the laws.

Today, education is perhaps the most important function of state and local governments. Compulsory school attendance laws and the great expenditures for education both demonstrate our recognition of the importance of education to our democratic society. It is required in the performance of our most basic public responsibilities, even service in the armed forces. It is the very foundation of good citizenship. Today it is a principal instrument in awakening the child to cultural values, in preparing him for later professional training, and in helping him to adjust normally to his environment. In these days, it is doubtful that any child may reasonably be expected to succeed in life if he is denied the opportunity of an education. Such an opportunity, where the state has undertaken to provide it, is a right which must be made available to all on equal terms.

We come then to the question presented: Does segregation of children in public schools solely on the basis of race, even though the physical facilities and other "tangible" factors may be equal, deprive the children of the minority group of equal educational opportunities? We believe that it does.

In *Sweatt* v. *Painter, supra,* in finding that a segregated law school for Negroes could not provide them equal educational opportunities, this Court relied in large part on "those qualities which are incapable of objective measurement but which make for greatness in a law school." In *McLaurin* v. *Oklahoma State Regents, supra,* the Court, in requiring that a Negro admitted to a white graduate school be treated like all other students, again resorted to intangible considerations: ". . . his ability to study, to engage in discussions and exchange views with other students, and, in general, to learn his profession."

494   OCTOBER TERM, 1953.

Such considerations apply with added force to children in grade and high schools. To separate them from others of similar age and qualifications solely because of their race generates a feeling of inferiority as to their status in the community that may affect their hearts and minds in a way unlikely ever to be undone. The effect of this separation on their educational opportunities was well stated by a finding in the Kansas case by a court which nevertheless felt compelled to rule against the Negro plaintiffs:

> "Segregation of white and colored children in public schools has a detrimental effect upon the colored children. The impact is greater when it has the sanction of the law; for the policy of separating the races is usually interpreted as denoting the inferiority of the negro group. A sense of inferiority affects the motivation of a child to learn. Segregation with the sanction of law, therefore, has a tendency to [retard] the educational and mental development of negro children and to deprive them of some of the benefits they would receive in a racial[ly] integrated school system." [10]

Whatever may have been the extent of psychological knowledge at the time of *Plessy* v. *Ferguson,* this finding is amply supported by modern authority.[11] Any lan-

---

[10] A similar finding was made in the Delaware case: "I conclude from the testimony that in our Delaware society, State-imposed segregation in education itself results in the Negro children, as a class, receiving educational opportunities which are substantially inferior to those available to white children otherwise similarly situated." 87 A. 2d 862, 865.

[11] K. B. Clark, Effect of Prejudice and Discrimination on Personality Development (Midcentury White House Conference on Children and Youth, 1950); Witmer and Kotinsky, Personality in the Making (1952), c. VI; Deutscher and Chein, The Psychological Effects of Enforced Segregation: A Survey of Social Science Opinion, 26 J. Psychol. 259 (1948); Chein, What are the Psychological Effects of

BROWN v. BOARD OF EDUCATION.   495

483   Opinion of the Court.

guage in *Plessy* v. *Ferguson* contrary to this finding is rejected.

We conclude that in the field of public education the doctrine of "separate but equal" has no place. Separate educational facilities are inherently unequal. Therefore, we hold that the plaintiffs and others similarly situated for whom the actions have been brought are, by reason of the segregation complained of, deprived of the equal protection of the laws guaranteed by the Fourteenth Amendment. This disposition makes unnecessary any discussion whether such segregation also violates the Due Process Clause of the Fourteenth Amendment.[12]

Because these are class actions, because of the wide applicability of this decision, and because of the great variety of local conditions, the formulation of decrees in these cases presents problems of considerable complexity. On reargument, the consideration of appropriate relief was necessarily subordinated to the primary question— the constitutionality of segregation in public education. We have now announced that such segregation is a denial of the equal protection of the laws. In order that we may have the full assistance of the parties in formulating decrees, the cases will be restored to the docket, and the parties are requested to present further argument on Questions 4 and 5 previously propounded by the Court for the reargument this Term.[13]   The Attorney General

---

Segregation Under Conditions of Equal Facilities?, 3 Int. J. Opinion and Attitude Res. 229 (1949); Brameld, Educational Costs, in Discrimination and National Welfare (MacIver, ed., 1949), 44–48; Frazier, The Negro in the United States (1949), 674–681. And see generally Myrdal, An American Dilemma (1944).

[12] See *Bolling* v. *Sharpe, post,* p. 497, concerning the Due Process Clause of the Fifth Amendment.

[13] "4. Assuming it is decided that segregation in public schools violates the Fourteenth Amendment

"(a) would a decree necessarily follow providing that, within the

496   OCTOBER TERM, 1953.

of the United States is again invited to participate.   The
Attorneys General of the states requiring or permitting
segregation in public education will also be permitted to
appear as *amici curiae* upon request to do so by Septem-
ber 15, 1954, and submission of briefs by October 1, 1954.[14]

It is so ordered.

---

limits set by normal geographic school districting, Negro children
should forthwith be admitted to schools of their choice, or

"(b) may this Court, in the exercise of its equity powers, permit
an effective gradual adjustment to be brought about from existing
segregated systems to a system not based on color distinctions?

"5. On the assumption on which questions 4 (a) and (b) are
based, and assuming further that this Court will exercise its equity
powers to the end described in question 4 (b),

"(a) should this Court formulate detailed decrees in these cases;

"(b) if so, what specific issues should the decrees reach;

"(c) should this Court appoint a special master to hear evidence
with a view to recommending specific terms for such decrees;

"(d) should this Court remand to the courts of first instance with
directions to frame decrees in these cases, and if so what general
directions should the decrees of this Court include and what procedures should the courts of first instance follow in arriving at the
specific terms of more detailed decrees?"

[14] See Rule 42, Revised Rules of this Court (effective July 1, 1954).

Sample Brief of *Brown v. Board of Education*

Name of Case:	*Brown v. Board of Education*
Citation:	347 U.S. 483, 74 S. Ct. 686, 98 L. Ed. 873
Date of Decision:	1954
Vote:	9-0
Author of Opinion:	Warren, C. J.
Legal Topics:	Constitutional Law; Civil Rights
Posture of the Case:	Consolidation of four cases brought to the Supreme Court (three cases by appeal, and one by writ of certiorari) from four states in which state law either required or permitted racial segregation of pupils in public schools. The lower courts in three of these cases upheld the constitutionality of school segregation laws; in the other case, the court struck down the law.
Facts:	All plaintiffs were black schoolchildren attending public schools segregated in accordance with state law. They had been denied admission to schools attended by white children under laws requiring or permitting segregation according to race. 347 U.S. at 488. Plaintiffs questioned the constitutionality of the "separate but equal" doctrine of *Plessy v. Ferguson,* 163 U.S. 537 (1896).
Question Presented:	Does segregation of children in public schools solely on the basis of race, even though the physical facilities and other "tangible" factors may be equal, deprive the children of the minority group of equal educational opportunities?
Answer:	Yes.
Court's Reasoning:	Where state has undertaken to provide public education for its citizens, public educational opportunities "must be made available to all on equal terms." 347 U.S. at 493. Evaluation of equality must include consideration of both tangible and intangible characteristics of the educational process. State-sanctioned separation of nonwhite students of similar age and qualifications solely because of their race has a detrimental effect upon the black children. "[T]he pol-

icy of separating the races is usually interpreted as denoting the inferiority" of the
black group. It has the tendency to retard the
educational and mental development of the
black children and to deprive them of some
of the benefits they would receive in a ra-
cially integrated school system. *Id.* at 494 &
nn. 10 & 11.

Significance: Held for the first time that state-mandated
racial separation (*de jure* racial segregation)
in public schools is inherently unequal and
therefore unconstitutional. Severely limited
but did not completely overrule *Plessy*.

APPENDIX F

Answers to Shepardizing Exercises

These are the results you should obtain in doing the sample Shepardizing exercises set out in Chapter 6. (See p. 109.)

1. Find a United States District Court case that distinguished the point of law summarized in headnote 7 of the N.E.2d version of *Trustees of Tufts College v. Volpe Construction Co., Inc.,* 358 Mass. 331, 264 N.E.2d 676 (1970).

   Answer: *Associated General Contractors of Massachusetts, Inc. v. Altshuler,* 361 F. Supp. 1293, 1307 (D. Mass. 1973).

2. Find a Colorado state court case citing *Mabra v. Schmidt,* 356 F. Supp. 620 (W.D. Wis. 1973).

   Answer: *Wesson v. Johnson,* 195 Colo. 521, 523, 579 P.2d 1165, 1167 (1978).

3. For this exercise, there is no fixed answer.

APPENDIX G

Alphabetical Listing of Case Digest Topics
(West Publishing Company)

Case digests are described in Chapter 1 ("Sources of the Law") and their use is explained in Chapter 4 ("Finding the Law"). See pages 13–15, 49–51, and 60–62. This appendix reprints an alphabetical listing of all the digest topics West Publishing Company uses in its case digest system. For a listing of these topics arranged according to subject matter, see Appendix H.

The numbers appearing next to the topics are assigned by West as codes for simplifying computerized research in West's data base, WESTLAW.

1	Abandoned and Lost Property	42	Assumpsit, Action of	80	Clubs
2	Abatement and Revival	43	Asylums	81	Colleges and Universities
3	Abduction	44	Attachment	82	Collision
4	Abortion and Birth Control	45	Attorney and Client	83	Commerce
5	Absentees	46	Attorney General	83H	Commodity Futures Trading Regulation
6	Abstracts of Title	47	Auctions and Auctioneers	84	Common Lands
7	Accession	48	Audita Querela	85	Common Law
8	Accord and Satisfaction	48A	Automobiles	86	Common Scold
9	Account	48B	Aviation	88	Compounding Offenses
10	Account, Action on	49	Bail	89	Compromise and Settlement
11	Account Stated	50	Bailment	89A	Condominium
11A	Accountants	51	Bankruptcy	90	Confusion of Goods
12	Acknowledgment	52	Banks and Banking	91	Conspiracy
13	Action	54	Beneficial Associations	92	Constitutional Law
14	Action on the Case	55	Bigamy	92B	Consumer Credit
15	Adjoining Landowners	56	Bills and Notes	92H	Consumer Protection
15A	Administrative Law and Procedure	57	Blasphemy	93	Contempt
16	Admiralty	58	Bonds	95	Contracts
17	Adoption	59	Boundaries	96	Contribution
18	Adulteration	60	Bounties	97	Conversion
19	Adultery	61	Breach of Marriage Promise	98	Convicts
20	Adverse Possession	62	Breach of the Peace	99	Copyrights and Intellectual Property
21	Affidavits	63	Bribery	100	Coroners
22	Affray	64	Bridges	101	Corporations
23	Agriculture	65	Brokers	102	Costs
24	Aliens	66	Building and Loan Associations	103	Counterfeiting
25	Alteration of Instruments	67	Burglary	104	Counties
26	Ambassadors and Consuls	68	Canals	105	Court Commissioners
27	Amicus Curiae	69	Cancellation of Instruments	106	Courts
28	Animals	70	Carriers	107	Covenant, Action of
29	Annuities	71	Cemeteries	108	Covenants
30	Appeal and Error	72	Census	108A	Credit Reporting Agencies
31	Appearance	73	Certiorari	110	Criminal Law
33	Arbitration	74	Champerty and Maintenance	111	Crops
34	Armed Services	75	Charities	113	Customs and Usages
35	Arrest	76	Chattel Mortgages	114	Customs Duties
36	Arson	76A	Chemical Dependents	115	Damages
37	Assault and Battery	76H	Children Out-of-Wedlock	116	Dead Bodies
38	Assignments	77	Citizens	117	Death
40	Assistance, Writ of	78	Civil Rights	117G	Debt, Action of
41	Associations	79	Clerks of Courts	117T	Debtor and Creditor
				118A	Declaratory Judgment

APPENDIX H

Subject Matter Listing of Case Digest Topics
(West Publishing Company)

Case digests are described in Chapter 1 ("Sources of the Law") and their use is explained in Chapter 4 ("Finding the Law"). See pages 13–15, 49–51, and 60–62. This appendix reprints a subject matter listing of all the topics West Publishing Company uses in its case digest system, arranged by West into seven major categories. West's categorical arrangement of digest topics forms a handy and comprehensive outline of the law. For a complete listing of West's topics arranged alphabetically, see Appendix G.

1. **PERSONS**
2. **PROPERTY**
3. **CONTRACTS**
4. **TORTS**
5. **CRIMES**
6. **REMEDIES**
7. **GOVERNMENT**

1. PERSONS

RELATING TO NATURAL PERSONS IN GENERAL

Civil Rights
Dead Bodies
Death
Domicile
Drugs and Narcotics
Food
Health and Environment
Holidays
Intoxicating Liquors
Names
Poisons
Seals
Signatures
Sunday
Time
Weapons

PARTICULAR CLASSES OF NATURAL PERSONS

Absentees
Aliens
Chemical Dependents
Children Out-of-Wedlock
Citizens
Convicts
Indians
Infants
Mental Health
Paupers
Slaves
Spendthrifts

PERSONAL RELATIONS

Adoption
Attorney and Client
Employers' Liability
Executors and Administrators
Guardian and Ward
Husband and Wife
Labor Relations
Marriage
Master and Servant
Parent and Child
Principal and Agent
Workers' Compensation

ASSOCIATED AND ARTIFICIAL PERSONS

Associations
Beneficial Associations
Building and Loan Associations
Clubs
Colleges and Universities
Corporations
Exchanges
Joint-Stock Companies and Business Trusts
Partnership
Religious Societies

PARTICULAR OCCUPATIONS

Accountants
Agriculture
Auctions and Auctioneers
Aviation
Banks and Banking
Bridges

1. PERSONS—Cont'd

PARTICULAR OCCUPATIONS
—Cont'd

Brokers
Canals
Carriers
Commerce
Consumer Credit
Consumer Protection
Credit Reporting Agencies
Detectives
Electricity
Explosives
Factors
Ferries
Gas
Hawkers and Peddlers
Innkeepers
Insurance
Licenses
Manufactures
Monopolies
Physicians and Surgeons
Pilots
Railroads
Seamen
Shipping
Steam
Telecommunications
Theaters and Shows
Towage
Turnpikes and Toll Roads
Urban Railroads
Warehousemen
Wharves

2. PROPERTY

NATURE, SUBJECTS, AND INCIDENTS OF OWNERSHIP IN GENERAL

Abandoned and Lost Property
Accession
Adjoining Landowners
Confusion of Goods
Improvements
Property

PARTICULAR SUBJECTS AND INCIDENTS OF OWNERSHIP

Animals
Annuities

Automobiles
Boundaries
Cemeteries
Common Lands
Copyrights and Intellectual Property
Crops
Fences
Fish
Fixtures
Franchises
Game
Good Will
Logs and Logging
Mines and Minerals
Navigable Waters
Party Walls
Patents
Public Lands
Trade Regulation
Waters and Water Courses
Woods and Forests

PARTICULAR CLASSES OF ESTATES OR INTERESTS IN PROPERTY

Charities
Condominium
Dower and Curtesy
Easements
Estates in Property
Joint Tenancy
Landlord and Tenant
Life Estates
Perpetuities
Powers
Remainders
Reversions
Tenancy in Common
Trusts

PARTICULAR MODES OF ACQUIRING OR TRANS-FERRING PROPERTY

Abstracts of Title
Adverse Possession
Alteration of Instruments
Assignments
Chattel Mortgages
Conversion
Dedication
Deeds
Descent and Distribution
Escheat
Fraudulent Conveyances

2. PROPERTY—Cont'd

PARTICULAR MODES OF AC-QUIRING OR TRANSFERRING PROPERTY—Cont'd

Gifts
Lost Instruments
Mortages
Pledges
Secured Transactions
Wills

3. CONTRACTS

NATURE, REQUISITES, AND INCIDENTS OF AGREEMENTS IN GENERAL

Contracts
Customs and Usages
Frauds, Statute of
Interest
Usury

PARTICULAR CLASSES OF AGREEMENTS

Bailment
Bills and Notes
Bonds
Breach of Marriage Promise
Champerty and Maintenance
Compromise and Settlement
Covenants
Deposits and Escrows
Exchange of Property
Gaming
Guaranty
Implied and Constructive Contracts
Indemnity
Joint Adventures
Lotteries
Principal and Surety
Rewards
Sales
Subscriptions
Vendor and Purchaser

PARTICULAR CLASSES OF IMPLIED OR CONSTRUCTIVE CONTRACTS OR QUASI CONTRACTS

Account Stated
Contribution

PARTICULAR MODES OF DISCHARGING CONTRACTS

Novation
Payment
Release
Subrogation
Tender

4. TORTS

Assault and Battery
Collision
Conspiracy
False Imprisonment
Forcible Entry and Detainer
Fraud
Libel and Slander
Malicious Prosecution
Negligence
Nuisance
Products Liability
Seduction
Torts
Trespass
Trover and Conversion
Waste

5. CRIMES

Abduction
Abortion and Birth Control
Adulteration
Adultery
Affray
Arson
Bigamy
Blasphemy
Breach of the Peace
Bribery
Burglary
Common Scold
Compounding Offenses
Counterfeiting
Criminal Law
Disorderly Conduct
Disorderly House
Disturbance of Public Assemblage
Dueling
Embezzlement
Embracery
Escape
Extortion and Threats
False Personation

5. CRIMES—Cont'd

False Pretenses
Fires
Forgery
Fornication
Homicide
Incest
Insurrection and Sedition
Kidnapping
Larceny
Lewdness
Malicious Mischief
Mayhem
Miscegenation
Neutrality Laws
Obscenity
Obstructing Justice
Perjury
Piracy
Prize Fighting
Prostitution
Rape
Receiving Stolen Goods
Rescue
Riot
Robbery
Sodomy
Suicide
Treason
Unlawful Assembly
Vagrancy

6. REMEDIES

REMEDIES BY ACT OR AGREEMENT OF PARTIES

Accord and Satisfaction
Arbitration
Submission of Controversy

REMEDIES BY POSSESSION OR NOTICE

Liens
Lis Pendens
Maritime Liens
Mechanics' Liens
Notice
Salvage

MEANS AND METHODS OF PROOF

Acknowledgment
Affidavits
Estoppel
Evidence
Oath
Records
Witnesses

CIVIL ACTIONS IN GENERAL

Action
Declaratory Judgment
Election of Remedies
Limitation of Actions
Parties
Set-Off and Counterclaim
Venue

PARTICULAR PROCEEDINGS IN CIVIL ACTIONS

Abatement and Revival
Appearance
Costs
Damages
Execution
Exemptions
Homestead
Judgment
Jury
Motions
Pleading
Process
Reference
Stipulations
Trial

PARTICULAR REMEDIES INCIDENT TO CIVIL ACTIONS

Arrest
Assistance, Writ of
Attachment
Bail
Deposits in Court
Garnishment
Injunction
Judicial Sales
Ne Exeat
Pretrial Procedure
Receivers
Recognizances
Sequestration
Undertakings

6. REMEDIES—Cont'd

PARTICULAR MODES OF REVIEW IN CIVIL ACTIONS

Appeal and Error
Audita Querela
Certiorari
Exceptions, Bill of
New Trial
Review

ACTIONS TO ESTABLISH OWNERSHIP OR RECOVER POSSESSION OF SPECIFIC PROPERTY

Detinue
Ejectment
Entry, Writ of
Interpleader
Possessory Warrant
Quieting Title
Real Actions
Replevin
Trespass to Try Title

FORMS OF ACTIONS FOR DEBTS OR DAMAGES

Account, Action on
Action on the Case
Assumpsit, Action of
Covenant, Action of
Debt, Action of

ACTIONS FOR PARTICULAR FORMS OR SPECIAL RELIEF

Account
Cancellation of Instruments
Debtor and Creditor
Divorce
Partition
Reformation of Instruments
Specific Performance

CIVIL PROCEEDINGS OTHER THAN ACTIONS

Habeas Corpus
Mandamus
Prohibition
Quo Warranto
Scire Facias
Supersedeas

SPECIAL CIVIL JURISDICTIONS AND PROCEDURE THEREIN

Admiralty
Bankruptcy
Equity
Federal Civil Procedure

PROCEEDINGS PECULIAR TO CRIMINAL CASES

Extradition and Detainers
Fines
Forfeitures
Grand Jury
Indictment and Information
Pardon and Parole
Penalties
Searches and Seizures

7. GOVERNMENT

POLITICAL BODIES AND DIVISIONS

Counties
District of Columbia
Municipal Corporations
States
Territories
Towns
United States

SYSTEMS AND SOURCES OF LAW

Administrative Law and Procedure
Common Law
Constitutional Law
International Law
Parliamentary Law
Statutes
Treaties

LEGISLATIVE AND EXECUTIVE POWERS AND FUNCTIONS

Bounties
Census
Commodity Futures Trading Regulation
Customs Duties
Drains
Eminent Domain
Highways
Inspection
Internal Revenue
Levees and Flood Control

7. GOVERNMENT—Cont'd

LEGISLATIVE AND EXECUTIVE POWERS AND FUNCTIONS—Cont'd

Pensions
Post Office
Private Roads
Public Contracts
Public Utilities
Schools
Securities Regulation
Social Security and Public Welfare
Taxation
Weights and Measures
Zoning and Planning

JUDICIAL POWERS AND FUNCTIONS, AND COURTS AND THEIR OFFICERS

Amicus Curiae
Clerks of Courts
Contempt
Court Commissioners
Courts
Federal Courts
Judges
Justices of the Peace
Removal of Cases
Reports
United States Magistrates

CIVIL SERVICE, OFFICERS, AND INSTITUTIONS

Ambassadors and Consuls
Asylums
Attorney General
Coroners
District and Prosecuting Attorneys
Elections
Hospitals
Newspapers
Notaries
Officers and Public Employees
Prisons
Registers of Deeds
Sheriffs and Constables
United States Marshals

MILITARY AND NAVAL SERVICE AND WAR

Armed Services
Military Justice
Militia
War and National Emergency

APPENDIX I

Titles in the *United States Code*

The *United States Code* is divided into numbered titles, each of which contains statutes pertaining to a particular subject matter. The *U.S.C.* titles and their corresponding numbers are listed below.

1. General Provisions
2. The Congress
3. The President
4. Flag and Seal, Seat of Government and the States
5. Government Organization and Employees
*6. [Surety Bonds]
7. Agriculture
8. Aliens and Nationality
9. Arbitration
10. Armed Forces
11. Bankruptcy
12. Banks and Banking
13. Census
14. Coast Guard
15. Commerce and Trade
16. Conservation
17. Copyrights
18. Crimes and Criminal Procedure
19. Customs Duties
20. Education
21. Food and Drugs
22. Foreign Relations and Intercourse
23. Highways
24. Hospitals and Asylums
25. Indians
26. Internal Revenue Code
27. Intoxicating Liquors

28. Judiciary and Judicial Procedure
29. Labor
30. Mineral Lands and Mining
31. Money and Finance
32. National Guard
33. Navigation and Navigable Waters
†34. [Navy]
35. Patents
36. Patriotic Societies and Observances
37. Pay and Allowances of the Uniformed Services
38. Veterans' Benefits
39. Postal Service
40. Public Buildings, Property, and Works
41. Public Contracts
42. The Public Health and Welfare
43. Public Lands
44. Public Printing and Documents
45. Railroads
46. Shipping
47. Telegraphs, Telephones, and Radio telegraphs
48. Territories and Insular Possessions
49. Transportation
50. War and National Defense; and Appendix

*This title has been superseded by the enactment of Title 31.

†This title has been superseded by the enactment of Title 10.

APPENDIX J

Titles in the *Code of Federal Regulations*

The *Code of Federal Regulations* is divided into numbered titles, each of which contains regulations pertaining to a particular subject matter. The *C.F.R.* titles and their corresponding numbers are listed below.

1. General Provisions
2. [Reserved]
3. The President
4. Accounts
5. Administrative Personnel
6. [Reserved]
7. Agriculture
8. Aliens and Nationality
9. Animals and Animal Products
10. Energy
11. Federal Elections
12. Banks and Banking
13. Business Credit and Assistance
14. Aeronautics and Space
15. Commerce and Foreign Trade
16. Commercial Practices
17. Commodity and Securities Exchanges
18. Conservation of Power and Water Resources
19. Customs Duties
20. Employees' Benefits
21. Food and Drugs
22. Foreign Relations
23. Highways
24. Housing and Urban Development
25. Indians
26. Internal Revenue
27. Alcohol, Tobacco Products and Firearms
28. Judicial Administration
29. Labor
30. Mineral Resources
31. Money and Finance: Treasury
32. National Defense
33. Navigation and Navigable Waters
34. Education
35. Panama Canal
36. Parks, Forests, and Public Property
37. Patents, Trademarks, and Copyrights
38. Pensions, Bonuses, and Veterans' Relief
39. Postal Service
40. Protection of Environment
41. Public Contracts and Property Management
42. Public Health
43. Public Lands: Interior
44. Emergency Management and Assistance
45. Public Welfare
46. Shipping
47. Telecommunication
48. Federal Acquisition Regulations System
49. Transportation
50. Wildlife and Fisheries

APPENDIX K

Researching Legislative History

Contents:

Introduction. Chapter 5 discusses legislative history as one of several guides for determining what a legislature intended when it enacted a statute you regard as ambiguous. (See pages 85–86.) As explained there, if a legislature's intent is not clear from the statutory language itself, researching the legislative documents generated at each stage of the process by which a bill becomes a law may shed light on what the legislature intended.

This appendix presents the essential information needed to conduct legislative history research. To identify the documents relating to a statute's legislative history and then to assess each document's relative importance as an indicator of legislative intent, you need at least a basic understanding of the link between the process of enacting laws and the documents the process produces at its various stages. This appendix therefore begins by summarizing the legislative process, using congressional procedures as the model, and describes the documents a legislature generates during the process.

Next, the appendix discusses the publications used to identify legislative documents and indicates how you can obtain the full texts of the documents once you have identified them. The appendix also outlines a basic strategy for doing legislative history research and concludes with some general remarks about the role of legislative history in interpreting statutes.

The discussion may seem long in relation to other topics covered in the book. The length does not mean, however, that legislative history research is either more difficult or substantially more important than other kinds of legal research. Rather, the length of this appendix results from its background discussion about legislative processes and documents. Many of the resources used in doing legislative history research are not self-explanatory; they generally presume a working knowledge of legislative processes and documents, even though this understanding often does not exist. For researchers who lack the necessary background, the research resources, which often amount to little more than shorthand lists, may be indecipherable. With the background information in this appendix, however, doing legislative history research should not prove any more difficult than doing research in other areas of law.

The legislative process followed by state legislatures (and by local legislative bodies, such as city councils) largely tracks the one Congress follows. At the state and local levels, however, legislatures generally produce fewer documents at each step of the process, and those documents they do produce usually contain less detail than their congressional counterparts. These characteristics make it more difficult—sometimes even impossible—to reconstruct meaningful legislative histories for state and local statutes. The idiosyncrasies of state legislative history research are discussed near the end of the appendix.

Finally, note that because our concern here is with statutory interpretation, the discussion in this appendix assumes your research relates to an existing statute. As used here, the term "legislative history research" means finding the documents that record a bill's journey to enactment as a statute. In other contexts, "legislative history research" sometimes refers to monitoring the status and progress of a bill pending in a legislature. The term can even encompass broad research into legislative activity relating to a specific topic, e.g., analyzing any bills Congress may have considered during the past five years regarding Social Security. Although this appendix focuses on legislative history research concerning existing statutes, if you understand how to do this kind of research, you can easily adapt your skills to monitoring current legislation or to examining generalized legislative activities; your goals will differ, but you will use the same research tools and legislative documents.

Legislative process: the background for legislative history research

As you read the following discussion of the legislative process, note the documents the process generates—*e.g.*, committee reports, transcripts of hearings and debates, and the various versions of legislative measures as they proceed through debate and amendment. These documents are the means by which you reconstruct the considerations that went into the statute you are trying to interpret.[52]

Step 1: Originating an idea. All legislation begins with an idea for legislative action. The idea can come from a variety of sources:

- individual constituents
- special interest groups, such as bar associations, the Council of State Governments, business associations, labor unions, or charitable organizations
- public policy or public interest research groups, such as the American Law Institute, the Brookings Institution, or the American Enterprise Institute
- special commissions set up to study and propose legislation
- individual legislators
- investigative or oversight hearings conducted by legislative committees to determine the need for legislation on particular subjects
- independent government agencies
- the executive branch

Some of these sources may prepare studies, issue reports or other statements (*e.g.*, a presidential message transmitting a legislative proposal to Congress), and keep files relating to their legislative proposals. If available to a researcher, these documents may shed light on what a statute's original proponents hoped to achieve through legislation.

After receiving a proposal, a legislator can advance it by introducing the proposal either as it was submitted or in a modified version. If the legislator redrafts the proposal, another document results that, because

---

[52]Researchers interested in further reading about the legislative process should see R. DOVE, ENACTMENT OF A LAW: PROCEDURAL STEPS IN THE LEGISLATIVE PROCESS, S. DOC. No. 20, 97th Cong., 2d Sess. (1981); G. FOLSOM, LEGISLATIVE HISTORY: RESEARCH FOR THE INTERPRETATION OF LAWS (1979); and E. WILLETT, HOW OUR LAWS ARE MADE, H.R. Doc. No. 120, 97th Cong., 1st Sess. (1981).

of differences in language between it and earlier documents, may later help refine the analysis of legislative intent.

Step 2: Introducing the proposal. The sponsoring legislator initiates the legislative process by introducing the proposal in the legislative chamber (House of Representatives or Senate) of which he or she is a member.[53] At this stage, the introduced version of the proposal is known as the *introduced print*. The legislator who sponsors the proposal may also offer an explanatory statement when introducing it.

Often, identical or nearly identical proposals, known as "companion bills," are introduced in both houses at approximately the same time. This technique, called "simultaneous introduction," can accelerate Congress' consideration of the proposals by allowing each chamber to review and debate the proposals simultaneously rather than consecutively. If simultaneous introduction occurs, only one proposal will ultimately survive, though it may incorporate provisions of companion bills.

There are four types of legislative proposals: bills, joint resolutions, concurrent resolutions, and simple resolutions. Because bills constitute the majority of legislative proposals that are introduced and become law, this appendix only focuses on the procedure by which Congress processes this form of proposal. The following list describes all four types of proposals, however, because you will encounter references to them as you research the legislative history of enacted bills.

- *Bills.* A bill is the form used for most legislation. With the exception of revenue bills, which must originate in the House, a bill may originate in either the House or the Senate. A bill in the House carries the prefix "H.R." followed by a unique, sequentially assigned number. The first bill introduced in the House during the two-year life span of a Congress[54] is designated "H.R. 1"; likewise, the 612th bill would be designated

---

[53]Congress and all state legislatures except the Nebraska legislature are organized bicamerally—that is, they consist of two chambers, each of which has its own procedural rules, committee structure, and leadership. Nebraska's legislature and most local legislatures (*e.g.*, city councils) are unicameral bodies. At the state level, the chambers of bicameral legislatures are sometimes known by names other than "House of Representatives" and "Senate"—for example, "House of Delegates" or "Assembly." The current edition of *The Book of the States*, a biennial publication of the Council of State Governments, provides information about various characteristics of each state legislature.

[54]The term "Congress" has two meanings: it refers to both the institution itself (*i.e.*, "the" Congress) and to the two-year term, starting in January of odd-numbered years, during which members of the institution meet (*i.e.*, "a" Congress). A Congress is usually divided into two sessions, each of which ordinarily lasts a year.

"H.R. 612." In the Senate, bills are designated with the prefix "S." followed by the appropriate sequential number.

Bills retain their identifying numbers until the two-year term of a Congress expires. A bill not enacted into law during the two-year Congress in which it is introduced does not carry over to the next Congress. If a legislator introduces the bill again—even in identical form—during a later Congress, the bill receives a new number.

To do legislative history research, you need to know the bill number. Because everything in a bill except its number is subject to change during the legislative process, the bill number provides the only means of tracing a bill through the various stages of consideration.

Bills are classified as either public or private. Public bills, which are far more common than private ones, seek to affect the general public. Private bills, by contrast, seek to affect only an individual or group, *e.g.*, to allow an individual to immigrate. Each chamber of Congress numbers its bills sequentially in a single series without regard to the public or private nature of the bills.

The discussion in this appendix assumes your research involves a public law resulting from passage of a public bill. Private laws, which result from private bills, usually do not require legislative history research: their highly specific focus means they rarely raise questions about legislative intent. In any event, private laws do not lend themselves to legislative history research because Congress, in passing private bills, generates few of the documents you normally find when researching histories of public laws.

• *Joint resolutions.* A joint resolution may originate in either the House or Senate. Despite what the title seems to imply, the term "joint" does not signify simultaneous introduction or consideration in both chambers.

When a joint resolution originates in the House, it is designated with the prefix "H.J. Res." followed by a unique, sequentially assigned number. A joint resolution originating in the Senate is designated "S.J. Res." and given its appropriate sequential number.

There is little practical difference between joint resolutions and bills. Except for joint resolutions proposing constitutional amendments, joint resolutions become law in the same way bills do.

- *Concurrent resolutions.* Congress uses concurrent resolutions to address matters involving the internal operations of both the House and Senate (such as establishing a joint standing committee) or to express a joint opinion on some subject. Despite its implication, "concurrent" does not refer to simultaneous introduction or consideration of a proposal.

  A concurrent resolution originating in the House is designated "H. Con. Res." followed by its unique sequential number. One originating in the Senate is designated "S. Con. Res." followed by its appropriate sequential number.

  Unlike bills and joint resolutions, concurrent resolutions are not approved by the President and therefore do not become law.

- *Simple resolutions.* Each chamber uses simple resolutions to address matters involving its own operations or as a means of making a unilateral statement. Simple resolutions are designated "H. Res." or "S. Res." (depending on the chamber in which they are introduced); a unique sequential number follows the prefix. Like concurrent resolutions, simple resolutions do not become law.

Step 3: Referral to committee. To handle its large volume of work, each chamber has established a system of committees to review, revise, and report on bills its members introduce. After a legislator introduces a bill and it receives its identifying number, the bill is printed in its introduced form and then referred to the committee or committees having jurisdiction over the bill's subject matter. At this stage, the bill appears in a documentary form known as a *referred print*.

Step 4: Committee consideration, hearings, and report. Once the appropriate committee receives the bill, the committee chair ordinarily refers the bill to a subcommittee for review. The vast majority of bills die in subcommittee, with most bills never receiving more than cursory examination at that level. As to those bills it does not summarily reject, the subcommittee may hold public *hearings* to allow experts or other interested individuals to state their views on the bill; the subcommittee is more likely to hold hearings when a bill deals with an especially important or controversial subject. Testimony at these hearings is recorded and transcribed, although not always printed (*i.e.*, published).

Whether or not the transcripts are printed, hearings have traditionally been identified principally by the number of the bill to which they pertain; they have not routinely received identifying numbers separate from the bill number. (Some committees, however, have created unique numbering systems for the published transcripts of their own hearings.) Other information used to identify a hearing includes the number of the Congress and session in which the hearing occurred (*e.g.*, 98th Congress, 1st Session),[55] the name of the committee or subcommittee holding the hearing, the dates of the hearing, and the short title the committee assigns to the hearing proceedings. In the 98th Congress (1983–84), the Senate began systematically identifying all its committee hearings in one sequentially numbered series over the course of a Congress, *e.g.*, "Senate Hearing No. 98-1," "Senate Hearing No. 98-2." The House has not yet adopted a similar numbering system for its hearings.

After the subcommittee completes its hearings on the bill, it meets in a "mark-up" session to discuss possible dispositions of the bill. The subcommittee can vote to table the bill at that point, a decision that indefinitely postpones further action and effectively kills the bill. If the subcommittee does not table the bill, it then decides whether to amend it and, if so, what amendments to make.[56] Finally, after approving any amendments, the subcommittee decides whether to send the bill to the full committee for further action. If the subcommittee decides to report the bill to the full committee, it normally prepares a *memorandum* containing its recommendations for favorable or unfavorable committee action on the bill.

After considering the subcommittee's memorandum, the full committee decides whether to table the bill. If it does not immediately table the bill, the committee goes through a process similar to the

---

[55]Hearings relevant to the bill you are researching may have occurred in earlier Congresses. A similar or identical bill may have been introduced in one or more preceding Congresses, and committees may have held hearings on that predecessor bill. Even though the predecessor bill was not enacted, testimony at the earlier hearings may offer additional insight into the legislature's intent in enacting the bill you are researching. Consequently, you should not limit your search for hearings to only those occurring in the Congress that enacted your bill. Similarly, a thorough search for the other legislative history documents described in this appendix would also extend beyond a single Congress. Footnote 65, *infra*, discusses techniques for identifying related documents from earlier sessions or Congresses.

[56]If the subcommittee amends the bill extensively, it may prepare a new version, called a "clean" bill, to incorporate the changes. A subcommittee member then introduces this new version into the chamber, where the bill receives its own number and is referred back to the subcommittee. After the clean bill returns to the subcommittee, it supersedes the original bill.

This technique of preparing and introducing clean bills can cause a researcher to prematurely terminate an inquiry into an enacted bill's legislative history. Because the clean bill's new number masks the bill's character as a successor to an earlier bill with a different number, a researcher may fail to connect the clean bill with the legislative history documents relating to the original bill from which it arose. You can avoid this error by routinely checking for predecessor bills. Information about predecessor bills appears near the beginning of the reports the committee ultimately issues on the corresponding clean bills.

subcommittee's—sometimes holding public hearings (with transcribed testimony), often considering amendments, and then deciding whether to report the bill to the full chamber (*i.e.*, the House or the Senate, as appropriate). The version of a bill reported out of a committee is known as a *reported print* or *calendar print*.

If the committee sends a bill to the full chamber, it also sends a *report*, which almost always recommends that the bill be enacted. On rare occasions, when the committee opposes the bill but decides not to table it, the committee may send the bill to the full chamber with a report recommending against enactment.

For purposes of discerning legislative intent, courts often view committee reports as the most meaningful guide to the legislature's reasons for enacting a bill. Committee reports typically include the text of the bill as reported out of the committee (indicating both the bill's original language and all committee amendments); a detailed analysis of each section of the bill; an explanation of the purpose of any committee amendments; an indication of what the bill is designed to accomplish and how it changes existing law; a recital of the full text of any laws being repealed; and the committee's explanation of its recommendation for action on the bill. Committee reports may also set forth the following: additional comments by individual committee members; one or more minority reports stating the views of committee members disagreeing with the committee's recommendations; and, if the bill resulted from an executive branch request for its introduction, copies of executive correspondence and similar documents related to the request.

Committee reports are assigned identifying numbers and then printed. Each chamber numbers its committee reports sequentially in a single series throughout the two-year term of a Congress.[57] Since 1969, report numbers have also included a prefix number indicating the number of the Congress during which the report was issued; for example, the 1,305th report the House issued during the 93rd Congress is designated "House Report No. 93-1305." The report number appears on the first page of the reported print of the bill and on subsequent versions of the bill.

Step 5: Consideration by the full chamber. After the committee reports a bill to the full chamber of which the committee is a part, the bill is placed on a "calendar," which serves as a consolidated list of all bills

---

[57]From the 16th Congress (1819–21) through the 46th Congress (1879–81), however, House Reports were numbered sequentially over the course of just a single session of a Congress, rather than over the two-year life of a Congress.

the chamber's various committees have reported as ready for the full chamber's consideration. Although a calendar establishes a presumptive order for considering reported bills, the chamber's leaders frequently exercise their authority to accelerate or delay a bill's consideration by the full chamber.

The chamber's consideration may involve *debate*, although in the overwhelming majority of instances, the chamber passes bills without extensive discussion. When debate occurs, it typically involves questions and answers by legislators about the bill's meaning and effect. During debate, legislators may also propose amendments, which the chamber may accept or reject. The floor debate is recorded, transcribed, and printed in the *Congressional Record* (a publication described at page 192).

After concluding its debate, the chamber votes on the bill. It may pass the bill, reject it, or (as an alternative to outright rejection) recommit the bill to committee for further consideration. As a practical matter, recommitment kills the bill.

If the chamber passes the bill, a legislative clerk, in a process known as "engrossment," prepares a precise copy of the bill that integrates all amendments. Once engrossed, the measure becomes known technically as an *act*, signifying that it is the act of one chamber; although now captioned as an "act," most people still refer to it as a "bill."

At this point, a legislative clerk sends the engrossed bill to the other chamber.

Step 6: Consideration by the second chamber. Upon arriving in the other chamber, the bill is reprinted and normally then referred to the appropriate committee or committees. This version of the bill is known as the *act print*; in the Senate, it may also be called the "Senate referred print" (indicating that the Senate has referred a House-passed bill to one of its committees). Although now in the second chamber, the bill retains the number assigned to it in the chamber in which it originated.

In its consideration of the bill, the second chamber engages in the same process the first chamber did. If its committee reports the bill to the floor, the second chamber may debate it and consider whether to amend it; eventually, the second chamber votes on the bill.

By its vote, the second chamber can do one of several things. It can defeat the bill by either rejecting it or recommitting it to its committee for further consideration (effectively killing the bill). It can pass the bill in the identical form in which the first chamber passed it, in which case the first chamber's enrolling clerk sends the final version of the bill to the printer, who prints what is known as the *enrolled bill*. As a third alternative, the second chamber can pass the bill with amendments. In that case, it engrosses (*i.e.*, prepares a precise written version of) its amendments and sends them, along with the first chamber's version of the bill, back to the first chamber with a request that it concur in the amendments.

Step 7: Reconsideration by the first chamber. When the first chamber receives the second chamber's amendments, it can concur in all, some, or none of them. Again, there may be recorded debate, especially if the amendments are substantial or controversial.

If the first chamber fully concurs in the amendments, an enrolled version of the final bill (incorporating the amendments) is printed. If the first chamber agrees to only some or none of the amendments, however, the bill dies unless both chambers agree on an identical version (after the bill has bounced back and forth between the chambers) or unless the chambers agree to create a conference committee that will attempt to resolve their remaining differences.

Step 8: Conference committee negotiations and further floor debate. A conference committee consists of selected legislators from both chambers. These legislators, known as "managers" or "conferees," may consider only those matters on which the two chambers disagree. The conferees may recommend accepting or rejecting all or some of the amendments in disagreement, or they may fashion their own compromises relating to the disputed matters.

After the conferees finish their negotiations, they prepare a *conference committee report* that includes the text of any compromise amendments and recommends how the chambers should vote on the bill. This report, often an important guide to legislative intent, is accompanied by a statement from the conference committee explaining how implementing its recommendations would affect the meaning of the bill.

The conference report is printed and generally issued only as a House Report because the Senate usually forgoes having it concurrently printed as a Senate Report. After printing, the conference report is sent to the floor of each chamber for further floor debate, which is printed in the *Congressional Record.* For the bill to become law, of course, both houses must reach complete agreement on an identical version of the bill, including amendments. If the two houses cannot reach an agreement, they can hold additional conference committee meetings, repeating the process described above. This cycle continues until both chambers fully agree on the bill or until at least one chamber declines to participate in further deliberations, in which case the bill dies.

If the two chambers reach an agreement on the bill, it is enrolled in its final form.

Step 9: Executive action. Once enrolled and signed by the presiding officer of each chamber, the bill goes to the president. It becomes law if the president signs it or fails to veto it within ten days, or if Congress by a two-thirds vote of each chamber overrides a presidential veto. A bill fails to become law if the president vetoes it and Congress either does not override the veto or by its adjournment prevents the president from returning the bill to Congress within ten days (a procedure known as a "pocket veto").

When signing a bill, the president may make a statement setting forth the executive branch's view of the legislation's meaning. In connection with vetoes other than pocket vetoes, the president is constitutionally required to return a vetoed bill to Congress with a message stating the president's objections to the bill. Presidential statements and messages generally do not figure significantly in substantive argument on legislative intent, but they occasionally summarize a bill's effect in a way that may usefully recapitulate what Congress intended.

Step 10: Publication of a law. If the bill becomes law, it is designated as public or private, assigned a number, and published in a form known as a *slip law*. Public and private laws are numbered sequentially in separate series throughout the two-year term of a Congress: for example, "Public Law 99-1" would designate the first public law passed by the 99th Congress, while "Private Law 99-1" would designate the first private law passed by the same Congress.[58] The law number is a core piece of information needed to research the legislative history of a statute.

After publication in slip law form, a public law is republished in the session laws (*Statutes at Large*) and then in the statutory code (*United States Code*); a private law is only republished in the session law compilation. (For a discussion of session laws and statutory codes, see Chapter 1.)

Summary of legislative process steps and resulting documents. Figure GG (pages 188–89) shows in summary form the relationship between the steps in the legislative process and the documents that are generated at each step. Not every bill will go through each step or yield every document listed. To conduct thorough legislative history research on a particular law, however, you should check for all of these steps and documents.

Other congressional documents. In doing legislative history re-

---

[58]Before the 82nd Congress (1951–52), all public and private laws were numbered consecutively in a single series and identified principally by consecutive chapter numbers, rather than by separate "public law" and "private law" numbers. In addition, these chapter numbers ran consecutively only throughout a single session, rather than over the two-year term of a Congress.

Legislative Step	Corresponding Documents
1. Originating an idea	• Transcripts and reports of investigative or oversight hearings; studies; presidential messages; etc. • Initial draft of legislative proposal
2. Introducing the proposal	• Introducing print of bill • Transcript of sponsoring legislator's supporting statement
3. Referral to committee	• Referred print of bill
4. Committee consideration	• Transcripts of committee and subcommittee hearings • Committee reports and subcommittee memoranda • Reported, or "calendar," print of bill (including committee amendments) for forwarding to full chamber
5. Consideration by the full chamber	• Transcripts of floor debates • Engrossed bill (incorporating amendments approved by the chamber)
6. Consideration in the second chamber (the same procedure the first chamber followed in steps 2 through 5)	• Act print of bill introduced and referred to committee (in the Senate, also called "Senate referred print") • Transcripts of committee and subcommittee hearings • Committee reports and subcommittee memoranda • Amendments reported from committee to full chamber • Amendments proposed during floor debate • Enrolled bill for executive action (if the second chamber does not approve any amendments to the bill) or engrossed amendments for return to the first chamber (if the second chamber approves amendments)

7. Reconsideration by the first chamber (if the second chamber amends the bill)

- Transcripts of floor debates
- Enrolled bill (if the first chamber concurs in the second chamber's amendments)

8. Conference committee negotiations and further floor debate (if the first chamber does not concur in the second chamber's amendments)

- Transcript of conference committee negotiations
- Compromise amendments
- Conference committee report for forwarding to both chambers
- Explanatory statement accompanying conference committee report
- Transcripts of chambers' floor debates
- Enrolled bill (if both chambers ultimately agree on a single version of the bill)

9. Executive action (if the chambers agree on a single version of the bill)

- Presidential statement accompanying signing of bill
- Presidential message accompanying veto

10. Publication of the law

- Slip law (first official published form of the law)
- Session law
- Statutory code version

Figure GG. Summary of Legislative Process Steps and Corresponding Documents

search, you will work principally with the documents already described, particularly the various versions of a bill as it moves through Congress, transcripts of hearings and debates, and reports. You may encounter references to a few other types of documents, however, and these are described below.

Committee prints. A committee print contains the results of a committee's research on a subject for which the committee has legislative responsibility. Committee prints can include statistical data, historical information, and factual studies, as well as legislative analyses of bills and any other information the committee finds particularly informative in connection with its general subject area responsibilities. The committee's research staff, the Library of Congress, or outside consultants prepare the material in committee prints as background information intended primarily for the committee's internal use. Because they frequently provide the factual and analytical underpinnings for recommendations contained in subsequent committee reports on bills, committee prints may afford significant insight into legislative intent.

Publication practices for committee prints vary widely: some committees number their prints sequentially, while other committees leave theirs unnumbered; moreover, some committees label their prints as such, while other committees do not. Also, some committee materials suitable for publication as committee prints are published as House or Senate Documents (discussed below) or as committee reports instead of, or in addition to, being published as committee prints. Beginning in the 98th Congress (1983–84), the Senate imposed some order on its system of publishing prints: it adopted sequential numbering for all Senate committee prints issued over the course of a Congress, *e.g.*, "Senate Print 98-1," "Senate Print 98-2." The House has not yet adopted a similar numbering system for its prints.

Investigative and oversight hearings. Committees sometimes hold investigative or oversight hearings not directly connected with pending legislation. In investigative hearings and some types of oversight hearings, committees gather information to determine the need to enact new laws or to modify existing laws. Committees also use oversight hearings to examine how well the executive branch and federal administrative agencies have followed Congress' intent in implementing legislation.

Investigative and oversight hearings generate hearings transcripts and committee reports like those resulting from hearings tied to pending legislation (discussed earlier under "Step 4"; see pages 182–84). The transcripts of investigative and oversight hearings may be published, although committee practices are erratic in this regard. Publication practices for the reports also vary, with committees issuing them as committee reports, committee prints, or House or Senate Documents.

House Documents and Senate Documents. These publications (spelled with an upper case "D") are a distinct category of congressional documents (lower case "d"). House and Senate Documents consist of a wide variety of miscellaneous materials, only some of which contribute to understanding legislative intent. The materials found in House and Senate Documents include presidential messages proposing or vetoing legislation; administrative agencies' reports to Congress; reports from federally chartered organizations, such as the Girl Scouts; and selected historical materials. House and Senate Documents can also consist of congressional materials that may have previously appeared in another form (such as committee prints or the transcripts and reports of investigative or oversight hearings) or materials that Congress decided not to issue in another, equally appropriate form.

Each chamber numbers its Documents sequentially over the two-year life of a Congress. A Document's numerical designation indicates the issuing chamber, the number of the Congress in which it was issued, and the Document's sequence number. Thus, for example, "House Document No. 93-339" designates the 339th Document the House issued during the 93rd Congress.

Publications for identifying federal legislative history documents

A wide variety of finding tools exists to help researchers discover relevant legislative history documents. These publications differ in their format and coverage; for example, several omit references to committee hearings and floor debates. Nonetheless, most of the finding tools overlap at least partly with respect to the types of documents they discuss and their dates of coverage, so there is no one right technique for coordinating their use. You may need to check several of the publications, depending on the information you are looking for. Which publications your library has available will also be an important consideration, of course, because few libraries will have all the available publications.

As you familiarize yourself with the publications discussed in this section, you may find the following generalizations helpful. First, although a few of the finding tools described here also reprint the full texts of some types of legislative documents, they principally serve to cite, index, or summarize legislative documents. By using the bibliographic references in the finding tools, researchers can then obtain the actual documents from other sources. (A later section of this appendix indicates the sources from which to obtain the legislative documents themselves.)

Second, most of the finding tools discussed in this section either contain or are themselves status tables that provide a chronological summary of what happened to a particular bill as it journeyed through the legislative process, e.g., whether a hearing was held on it, whether the bill was amended, whether floor debate occurred. Using the information in the tables, you can quickly determine which congressional documents exist in connection with the bill you are researching. Figures HH and II show two examples of status tables.

As a final generalization, the finding tools published by commercial organizations are often better indexed, more detailed, and more rapidly supplemented than are the finding tools published by the government.

The remainder of this section describes the main finding tools used in legislative history research. Those published by the government are discussed first, followed by a discussion of the commercial publications. The descriptions are intended to help you develop a sense of the strengths and weaknesses of the various publications. Not every detail in the descriptions need be immediately absorbed; once you have a general feel for the coverage of each publication, you can decide which ones to use in researching a particular legislative history problem, taking into account not only the publications' functions, but their availability and your preferences as well. Figure JJ (pages 204–05) can also help you decide which finding tools to use: it correlates legislative history documents with the finding tools that cite, index, and summarize them. In addition, the appendix section entitled "A basic strategy for federal legislative history research" sets forth a methodology for integrating the numerous resources into a unified research procedure.

Government-published finding tools

Congressional Record. This periodical, published by the Government Printing Office, serves two important functions for researchers evaluating legislative intent.[59] First, it contains an official record of the legislative actions and debates on the floor of each chamber. Second, the *Record* contains two helpful status tables—*History of Bills Enacted*

---

[59]The *Congressional Record*'s coverage begins with the first session of the 43rd Congress (1873) and continues to the present. Three predecessor publications provide coverage back to the first session of the First Congress: the *Annals of Congress* (1789–1824); the *Register of Debates* (1824–37); and the *Congressional Globe* (1833–73).

07-05-83 Reported to Senate from the Committee on Armed
          Services with amendment, S. Rept. 98-174
07-11-83 Measure called up by unanimous consent in Senate
07-11-83 Measure considered in Senate
07-12-83 Measure considered in Senate
07-13-83 Measure considered in Senate
07-13-83 Tabled Motion to recommit to Committee on
          Armed Services with instructions, roll call #189
          (53-41)
07-14-83 Measure considered in Senate
07-15-83 Measure considered in Senate
07-16-83 Measure considered in Senate
07-18-83 Measure considered in Senate
07-19-83 Measure considered in Senate
07-19-83 Cloture motion filed in Senate on committee
          amendment
07-19-83 Cloture motion filed in Senate on Measure
07-20-83 Measure considered in Senate
07-20-83 Cloture motion filed in Senate on committee
          amendment (Second Motion)
07-20-83 Cloture motion filed in Senate on Measure (Second
          Motion)
07-21-83 Measure considered in Senate
07-21-83 Cloture motion on committee amendment rejected
          in Senate, roll call #214(55-41) (First Motion)
07-21-83 Cloture motion on Measure vitiated in Senate
          (First Motion)
07-21-83 Cloture motion filed in Senate on committee
          amendment (Third Motion)
07-21-83 Cloture motion filed in Senate on Measure (Third
          Motion)
07-22-83 Measure considered in Senate
07-25-83 Measure considered in Senate
07-26-83 Measure considered in Senate
07-26-83 Measure passed Senate, amended, roll call #221
          (83-15)
07-26-83 See H.R. 2972 for similar provisions of Title II
07-26-83 See S. 1107 for similar provisions of Title III
07-29-83 Measure called up by unanimous consent in House
07-29-83 Measure considered in House
07-29-83 Measure passed House, amended(Inserted provi-
          sions of H.R. 2969 as passed House)
07-29-83 Conference scheduled in House
08-01-83 Conference scheduled in Senate
08-01-83 Motion that certain portions of Conf. Comm. Meet-
          ing be closed to the public passed
          Hse.,r.c.#299(396-10)
08-15-83 Conference report filed in Senate, S. Rept. 98-213
09-12-83 Conference report filed in House, H. Rept. 98-352
09-13-83 Senate agreed to conference report, roll call #244
          (83-8)
09-15-83 House agreed to conference report, roll call #339
          (266-152)
09-15-83 Measure enrolled in House
09-15-83 Measure enrolled in Senate
09-19-83 Measure presented to President
09-24-83 Public Law 98-94

Figure HH. Sample Status Table: Extract from *Digest of Public General Bills and Resolutions*

HISTORY OF BILLS ENACTED INTO PUBLIC LAW (93D CONG., 2D SESS.)

(Cross-reference of bill number to public law number may be found on p. D882)

Title	Bill No.	Date introduced	Committee House	Committee Senate	Date reported House	Date reported Senate	Report No. House	Report No. Senate	Page of Congressional Record of passage House	Page of Congressional Record of passage Senate	Date of passage House	Date of passage Senate	Public Law Date approved	Public Law No.
Designating the Mansfield Lake, Ind., as the "Cecil M. Harden Lake."	S. 1561	Apr. 12 1973	PW	PW	Nov. 19	Dec. 13 1973	93-1481	93-624	37860	41551	Dec. 3	Dec. 14 1973	Dec. 14	93-521
Authorizing continued use of certain lands within the Sequoia National Park, Calif., for a hydroelectric project.	H.J. Res. 444 (S.J. Res. 237)	Mar. 20 1973	IIA	IIA	Sept. 17	Oct. 4	93-1360	93-1236	34108	37075	Oct. 7	Nov. 22	Dec. 14	93-522
To assure that the public is provided with safe drinking water.	S. 433 (H.R. 13002)	Jan. 18 1973	IFC	Com	June 20 1973	July 10	93-231	93-1185	36412	20814	Nov. 19	June 22 1973	Dec. 16	93-523
To deduct from gross tonnage, in determining net tonnage, those spaces in vessels used for waste materials.	S. 1353	Mar. 22 1973	MMF	Com	Sept. 30	Mar. 12	93-1392	93-730	37920	6696	Dec. 3	Mar. 13	Dec. 18	93-524
Repealing requirement that only certain officers with aeronautical ratings may command flying units of the Air Force.	S. 3906	Aug. 15 1973	AS	AS	Sept. 30	Aug. 15	93-1388	93-1094	38644	28725	Dec. 9	Aug. 16	Dec. 18	93-525
To protect and preserve tape recordings and other materials involving Richard M. Nixon which were produced during his tenure as President.	S. 4016	Sept. 18	HA	GO	Nov. 27	Sept. 26	93-1507	93-1181	37906	33975	Dec. 3	Oct. 4	Dec. 19	93-526
To increase pension rates and annual income limitations for eligible veterans and their survivors.	S. 4040	Sept. 24	VA	VA	Nov. 26	Oct. 3	93-1499	93-1226	38645	34008	Dec. 9	Oct. 7	Dec. 21	93-527
Amending the antitrust laws with regard to the conduct of consent decree procedures.	S. 782	Feb. 6 1973	Jud	Jud	June 30 1973	Oct. 11	93-1463	93-298	36365	24605	Nov. 19	July 18 1973	Dec. 21	93-528
To rescind certain budget authority recommended in Presidential messages transmitted through November 13 pursuant to the Impoundment Control Act of 1974.	H.R. 17505	Nov. 25	App	....	Nov. 26	....	93-1501	....	38202	38942	Dec. 4	Dec. 10	Dec. 21	93-529
Authorizing purchase of property located within the San Carlos, Ariz., mineral strip.	H.R. 7730	May 10 1973	IIA	IIA	Sept. 11 1973	Oct. 4	93-465	93-1234	42233	34300	Dec. 18 1973	Oct. 8	Dec. 22	93-530
Providing a final settlement to the dispute over certain reservation lands held jointly by the Navajo and Hopi Indian Tribes.	H.R. 10337	Sept. 18 1973	IIA	IIA	Mar. 13	Sept. 25	93-909	93-1177	16800	37749	May 29	Dec. 2	Dec. 22	93-531
Relating to former Speakers of the House of Representatives.	H.R. 17026	Oct. 2	PW	PW	Oct. 3	Dec. 4	93-1425	93-1306	34135	38469	Oct. 7	Dec. 9	Dec. 22	93-532
Providing for greater disclosure of the nature and costs of real estate settlement services.	S. 3164 (H.R. 9989)	Mar. 13	BC	BHUA	July 3	May 22	93-1177	93-866	28283	24928	Aug. 14	July 24	Dec. 22	93-533
To allow the Federal Government to make advance subscription payments for audio-visual as well as for printed materials.	H.R. 7072	Apr. 16 1973	GO	GO	Aug. 23	Dec. 11	93-1338	93-1330	34105	39399	Oct. 7	Dec. 12	Dec. 22	93-534
To establish the Cascade Head Scenic-Research Area in Oregon.	H.R. 8352	June 4 1973	IIA	IIA	July 31	Aug. 13	93-1247	93-1089	26790	28677	Aug. 5	Aug. 16	Dec. 22	93-535

Figure II. Sample Status Table: Extract from Congressional Record's Table Entitled "History of Bills Enacted into Public Law"

into Public Law and *History of Bills and Resolutions*—that summarize the legislative histories of bills and resolutions.

The *Congressional Record* appears in two versions: a paperback edition published daily whenever at least one chamber of Congress is in session, and a permanent hardbound edition published at the end of each congressional session to cumulate, with some modifications, the daily editions issued over the course of the session. Both versions include nearly verbatim transcripts of floor debates and speeches. Although they do not provide a complete record of non-debate materials, both versions of the *Congressional Record* also reprint the texts of some types of legislative history documents, such as presidential messages to Congress, conference committee reports, and *selected* bills.

Since the 80th Congress (1947-48), each daily edition of the *Record* has included the *Daily Digest*, which summarizes the day's legislative activities and shows the legislative status of bills acted on during the day the particular *Digest* covers. At the end of each session of Congress, the *Daily Digests* appearing in the daily editions of the *Record* cumulate in a separate hardbound volume that includes a status table called *History of Bills Enacted into Public Law*. This table lists all enacted bills according to their corresponding public law numbers and shows some of the steps, such as introduction and passage, in the bills' progress through Congress. Although helpful, this table is less complete than the *Record*'s *History of Bills and Resolutions* table (discussed below).

Every two weeks, the daily edition of the *Congressional Record* provides a non-cumulative index to the daily editions issued during the preceding two-week period. This index, entitled the *Congressional Record Index* (though sometimes called "Index to the Proceedings"), provides access by subject, names of legislators, and titles of legislative proposals. The *Index* includes a comprehensive status table entitled *History of Bills and Resolutions*. This table lists, by bill and resolution number, those bills and resolutions either chamber acted on during the preceding two weeks and summarizes each measure's legislative history since its introduction. The table cites committee reports and the pages in the *Record* where transcripts of relevant floor debates appear; however, like the *Record*'s other table, it does not cite committee hearings.

At the end of each congressional session, the bi-weekly *Congressional Record Index* cumulates in a separate hardbound volume as part of the permanent edition of the *Record*. This permanent index volume contains a final *History of Bills and Resolutions* table that cumulates all the bi-weekly *History* tables that appeared in the *Index* during the preceding session. In using the *History* tables to research a bill introduced but not enacted during the first session of a Congress, you need to check the cumulated *History* tables for both sessions of the Congress.

The permanently bound cumulation of the *Congressional Record*'s daily editions involves some modifications to the previously published material, including different pagination. Legislators may revise how their remarks will appear in the permanent edition. In addition, since the second session of the 83rd Congress (1954), the permanent edition has omitted an appendix that appears in the daily editions under the heading "Extension of Remarks"; that appendix reprints miscellaneous legislative material, such as legislators' statements not actually delivered on the floor of Congress, and non-legislative material, such as a constituent's letter or a topical newspaper article. Once the permanent edition is available, it is considered the authoritative version of the *Record*. If a citation to the *Record* refers to the daily rather than the permanent edition, it should parenthetically indicate "Daily ed." and the date of the daily edition.

House and Senate Journals. Starting with the First Congress in 1789, each chamber has kept its own *Journal*, which summarizes the chamber's legislative proceedings and reprints presidential messages to Congress. The *Journals* are published at the end of each session in separate bound volumes for each chamber. Unlike the *Congressional Record*, the *Journals* do not contain transcripts of debates on the floor of the chambers.

You locate material in a *Journal* by using either its bill number index or subject index. The bill number index is entitled "History of Bills and Resolutions" (not to be confused with the *Congressional Record* table of the same name) and it doubles as a status table. It shows, in numerical order, the legislative history of each bill the chamber considered during the session the particular *Journal* covers.

Calendars. Each chamber and most committees publish daily agendas of their activities while Congress is in session. These calendars are prepared principally to provide legislators with current information on pending legislation, but they are also widely distributed to law libraries.

For legislative history research, the most useful feature of calendars is generally the House of Representatives' calendar table entitled *Numerical Order of Bills and Resolutions Which Have Passed Either or Both Houses, and Bills Now Pending on the Calendar*. This status table appears as part of the daily House calendars, and each table cumulates all previous tables. In the version published after a Congress adjourns at the end of its second session, the *Numerical Order* table cumulates legislative history information about all bills that were acted on by either chamber or that were reported to the floor by the chambers' standing committees during both sessions. The table also cross-references identical bills or bills that refer to one another. The final version of the calendar contains a subject index; a cumulative index to the daily House calendars is published weekly.

The *Numerical Order* table does not cover all introduced bills, only those receiving legislative action. It is therefore less complete than the *History of Bills and Resolutions* table in the *Congressional Record*. However, the final cumulative *Numerical Order* table for each congressional session is available before the cumulative status tables that accompany the permanent year-end edition of the *Congressional Record.*

The House calendars also contain a status table called *Bills Through Conference*, which provides information (such as names of conferees, conference report numbers, and public law numbers) about bills reported from conference committees. Because this table is arranged by the date on which the chambers agreed to a conference, rather than by bill number, you need to find this date from some other source before you can use the table.

Unlike the House calendars, the Senate calendars have little value to legislative history researchers because they do not contain an index or a *Numerical Order* table.

Digest of Public General Bills and Resolutions. Prepared by the Congressional Research Service of the Library of Congress since the second session of the 74th Congress (1936), this publication provides perhaps the most detailed descriptions of all public bills and resolutions introduced in Congress, as well as of all public laws enacted. Following each description, the *Digest* provides a status table showing the progress through Congress of all public bills and resolutions reported from committees to the chambers. The citations in the tables include references to committee reports issued on the measures, but do not indicate whether hearings were held.

Four indexes provide access to the *Digest*: by sponsor or co-sponsor; by the bill numbers of other, identical bills introduced in either chamber; by short title; and by subject matter. The *Digest* cumulates periodically throughout a congressional session, with supplements appearing between cumulations; a final cumulative version is issued at the session's conclusion.

Cumulative Index of Congressional Committee Hearings. This multi-volume series of indexes prepared by the Library of the United

States Senate lists House and Senate hearings transcripts contained in the Senate library collection. Hearings are listed by subject (using key words from hearing titles), by committee, and by bill number. The *Index* also indicates the dates on which the hearings were held. The usefulness of the *Index* is limited by its restriction to only those hearings in the Senate library, which does not include all congressional hearings in its collection.

The *Index* provides coverage from the 41st Congress (1869–71) through the 96th Congress (1979–80); each volume in the series covers a specific period, and later volumes do not cumulate earlier ones. The Government Printing Office discontinued publication of the series in 1980. Where available, the *CIS U.S. Congressional Committee Hearings Index* and the *CIS/Index*, published by Congressional Information Service (a commercial publisher discussed later in this appendix), now provide comprehensive coverage of committee hearings by duplicating and significantly expanding the Senate library's *Index*.

History notes accompanying officially published statutes. Slip laws, *Statutes at Large*, and the *United States Code* provide brief notes summarizing the legislative histories of federal statutes. Slip laws and *Statutes at Large* began including legislative history information in 1963. The notes now appear at the end of each public law; for each law, the notes provide relevant references to House and Senate Reports, the *Congressional Record*, and the *Weekly Compilation of Presidential Documents*.[60] From volume 77 (1963) through volume 88 (1974), the legislative history information in *Statutes at Large* appeared in a section called "Guide to Legislative History of Bills Enacted Into Public Law" instead of at the end of individual laws. Since the first session of the 58th Congress (1903), *Statutes at Large* has also indicated at the outset of each public law its corresponding bill number.[61]

In the *United States Code*, the history notes appear at the end of each statute and briefly describe each amendment to the statute; the notes do not cite any related congressional documents, such as committee reports. Another entry following each statute in the *United States Code* indicates the public law numbers (or chapter numbers, for the period when those were used instead of public law numbers) and the *Statutes at Large* citations for the original statute and all amendments.

---

[60]Published since 1965, the *Weekly Compilation* is an official weekly publication containing material the White House issues, such as presidential messages, speeches, and statements made upon signing bills into law.

[61]To find bill numbers for laws enacted before 1903, see E. NABORS, LEGISLATIVE REFERENCE CHECKLIST: THE KEY TO LEGISLATIVE HISTORIES FROM 1789–1903 (1982).

Numerical List and Schedule of Volumes. This two-part index prepared by the Superintendent of Documents enables researchers to locate documents in the *Serial Set*.[62] The *Numerical List* allows a researcher who knows the number of a House or Senate Report or Document to determine which volume of the *Serial Set* contains the material. The *Schedule of Volumes* lists *Serial Set* volumes in numerical order and shows researchers what materials each volume includes.

Monthly Catalog of United States Government Publications. This publication, issued under various titles since 1895 and under its current title since 1951, is a comprehensive catalog of federal government documents available to the public. It contains information analogous to that found in a card catalog, briefly describing the documents and indicating from what sources they can be obtained. The *Catalog* lists many documents relevant to legislative history research, including committee hearings, committee prints, House and Senate Reports, and House and Senate Documents.

To use the *Catalog*, you first check one of its several indexes; material is indexed by author, subject, and title, among other ways. The index provides a unique locator number you then use to find the information about the document in the bibliographic section of the *Catalog*.

Commercially published finding tools

Congressional Information Service (CIS). Established in 1970, this commercial publisher provides the most thorough coverage and detailed indexing available of legislative history documents. CIS's mate-

---

[62]The *Serial Set* is an ongoing compilation of congressional and other governmental and historical documents. Prepared under the direction of Congress, the *Serial Set* contains many documents relevant to legislative intent, particularly House and Senate Reports.

The *Serial Set*'s coverage began in 1817, with documents from the Fifteenth Congress, and it continues to the present. A companion publication, *American State Papers*, compiles documents from the First through Fourteenth Congresses (1789–1817). Today, the *Serial Set* consists of hundreds of thousands of documents bound in thousands of volumes.

Congress decides what documents to include in the *Serial Set*, and selection practices have varied. The set has always included House and Senate Reports and Documents; on the other hand, bills and resolutions, committee hearings, and committee prints have generally been excluded. Other congressional materials, such as the *Journals* of the House and Senate, have appeared episodically.

In using the *Serial Set*, you may notice gaps in the volume numbers. From 1913 to 1978, only five libraries, all in federal government agencies in the District of Columbia, received every volume of the *Serial Set*. The versions found in all other libraries omitted various volumes. The missing material can be found in Congressional Information Service's *CIS US Serial Set on Microfiche*, which duplicates the complete version of the *Serial Set* sent to the five Washington libraries. (CIS, a commercial publisher of legislative history materials, is discussed later in this appendix.)

rials fall into three categories: indexes; summaries, *i.e.*, abstracts, of the documents that CIS indexes; and a microfiche collection of the full texts of CIS-indexed documents. CIS is the only publisher that attempts to provide access to *all* the documents relevant in legislative history research.

CIS covers congressional documents published after 1969 in *CIS/Index to Publications of the U.S. Congress*, commonly known as *CIS/Index*. For documents published through 1969, CIS provides separate indexing services: committee hearings are indexed and briefly annotated in *CIS U.S. Congressional Committee Hearings Index*; committee prints are indexed and briefly annotated in *CIS U.S. Congressional Committee Prints Index*; and House and Senate Reports, House and Senate Documents, and other congressional materials in the *American State Papers* and the pre-1970 volumes of the *Serial Set*[63] are indexed in *CIS U.S. Serial Set Index*. For pre-1970 documents, these CIS publications provide the most detailed indexing available. They are organized and used much like the *CIS/Index*.

The *CIS/Index* consists of two sections. Its comprehensive index section categorizes documents several ways: by subject, by author, by name of committee or subcommittee chairperson, by names of witnesses testifying at committee hearings, by subcommittee name, by title, by bill number, and by House and Senate Report and Document number. The abstracts section provides concise but detailed synopses of documents, outlining each document's contents and indicating its title and other identifying information necessary to retrieve the document.

To use the *CIS/Index*, you start by checking one or more of its indexes, which will provide you with CIS-assigned accession numbers indicating where to find the corresponding discussions in the abstracts section. Then, by reading the abstracts, you can assess whether to read the document itself. If you decide to read the document, you will have to obtain it from a source outside the *CIS/Index* itself, *e.g.*, a library, the agency issuing the document, the Government Printing Office, or CIS's separate document collections.

Both the index and abstracts sections of the *CIS/Index* are issued monthly. CIS cumulates the indexes every three months. At the end of the year, CIS cumulates both the indexes and the abstracts in a permanently bound edition entitled *CIS/Annual*. Approximately every four years, CIS publishes a multi-year *Index* volume cumulating the index sections, but not the abstracts sections, from the *CIS/Annuals* published since the previous multi-year *Index*.

[63]*See* note 62, *supra*.

Each *CIS/Annual* includes a legislative history section with thorough legislative history tables for all public laws enacted during the year (except those of a ceremonial nature, *e.g.*, a measure congratulating an Olympic team).[64] These history tables are particularly valuable for two reasons: their citations include hearings, which many other finding tools omit, and they refer to all related congressional documents, even those from earlier sessions or Congresses.[65] If relevant documents are issued after CIS publishes its annual edition of the *CIS/Index*, CIS provides a revised legislative history in the *CIS/Annual* for the year in which the documents appeared; therefore, when you use the *CIS/Annual* legislative history section, you should also check later *Annuals* for revised histories. Starting in 1984, the legislative history tables in *CIS/Annual* include summaries of legislative documents in addition to their citations.

Congressional Index. This index, published by Commerce Clearing House ("CCH"), is highly regarded for the speed with which it issues well-indexed, basic information about congressional activity. The *Congressional Index* features weekly reporting while Congress is in session and up to six weeks after adjournment.

Because it provides continuous supplementation, CCH publishes the *Congressional Index* in a looseleaf format; to house the latest pages as they become available, CCH provides a two-volume set of binders for each Congress, with one volume for the House and another for the Senate. Although the *Index* is intended principally as a tool for monitoring current congressional activity, sets of the *Index* covering previous Congresses offer information useful for doing legislative history research.

---

[64]For the 97th Congress (1981–82) and the first session of the 98th Congress (1983), the separately available looseleaf *CIS Legislative History Service* provided additional, expanded coverage for major public laws. CIS discontinued this short-lived service in 1984, but immediately broadened the scope of its *CIS/Annual* legislative history tables.

[65]If you do not have access to CIS's legislative history tables, you may be able to identify earlier related documents in two other ways. First, the legislative documents you find as you research the history of a statute may contain references to related legislative documents from an earlier session or Congress. For example, witnesses testifying at a hearing on the bill that became your statute may refer to similar or identical bills about which they testified on previous occasions. Committee reports or floor debates may yield similar references to predecessor bills. By looking up the bill number of a predecessor proposal in a status table or index arranged by bill number, you can identify related hearings, committee reports, floor debates, and other legislative documents.

Second, you can identify related documents by using a subject matter index. Once you determine the subject headings under which the bill that became your statute is indexed, search under those headings in subject matter indexes covering earlier sessions or Congresses. This search will lead you to related bills whose bill numbers you can use to identify other related legislative documents.

The *Congressional Index* provides indexes for all public bills introduced. The indexes are arranged by author (*i.e.*, sponsoring legislator) and subject. The subject index has three parts: the main subject index and two supplemental subject indexes that cover new developments. To ensure your research in the subject index is complete, you need to check all three parts.

In its "House Bills" and "Senate Bills" sections, the *Congressional Index* very briefly highlights the contents of all introduced bills. The *Congressional Index* sections entitled "Current Status of House Bills" and "Current Status of Senate Bills" contain status tables of public bills on which a committee has commenced hearings or which a committee has reported to the floor. The status tables include references to committee hearings (also noting whether transcripts have been printed) and other relevant documents (except floor debates). Other sections of the *Congressional Index* provide the following information: legislators' voting records; a list of when particular committees held hearings on specific subjects and legislation; a list of public bills enacted, including a separate subject index for the list and information about presidential vetoes; a table of companion bills; legislators' biographies; and rosters of committee and subcommittee members (a useful resource if you have to obtain a congressional document from a committee or subcommittee member).

U.S. Code Congressional and Administrative News. West Publishing Company has issued this publication, informally referred to as *USCCAN*, since 1941. In addition to serving as an unofficial and more quickly available version of *Statutes at Large* by promptly publishing newly enacted public laws, *USCCAN* includes several features useful for doing legislative history research. It reprints the texts of *selected* committee reports on bills enacted into law and the texts of presidential messages to Congress. (West sometimes edits the reports, indicating deletions with asterisks.) *USCCAN* also provides status tables summarizing the legislative histories of new public laws.

West issues *USCCAN* monthly in paperbound pamphlets; the index and tables found in each pamphlet cumulate. At the end of a congressional session, West cumulates the pamphlets into a permanent hardbound multi-volume annual edition. Since the second session of the 88th Congress (1964), West has reprinted and indexed presidential messages in the paperbound pamphlets only.

USCCAN's principal legislative history table (which *USCCAN* designates "Table 4") indicates, in order of public law number, the following information about each public law: public law number; *Statutes at Large* citation; bill number; House and Senate Report numbers; committees that reported the bill; and dates the House and Senate considered and passed the law, including the volume number and year of the *Congressional Record* that reports the chambers' actions. The table does not refer to committee hearings. The information from the legislative history table also appears in non-tabular form at the outset of those committee reports that *USCCAN* reprints.

History notes accompanying unofficially published statutory codes. Legislative history notes in *United States Code Annotated* and *United States Code Service* duplicate the notes (discussed at page 198) that accompany the official statutory code, *United States Code.* The commercial publishers, however, frequently add cross-references to other publications that may assist in evaluating legislative intent. For example, West Publishing Company's *United States Code Annotated* cross-references legislative history information in its *United States Code Congressional and Administrative News.*

Computerized data bases. Several commercial publishers, including Congressional Information Service and Commerce Clearing House, offer computerized data bases of information that can be useful in researching legislative history. Because of the volume of material involved and the publishers' desire to offer prompt access to timely information, the data bases generally provide only abstracts and summaries of congressional documents. As a separate service to subscribers, some of the publishers will, for an additional fee, send full-text copies of documents upon request.

Some of the data bases only contain information for monitoring pending legislation, although a few cover longer periods. For example, through its AcCIS data base, Congressional Information Service provides online access to its full *CIS/Index* coverage from 1970 to the present. Similarly, Capitol Services International provides coverage of the *Congressional Record* since 1976 through its CRECORD data base.

Because of their expense, data bases with legislative history information may not be available in your library. If you do have access to such a data base, you should carefully review the user's manual provided with it. For further information about legislative history data bases and suggestions for using them effectively, you may want to consult Knowledge Industry Publications' *Online Search Strategies* (1982), edited by Ryan Hoover.

Summary. Figure JJ (pp. 204–05) summarizes the coverage of the principal finding tools used in legislative history research.

LOOK IN

TO FIND	CCH Congressional Index (sections on House and Senate committee hearings)	CCH Congressional Index ("Current Status" tables)	CCH Congressional Index ("House Bills" and "Senate Bills" sections)	CIS/Index; CIS/Annual	CIS U.S. Congressional Committee Hearings Index	CIS U.S. Congressional Committee Prints Index	CIS U.S. Serial Set Index	Congressional Record ("History of Bills Enacted Into Public Law" table)	Congressional Record ("History of Bills and...
Presidential messages proposing legislation: indexed				•					
Bill number: cited				•				•	
Bills: summarized			•						•
Status tables arranged by bill number		•							•
Amendments to bills: cited		•		•					•
Committee hearings: cited		•		•					
Committee hearings: indexed	•			•	•				
Committee hearings: summarized				•					
Committee reports: cited		•		•				•	•
Committee reports: indexed				•			•		
Committee reports: summarized				•					
Committee prints: cited				•					
Committee prints: indexed				•		•			
Committee prints: summarized				•					
House and Senate Documents: cited				•					
House and Senate Documents: indexed				•			•		
House and Senate Documents: summarized				•					
Floor debates: citations to Congressional Record				•					•
Enacted bills (public laws): public law number cited		•							•
Public laws: summarized				•					
Status tables arranged by public law number				•				•	
Presidential signing statements and veto messages: cited				•					
Presidential signing statements and veto messages: indexed				•			•		

Figure JJ.   Summary of Principal Finding Tools that Cite, Index, and Summarize L

Digest of Public General Bills and Resolutions	House Calendar ("Bills Through Conference" table)	House Calendar ("Numerical Order" table)	Journals of the House and Senate	Monthly Catalog of U.S. Government Publications	Serial Set ("Numerical List and Schedule of Volumes")	Slip laws	Statutes at Large	U.S. Code Congressional & Administrative News	Weekly Compilation of Presidential Documents; Public Papers of the Presidents	Comments
			•					•	•	Finding tools indexing House and Senate Documents cover messages reprinted as Documents. Since 1964, *USCCAN* has indexed messages in its paperbound volumes only.
•						•	•	•		For bills before 1903, check E. Nabors, *Legislative Reference Checklist* (1982).
•										*Digest* summaries are detailed; CCH and *Record* summaries are extremely brief.
•		•	•							*Journals'* bill number indexes double as status tables.
•			•							
				•						CIS indexing is the most thorough.
										CIS U.S. Congressional Committee Hearings Index very briefly annotates hearings.
•	•	•	•			•	•	•		"Bills Through Conference" table only cites conference committee reports.
				•	•					CIS indexing is the most thorough.
										Prints issued or reissued as House or Senate Reports or Documents also treated in finding tools for Reports and Documents.
				•						See preceding comment. CIS indexing is the most thorough.
										Prints issued or reissued as House or Senate Reports or Documents also treated in finding tools for Reports and Documents. *CIS U.S. Congressional Committee Prints Index* very briefly annotates prints.
				•	•					CIS indexing is the most thorough.
										Citations are included in *CIS/Annual* legislative history tables as of 1984.
	•	•	•							
•										*Digest* summaries are detailed; summaries in CIS history tables are brief.
•							•			
							•	•		All cites are to *Weekly Compilation of Presidential Documents*. Cites in *USCCAN* appear after reprints of laws.
				•	•			•	•	Starting in 1964, *USCCAN* indexes in paperbound volumes only. *Serial Set* "Numerical List" indexes veto messages issued as House or Senate Documents.

▪cuments

Obtaining the texts of federal legislative documents

Copies of federal legislative documents are available in most major law libraries and in other libraries designated as federal depositories. The federal depository library program, administered by the U.S. Government Printing Office ("GPO"), provides free public access to government publications. Each state has several depository libraries, which range from local public libraries to large university libraries. You can find the depository library nearest you by asking a librarian or by checking the list of depository libraries in *Government Depository Libraries*, a committee print issued by the Joint Committee on Printing and available from the GPO.[66]

For two reasons, not all libraries, even depository libraries, will have copies of every legislative document as a result of government distribution. First, the GPO has not always distributed certain types of documents; for example, although Congress established the depository library program in 1857, the GPO has distributed committee hearings as depository items since only 1938. Second, although some depository libraries (called "regional" depositories) receive all government documents distributed under the program, other libraries (designated "selective" depositories) do not. If the library also subscribes to Congressional Information Service's microfiche collections, however, it will have a comprehensive holding of legislative documents.

In retrieving legislative documents in a library, you need to realize that because of the overwhelming volume of government materials sent to libraries that receive legislative documents as depository items, many libraries do not catalog these documents in their regular card catalogs. To locate legislative materials, therefore, you may have to ask a librarian for assistance.

If your library does not have a legislative document you need, you can often obtain it in other ways, particularly if the document is not especially old. You can ask your librarian to obtain the document through an inter-library loan or, perhaps, to purchase it for your library's permanent collection. You may be able to purchase the document yourself from the GPO[67] or through the "documents on demand" service of a commercial publisher, such as Congressional Information Service or Com-

---

[66]The GPO's address is Superintendent of Documents, U.S. Government Printing Office, Washington, D.C. 20402.

[67]When purchasing documents from the GPO, you can obtain helpful ordering information in the *Monthly Catalog of United States Government Publications*, discussed at page 199, *supra*.

merce Clearing House. In addition, you may be able to obtain a copy of the document directly from Congress by contacting the sponsoring legislator, the clerk of the committee that issued the document, the clerk of the House, or the secretary of the Senate; in practice, though, you may find it easier or quicker to ask your own Representative or Senator to obtain a copy of the document for you.

The rest of this section indicates how to obtain the texts of specific types of legislative documents when researching in a library whose collection includes the documents you need. Most of the publications listed in this section as including the texts of legislative documents have already been described in the preceding section, where their indexing features and status tables were discussed.

Legislative proposals. Proposals for new legislation originate from a wide range of sources; documents associated with these proposals will therefore be located in a variety of places. (See page 179.) Presidential messages accompanying proposals initiated by the president are issued individually as House Documents and, sometimes, also as Senate Documents. (Resources that reprint House and Senate Documents are listed below.) Presidential messages proposing legislation also appear in the *Congressional Record*, the *Weekly Compilation of Presidential Documents*, the *Public Papers of the Presidents* series,[68] the *Journal* of the chamber receiving the message, and in *United States Code Congressional and Administrative News*. (Since 1964, the messages in *USCCAN* have appeared in the paperbound volumes only.)

When legislative proposals result from committee investigations, the reports or transcripts of the committee investigative hearings may be printed and issued individually. The hearings will be labelled as such; the reports may be issued as committee reports or prints or as House or Senate Documents (see below).

Bills. These are issued individually in slip form. Texts of bills are also included in the transcripts of related hearings and may be available as committee prints. (See below.) In addition, bills are sometimes reprinted in committee reports or in the *Congressional Record*. Compromise bills negotiated by conference committees appear in the conference committees' reports (see below). Through its *Congressional Bills,*

---

[68]The *Public Papers of the President* series includes the same types of presidential materials as the *Weekly Compilation of Presidential Documents*, but is not published as frequently. *See* note 60, *supra*. Although the *Public Papers* series does not collect the papers of every President, it provides access to many presidential papers that antedate the *Weekly Compilation*.

Resolutions and Laws collection, CIS provides microfiche copies of original, amended, and revised versions of all bills; coverage currently extends back to the 78th Congress (1943–44), and CIS plans to add coverage of earlier Congresses.

Amendments to bills. Committee amendments to bills are found in committee-reported prints of bills and in accompanying committee reports (see below). Amendments offered from the floor of the chambers appear in the *Congressional Record*. CIS provides copies of amended bills through its *Congressional Bills, Resolutions and Laws* microfiche collection.

Committee hearings. Transcripts of hearings are issued individually in paperbound pamphlet or book form. Hearings transcripts are also available in the *CIS/Microfiche Library* (which covers hearings held from 1970 to the present) and in *CIS U.S. Congressional Committee Hearings on Microfiche* (covering hearings held from approximately 1833 to 1969).

Committee reports. These documents are issued individually as paperbound pamphlets or books and are also included in the *Serial Set*. Reports of conference committees are individually issued as House and sometimes Senate Reports and reprinted in the *Congressional Record* when either chamber acts on the reports; they are also reprinted in the House *Journal* whenever the House acts on the reports and, until the late 1970's, were reprinted in the Senate *Journal* whenever the Senate acted. In addition, West's *U.S. Code Congressional and Administrative News* reprints selected reports, although West sometimes edits the texts for length. Committee reports are also available in the *CIS/Microfiche Library* (covering reports issued from 1970 to the present) and in *CIS U.S. Serial Set on Microfiche* (covering reports issued from 1789 to 1969).

Committee prints. These materials are issued individually in paperbound form and are also available in the *CIS/Microfiche Library* (covering prints issued from 1970 to the present) and in *CIS U.S. Congressional Committee Prints on Microfiche* (covering prints issued from 1830 to 1969). Prints are sometimes reissued as committee reports or as House or Senate Documents. If so, they are generally available to the same extent as other reports and Documents.

House and Senate Documents. These are issued individually in paperbound form and are also included in the *Serial Set*. In addition, they are available in the *CIS/Microfiche Library* (covering Documents issued from 1970 to present) and in *CIS U.S. Serial Set on Microfiche* (covering Documents issued from 1789 to 1969).

Floor debates. Nearly verbatim transcripts of both chambers' floor debates appear in the *Congressional Record* and its predecessor publications. The *Congressional Record* and its predecessors are also available on microfiche from CIS.

Enacted bills (public laws). The texts of public laws initially appear individually in slip law form. Shortly afterward, public laws are published, in order of their enactment, in *United States Code Congressional and Administrative News* (first in paperbound advance sheets and later in the permanent hardbound volumes) and in the advance sheets for *United States Code Service*. At the end of each session of Congress, public laws are collected chronologically in the official session laws, *Statutes at Large*. In addition, CIS makes slip laws and *Statutes at Large* available on microfiche. Finally, public laws are arranged by subject matter and republished in the official *United States Code* and the unofficial *United States Code Annotated* and *United States Code Service*.

Presidential statements and veto messages. Presidential statements made upon signing public laws are reprinted in the *Weekly Compilation of Presidential Documents* and the *Public Papers of the Presidents* series. Presidential veto messages sent to Congress upon vetoing bills are issued individually as House and Senate Documents and reprinted in the *Weekly Compilation*, the *Public Papers* series, the *Congressional Record*, the *Journal* of the chamber in which the bill originated, and *United States Code Congressional and Administrative News*. (Since 1964, the messages in *USCCAN* have appeared in the paperbound volumes only.)

A basic strategy for federal legislative history research

Because of the wide array, varying availability, and differing coverage of federal legislative history publications, a researcher can follow a large number of paths in searching for legislative intent. Yet, as with other legal research, effective and efficient legislative history research requires some system for selecting which path will likely prove most fruitful. Certain research steps are common to all federal legislative history research projects, and bearing these steps in mind should keep your research on track. The steps, explained in this section, are:

- Find the bill number or public law number.
- Look for a previously compiled legislative history.
- If a compiled history is unavailable, or if it needs supplementing, use the bill number or public law number to find refer-

ences to legislative history documents in one or more status tables or indexes.

● Obtain and review the full texts of the documents cited.

Nearly every publication for identifying federal legislative history documents is arranged by either bill number or public law number. Consequently, you first need to find the number of the bill or public law corresponding to the statutory provision you are researching. The easiest way to find a public law number is to check the parenthetical information provided at the end of the statutory provision as it appears in the *United States Code*, *United States Code Annotated*, or *United States Code Service*. (Along with the public law number, you will also find the corresponding *Statutes at Large* citation there.)

To find a bill number, check the slip law or its reprint in *Statutes at Large* or *United States Code Congressional and Administrative News*; the bill number will be listed in the margin near the beginning of the law. If you do not have access to *Statutes at Large* or *USCCAN*, you can find the bill number by looking up the public law number in a status table arranged in public law number order. Status tables arranged this way include the legislative history tables in *CIS/Annual*, the "Public Laws" table in the *Digest of Public General Bills and Resolutions*, and the table entitled *History of Bills Enacted into Public Law* found in the hardbound version of the *Daily Digest* section of the *Congressional Record*. The CCH *Congressional Index* also cross-references public law and bill numbers in its "Enactments-Vetoes" list. To find bill numbers corresponding to laws passed before 1903, when bill numbers first appeared in *Statutes at Large*, check E. Nabors, *Legislative Reference Checklist: The Key to Legislative Histories from 1789–1903* (1982).

As your next step, look for a "compiled" legislative history of the statute in which you are interested. A compiled legislative history collects in one place the full texts of legislative documents pertaining to a particular statute, thus eliminating the need to identify and obtain the documents one at a time.[69] Compiled histories can obviously save considerable research effort, but even when available, their quality varies; some compiled histories may not include all relevant documents. Therefore, you still need to familiarize yourself with all the potentially

[69]For statutes enacted in 1984 and later, the tables in the legislative histories section of *CIS/Annual* provide the most helpful alternatives to compiled legislative histories. Since 1984, these CIS tables have collected *summaries* of the contents of congressional documents relating to particular statutes, thus giving more information about the documents than appears in the status tables of other finding tools (which generally just cite the documents).

available types of legislative documents and with the finding tools discussed in the appendix section entitled "Publications for identifying federal legislative history documents." This familiarity will allow you to evaluate the thoroughness of a compiled legislative history and to fill any gaps in its coverage.

Several commercial and public organizations publish compiled legislative histories on federal statutes. For example, among commercial publishers, Commerce Clearing House has made compiled legislative histories available through its *Public Laws—Legislative Histories on Microfiche* since the 96th Congress (1979–80). The Library of Congress' Congressional Research Service and other federal government agencies sometimes compile legislative histories of selected federal statutes. For instance, the U.S. Food and Drug Administration has compiled a legislative history on the Federal Food, Drug, and Cosmetic Act. In addition, special interest groups and public policy research organizations sometimes compile legislative histories on statutes in which they are interested.

There are several ways to determine the availability of compiled legislative histories. Nancy Johnson's *Sources of Compiled Legislative Histories* (1979 and latest supplement) lists, by public law number, compiled legislative histories for federal statutes and indicates the publisher and scope of each history. Another widely available list of compiled legislative histories is the *Union List of Legislative Histories* (5th ed. 1985). Prepared by the Law Librarians' Society of Washington, D.C., this list indicates compiled histories found in the collections of various libraries and that might be available through inter-library loans. A law librarian can advise you further about the availability of compiled histories.

If you cannot find a comprehensive compiled legislative history, you will have to compile your own. This task involves two steps. First, look up the bill number or public law number in one or more of the status tables and indexes discussed at pages 191 to 205. For example, a public law number provides access to the information in the *CIS/Annual* legislative history tables, while a bill number allows you to use the *History of Bills and Resolutions* table in the *Congressional Record*, the "Other Measures Receiving Action" table in the *Digest of Public General Bills and Resolutions,* or the "Current Status" tables in CCH's *Congressional Index.* These and other status tables will provide citations to legislative documents pertaining to the statute you are researching. The documents cited will depend on which status table you use; for instance, several tables omit references to hearings, committee prints, and floor debates. Figure JJ (pages 204–05) shows in tabular form which status tables refer to which types of legislative documents.

As you become familiar with researching legislative history, you will discover that, as a practical matter, you can find nearly all the citation information you need by checking as few as two of the many available status tables and indexes. In this regard, the resources mentioned by title in the preceding paragraph are excellent; for example, tables and indexes published by Congressional Information Service, in combination with the *History of Bills and Resolutions* table in the index to the *Congressional Record*, provide citations to all relevant legislative documents you are likely to need. (In fact, beginning with laws enacted in 1984, the legislative history tables accompanying *CIS/Annual* provide comprehensive citations to *all* types of legislative documents, including *Congressional Record* page references to floor debates, which CIS tables previously omitted.)

Second, after checking a status table or index, you complete your legislative history research by using the information from the status table or index to obtain the full texts of the documents so you can review them for yourself. Even if your research leads you to a summary or abstract of a relevant legislative document, you will still need to read the document to determine its actual significance. The preceding section of the appendix indicated how to obtain the full texts of legislative documents.

Researching the legislative history of state statutes

Although you use different resources, legislative history research in state statutes (and in local ordinances) roughly parallels the process for federal legislative history research. As with federal statutes, the objective is to find and analyze legislative documents generated at the various steps leading up to a measure's enactment: introduction of the proposal; referral to committee; hearings; floor debate; and so forth. At the state level, though, the documents are generally less detailed and more difficult to locate. They may even be completely inaccessible.

Most state legislative bodies do not transcribe their floor debates. At most, an official journal records minutes of the legislative sessions, frequently indicating only the introduction of bills and the votes on the bills and proposed amendments to them. Also, committees usually do not publish their reports or hearings for general distribution. Moreover, even when a state legislature maintains files on enacted legislation, the documents in the files may not be indexed or collected in any discernible order. Often, the only meaningful legislative documents in a legislative file are various versions of a proposal as it moves from introduction to enactment.

Despite the difficulties involved in researching legislative history at the state level, it may be possible to reconstruct the history of a state statute by trying the following approach.[70]

Start by looking for a compiled legislative history for your statute. If you are researching the legislative history of an especially noteworthy statute or of a uniform statute, *e.g.*, the Uniform Commercial Code, a legislative history may already have been compiled, collecting the texts of relevant documents. A law librarian, particularly one at the legislature's reference bureau (if your legislature has one) or at the state's official law library, can help you locate whatever compiled legislative histories may be available. Associations of local law librarians sometimes prepare "union lists" of compiled legislative histories contained in the collections of area law libraries and that might be available through inter-library loans. If an administrative agency has responsibility for implementing the statute you are researching, you may also be able to locate a compiled legislative history at the agency. Finally, the state bar association, lobbyists, or local political activists with an interest in the statute you are researching may have collected the documents or be able to direct you to them.

You should also try to determine whether your statute was originally proposed or drafted by an organization, such as a law revision commission or judicial council, responsible for recommending new legislation or amendments to existing legislation. If it was, the organization may have issued a report explaining its proposals. In evaluating legislative intent, courts often view these reports as functionally equivalent to reports is-

---

[70]This approach assumes that your routine research into the statute (*e.g.*, checking case annotations in the annotated code, Shepardizing the statute) has already led you to cases and other authorities, such as attorney general opinions or law review articles, interpreting your statute. The suggestions in this section also assume that your review of those materials has not definitively answered your questions about a perceived ambiguity in the statute and that you now need to research legislative history as a guide to intent. (If a case with mandatory precedential value clearly answered your questions about statutory meaning, you would presumably not need to engage in legislative history research—unless, of course, you conclude the court wrongly decided the earlier case and you want to argue that the court should overrule its precedent.)

As you read these cases and other authorities, you should note any relevant legislative documents they cite. By recording the citations as you go, you will have a convenient starting point if you subsequently discover you need to examine legislative history; this is especially important in legislative history research at the state level because of the dearth of status tables, indexes, and other legislative history finding tools analogous to those at the federal level. As an added benefit, your notes will help you sense which types of legislative documents might persuade a court when it considers an argument relying on legislative history.

sued by legislative committees, especially when no legislative committee has issued a report. Annotated statutory codes sometimes cite, or even excerpt, reports of non-legislative agencies; also, a state law librarian or a legislative reference bureau librarian can often help you find the reports.

If you have to identify and collect legislative documents yourself because a complete compiled legislative history is unavailable, you can determine the types of legislative history documents available in your state by checking Mary Fisher's *Guide to State Legislative Materials* (3d ed. 1985). This publication indicates for each state the available legislative materials and where to locate them. Learning more about how your legislature enacts laws can also help you figure out what types of legislative history documents it routinely creates. Your legislature may publish a book or pamphlet explaining how it operates, or you can ask a staff member at the legislative reference bureau, your local legislator, or a member of your legislator's staff for information. Finally, you may find helpful suggestions in a legal research guide specifically tailored to your jurisdiction; your law library's card catalog should indicate, under the heading "legal research," if such a guide exists for your state.

As a general matter, to compile a legislative history on a state statute, you need to obtain the legislature's file on the measure.[71] To obtain the file, you normally need to know the session law number corresponding to your statute: for bills enacted into law, legislatures usually store their bill files in session law number order. A staff member of a legislative reference or drafting bureau or the clerk of a legislative chamber can help you find bill files.

Once you locate a legislative file on the bill that became the law in whose history you are interested, its contents should help you determine who sponsored the bill and to which committee or committees the bill was referred. By talking to the bill's sponsor or other legislators involved in the bill's enactment, you may gain access to personal or committee files related to the bill. In addition, although courts generally will not consider individual legislators' statements about what an entire legislature intended in enacting a bill, talking to legislators may provide helpful background information or insights that will enhance your own understanding of the statute.

In the end, though, parsing the language of legislative proposals remains the principal means of determining legislative intent behind am-

---

[71]Frequently, you can uncover all the legislative documents underlying a state statute only at the legislature itself (specifically, its central library or legislative reference or drafting bureau) or at the state's official law library.

biguous state statutes. Because state legislatures do not systematically create or widely distribute legislative documents such as committee reports or hearings transcripts, and because states generally have few, if any, status tables, indexes, or other legislative history finding tools to provide access to the documents that may be available, researchers must discern legislative intent largely by scrutinizing and comparing language differences in the various drafts of a bill. In addition to keeping drafts in their own bill files, some state legislatures distribute at least selected versions of bill drafts to major libraries in the state.

The role of legislative history research

Given the widespread use of legislative history in statutory interpretation, knowing how to conduct legislative history research is an essential skill. Nonetheless, a longstanding controversy exists regarding the use of legislative history in interpreting both federal and state statutes, and you will work more effectively with legislative materials if you recognize and accommodate the divergent views on the subject. This section summarizes the principal elements of the dispute.

The question at the heart of the controversy is whether examining the documents a legislature generates during the enactment of a statute is actually an appropriate way to ascertain legislative intent. After all, the argument goes, the legislature enacted (and the executive signed into law) only the statute, not the documents relating to its pre-enactment consideration. In a frequently cited concurring opinion, United States Supreme Court Justice Robert Jackson stated the case against using legislative history in interpreting statutes:

> It is the business of Congress to sum up its own debates in its legislation. Moreover, it is only the words of the bill that have presidential approval, where that approval is given. It is not to be supposed that, in signing a bill, the President endorses the whole Congressional Record. For [the Court] to undertake to reconstruct an enactment from legislative history is merely to involve the Court in political controversies which are quite proper in the enactment of a bill but should have no place in its interpretation.[72]

In addition to concerns about keeping the institutional responsibilities of the judicial and legislative branches distinct, pragmatic considerations have caused some commentators to urge a circumscribed role

---

[72]Schwegmann Bros. v. Calvert Distillers Corp., 341 U.S. 384, 396 (1951) (Jackson, J., concurring).

for legislative history. In particular, these commentators argue that three problems attend the legislative documents generated in the enactment process: (1) they are not always accessible to researchers inquiring into a statute's meaning; (2) they may not have been taken into account by a significant number of legislators; and (3) they lack reliability.[73]

Accessibility remains a substantial problem in connection with legislative history research into state statutes. The accessibility of federal legislative history documents, however, has improved in recent years because of these materials' wider distribution, often by private publishers.

With respect to the second objection, concern has not diminished over the impossibility of knowing whether enough legislators took account of a given legislative document for the document to be considered a meaningful indicator of legislative intent. For example, a researcher can never know with certainty how many legislators read a committee report or heard a statement during floor debate. Even if that information could be known, it would remain a mystery whether the legislators, when drafting or voting on a bill, actually relied on what they read or heard and, if they did, what form their reliance took. A legislator may, for instance, vote for a bill despite sharp disagreement with many statements in the bill's accompanying report or made during floor debate.

Ultimately, though, the unreliability of legislative documents remains the major objection to their use as guides to legislative intent. Legislative documents vary widely in their reliability, depending on the circumstances surrounding their origin. For example, a document (such as a transcript of a debate) may contain statements by legislators unfamiliar with the bill under consideration. In other cases, excessive exuberance may cause a bill's supporters to distort their recorded statements about the bill's meaning as they seek to persuade colleagues to support the measure. At the extreme, legislators or their staffs may intentionally manipulate the contents of legislative documents; for instance, they might knowingly insert into a committee report some explanatory or background material that supports provisions the

---

[73]See, e.g., id. at 396-97; F. DICKERSON, THE INTERPRETATION AND APPLICATION OF STATUTES 141-42 (1975). Professor Dickerson's book provides a detailed analysis of the arguments for and against using legislative history to interpret statutes. Much of the discussion in this section of the appendix draws on Professor Dickerson's book, an excellent treatise for readers seeking an in-depth treatment of the subject. See also A. MIKVA & P. SARIS, THE AMERICAN CONGRESS 251 (1983).

committee in fact deleted from the bill.[74] Such manipulation seeks to lead a court to later discern from the legislative document an intent that did not actually underlie the statute.[75]

Despite these and other objections to the use of legislative documents in interpreting statutes, courts continue to turn to legislative history with considerable frequency when they must resolve ambiguity in statutory language. An ability to work with legislative history materials therefore remains a necessary skill for legal researchers.

In doing this type of research, it is important to realize that not all types of legislative documents enjoy equal respect as guides to intent. As a *general* matter, committee reports and statements by sponsoring legislators are regarded as the best indicators of intent: courts usually presume that sponsors and committees responsible for overseeing a bill's progress through the legislative process have the clearest understanding of the measure's meaning.[76] Other legislative documents, such as committee hearings and floor debates, are often considered less reliable indicators of a legislature's intent, largely because a significant number of legislators may not have heard or read the testimony or colloquies before voting on the measure to which they relate. Nonetheless, courts sometimes rely on these types of documents in interpreting statutes.[77]

Putting the debate in perspective. The controversy surrounding the role of legislative history as a guide to legislative intent raises two practical problems for legal researchers. First, how do you decide whether extensively researching legislative history will be worthwhile for a given statutory problem? Second, assuming you decide to pursue comprehensive legislative history research, what use should you make of the results when presenting an argument to a court?

At the state level, the paucity of legislative documents often answers the first question: the general inaccessibility of the documents frequently precludes extensive legislative history research. In deciding

---

[74]*See, e.g.,* C. CURTIS, IT'S YOUR LAW 53 (1954); F. DICKERSON, *supra* note 73, at 155-56; A. MIKVA & P. SARIS, *supra* note 73, at 236; E. REDMAN, THE DANCE OF LEGISLATION 151-52, 157-58 (Touchstone ed. 1973).

[75]C. CURTIS, *supra* note 74, at 53; A. MIKVA & P. SARIS, *supra* note 73, at 236; E. REDMAN, *supra* note 74, at 152.

[76]*See, e.g.,* Schwegmann Bros., 341 U.S. at 395 (Jackson, J., concurring). *See also* C. CURTIS, *supra* note 74, at 51–52.

[77]*See, e.g.,* Grove City College v. Bell, 104 S. Ct. 1211 (1984) (relying on committee hearings and floor debates). For an in-depth discussion of which legislative documents courts are most apt to find persuasive, see G. FOLSOM, *supra* note 52, at 30–41. *See also* C. CURTIS, *supra* note 74, at 51–52.

how far to pursue legislative history research in other instances, though, you need to weigh various factors. First, the advocate on the other side of your dispute might research legislative history comprehensively and, because a court might decide to rely on legislative documents, you should be equally prepared.

Another factor to weigh, however, is the availability of other interpretative aids, such as treatises or law review articles, that may shed helpful light on the meaning of your statute. In some cases, these other publications will be easier to locate or read than legislative documents. Moreover, depending on the quality of their analyses, these non-legislative publications may be just as persuasive to a court.[78]

In deciding how far to pursue legislative history research, yet another consideration is the variable willingness of judges to consider arguments based on this type of research. Some judges, such as Justice Jackson, think courts should rarely base their decisions on statements in legislative documents.[79] If you confronted a problem of statutory interpretation in connection with a case pending before a judge who had expressed antipathy towards considering legislative history, you might want to concentrate your research on other sources. Still, a judge's general attitude will not always accurately predict how that judge will respond to or use legislative history in a particular case. Even Justice Jackson, who favored strictly limiting judicial consideration to committee reports only, admitted that he "sometimes offended against that rule."[80]

The importance of the problem you are researching also influences a decision about how far to pursue legislative history research.[81] Legal research is no place to cut corners, and a reluctance to do the necessary work involved in identifying, retrieving, and analyzing legislative documents should not cause researchers to avoid legislative history research where it might prove fruitful. Nonetheless, the varying accessibility of legislative documents, the debate over the proper weight to attach to them, and the availability of other guides to legislative intent mean that you may be able to resolve many statutory problems, particularly in relatively routine matters, without extensive legislative history research.

---

[78]Cf. Hirschey v. Fed. Energy Reg. Comm'n, 777 F.2d 1, 7 (D.C. Cir. 1985) (Scalia, J., concurring) (suggesting that committee reports and law review articles of comparable quality should be accorded equal weight).
[79]See, e.g., Schwegmann Bros., 341 U.S. at 395-96 (Jackson, J., concurring).
[80]Id.
[81]See F. DICKERSON, supra note 73, at 164 n.68.

In the end, though, the determining factor in deciding how deeply to delve into legislative history will generally be the same guideline that applies to all types of legal research: if you think additional research will shed significant new light on the issues in your problem, keep going. (See Chapter 8.)

In connection with those statutory problems you decide warrant legislative history research, you will have to decide what use to make of any documents you uncover that address your issues. At the least, the legislative documents may enhance your background understanding of the statute, even if you choose not to cite them. As a practical matter, however, despite the general rule that committee reports and sponsoring legislators' statements are significantly more respected than other documents as indicators of legislative intent, you may want to cite *any* relevant documents that support your position. Courts are sufficiently inconsistent in their reliance on legislative history that virtually every kind of legislative document has been used at some point as support for a judicial decision.

APPENDIX L

Definitions of Terms
Frequently Encountered in Legal Research

action—One term for a lawsuit. "Bringing an action" is the same thing as filing a lawsuit in a court. See also case, cause of action, lawsuit.

adjudication—A formal decree or pronouncement of judgment by a court.

advance sheets—Paperbound pamphlets containing the most recent court decisions published in a given case reporter series. Periodically, several advance sheets are collected and published in a hardbound version as a new case reporter volume, at which time the old advance sheets are no longer needed.

affidavit—A written statement of facts made under oath before someone authorized by law to administer oaths. The person making the statement is called an "affiant."

allegation—What a party to an action states, in a pleading, that he or she intends to prove.

annotations—This term has two different meanings. (1) In statutory research, the term is used to refer to brief summaries of court decisions interpreting and applying statutes. These summaries appear in annotated statutory compilations, after the reprinted text of individual statutes to which they relate. (2) "Annotations" is also used to refer to articles, prepared and published by

Lawyers Cooperative Publishing Company in its *American Law Reports Annotated* ("A.L.R.") series, analyzing points of law raised in selected court decisions, statutes, and administrative regulations.

answer—The pleading by which a defendant responds to a plaintiff's complaint. See complaint, pleading.

appellant—The party in an action who appeals a court's decision or judgment to a higher court. Some courts use the term "petitioner" instead of "appellant." See petitioner. Compare appellee.

appellee—The party in an action against whom an appeal is taken. The appellee is usually but not always the winner in the lower court. Further, because an appeal may involve multiple issues decided by the lower court, a given party may be an appellant with respect to some issues and an appellee with respect to others. A party's status as appellant or appellee has no necessary correlation to his or her original status as a plaintiff or defendant in the lower court. Finally, some courts use the term "respondent" instead of "appellee." Compare appellant.

authority—A statute, court decision, constitutional provision, administrative regulation or decision, or a publication about the law. There are two kinds of legal authorities: primary and secondary. *Primary authorities* consist of the law itself, as expressed in constitutions, statutes, court decisions, and administrative regulations and decisions. Primary authorities are either *mandatory* (which must be followed by all courts within a given jurisdiction) or *persuasive* (which offer guidance but need not be followed, e.g., a decision of the Ohio Supreme Court might be regarded as persuasive by the Arizona Supreme Court when it considers a similar kind of issue or case in its own jurisdiction, but it would not bind the Arizona court). *Secondary authorities* are everything else—essentially, writings or commentaries *about* the law found in primary sources. Secondary authorities, which include such publications as legal encyclopedias and law reviews, are not binding.

black letter law—A colloquial term for summary statements of fundamental and widely accepted principles of law.

Blue Book—The informal designation of *A Uniform System of Citation*, a joint publication of the law reviews of Columbia Law School, Harvard Law School, the University of Pennsylvania Law School, and Yale Law School, explaining proper citation format. See Chapter 2.

brief—This term has two different meanings: (1) a written document prepared by counsel to file in a legal proceeding, setting forth the pertinent facts, the applicable law, and an argument supporting counsel's position and challenging the opponent's position; and (2) a summary or abstract of a court decision, usually prepared by a law student to assist in understanding the decision's significance.

case—One term for a lawsuit. See also action, cause of action, lawsuit.

"Case" is also used to refer to a court's decision.

cause of action—Any civil or criminal question litigated or contested before a court of justice; the basis for a lawsuit, *e.g.*, breach of contract, trespass, assault. The phrase is also frequently used as another term for a lawsuit. See also action, case, lawsuit.

citation—The title or other identification of a primary or secondary legal authority, such as a constitution, statute, court decision, or treatise. Lawyers use citations to establish or support propositions they assert in their oral and written legal arguments.

citator—A reference work used in legal research to update certain legal authorities by tracing their subsequent history and treatment, *e.g.*, later judicial history and interpretation of reported court decisions and later judicial and legislative treatment of statutes. The title of the citators used in American legal research is *Shepard's Citations*. See Chapter 6.

cite—In legal research, argumentation, and writing, the term means to provide a citation; also frequently used as a shortened form of "citation." See citation.

civil action—Every action other than a criminal action; an action based on a private wrong, as opposed to a crime, which is considered a wrong to the public in general. Compare criminal action.

claim—A statement or declaration of a legal right. Often used interchangeably with the term "allegation." See allegation.

code—A compilation of statutes or administrative regulations arranged by subject matter or topic.

common law—Principles and rules of law developed, modified, and applied by courts rather than by legislatures (which create statutory law). Common law is sometimes referred to as "judge-made law" or "case law."

complainant—The person who files a complaint; another term for "plaintiff" or "petitioner." See complaint, petitioner, plaintiff.

complaint—The pleading with which a plaintiff starts an action. In a criminal action, the complaint is called an "indictment" or "information." See pleading.

concurring opinion—When a court has a panel of judges ruling on a single case, a judge agreeing with the conclusions, result, or outcome stated in the opinion of the court but disagreeing with the court's rationale may write a separate opinion (called a "concurring opinion") agreeing with the result but stating different reasons for reaching it. Concurring opinions are *not* the law of the case nor binding as precedent, but they may provide a legal researcher with useful insight into the manner in which a court might interpret or apply the case in the future.

count—A statement or declaration of a legal right. Often used interchangeably with the terms "allegation," "claim," and "cause of action." See allegation, claim, and cause of action.

criminal action—A lawsuit in which the government, as prosecutor, tries to persuade a judge or jury to punish a person for violating a criminal statute.

damages—Money given to a person in a lawsuit because of someone else's unlawful conduct. There are two broad categories of damages: *compensatory* damages are awarded to repay a person for an injury or loss he or she has suffered, and *punitive* (or *exemplary*) damages are imposed solely to punish

someone for an injury or loss he or she inflicted on another person.

decision—A court's or other tribunal's disposition (*e.g.*, affirmance, reversal) of a case. Although technically different from an opinion, the two terms are often loosely used as synonyms. See and compare opinion.

defendant—The person defending against or denying the allegations in a complaint, indictment, or information. There can be more than one defendant in a lawsuit.

defendant in error—Another term for an appellee. See appellee.

dictum—See definition in Appendix M.

digests—Legal research reference works containing very brief summaries of reported court decisions, with the summaries arranged by subject matter so that all case summaries on a single point of law are collected together, regardless of the date of issuance of the individual court decisions. See pages 13–15.

dissent—When a court has a panel of judges ruling on a single case, judges disagreeing with the majority's decision may express their views in a dissenting opinion, which may disagree with all or only part of the majority opinion. Dissents are *not* the law of the case nor binding as precedent, but they may provide legal researchers with useful summaries of competing interpretations of specific legal principles or doctrines, and help them in doing their analyses of the strengths and weaknesses of the majority decision.

enjoin—To require or command someone to do, or not to do, some act. See injunction.

headnote—A one-paragraph summary of a specific point of law decided in a case. Headnotes appear at the beginning of a case, and are usually written by the editors of the publisher of the case reporter in which the decision appears. Sometimes, however, the judges themselves or other court personnel will prepare these summaries. See Appendix D.

indictment—A criminal complaint issued by a grand jury at the request of a prosecutor and charging a person with a crime. See complaint. Compare information.

information—A criminal complaint issued by a prosecutor (*e.g.*, a district attorney) rather than by a grand jury, and charging a person with a crime. See complaint. Compare indictment.

injunction—An order from a court requiring or commanding someone to do, or not to do, some act. See enjoin, relief, remedy.

jurisdiction—This term has two different meanings: (1) the authority of a court or other tribunal to take cognizance of a case and to render a decision in it that is legally binding on certain persons or property; and (2) a geographical territory (*e.g.*, a state) in which a particular body of law applies.

Key Number—The name given by West Publishing Company to its digest system of indexing court decisions. West identifies thousands of narrow, separate points of law discussed in court decisions, designates those points as "sub-topics" under its broader digest topics (see Appendices G and H), and then assigns a permanent "Key Number" to each sub-topic. These topics, sub-topics, and Key Numbers comprise the digest system West uses for indexing its case reporters. Key Numbers remain constant throughout all West digests and reporters, *i.e.*, all cases dealing with a given point of law will be summarized in West's digests under the same topic, sub-topic, and Key Number. Use of digests and Key Numbers is discussed at pages 49–51, 53, 56–

58, 59.

Publishers of non-West case reporters and digests use a similar indexing system, but there the functional equivalent of a Key Number is called a "section number," or occasionally a "paragraph number."

lawsuit—A legal proceeding brought in a court in which one or more persons tries to make one or more other persons do something or stop doing something, and/or to pay damages. Other terms sometimes used interchangeably with "lawsuit" are "action," "case," and "cause of action."

liability—Legally enforceable responsibility of one person to pay damages as a result of committing an injurious act or of owing an obligation or debt. See damages.

mandatory authority—See authority.

motion—A request made to a court asking that it do something in a lawsuit. In making a motion, a person is said to "move" the court to do something. Example: "Plaintiff moves the court to have the defendant held in contempt for refusing to answer the question."

opinion—A statement by a judge or court or other tribunal of the rationale followed in reaching the result (*e.g.*, reversal, affirmance) in a particular case. See also concurring opinion, dissent, per curiam (Appendix M), and plurality opinion.

parallel citation—The title or identification (see citation) of a single court decision's verbatim republication in a second or third source.

party—A participant in a transaction or proceeding, *e.g.*, party to a contract, party to a lawsuit. In a lawsuit, the most common parties are plaintiffs and defendants, although there are also other kinds of parties, such as third-party plaintiffs, third-party defendants, and intervenors.

persuasive authority—See authority.

petition—A formal written application to a government body requesting that the tribunal exercise its authority to achieve a particular effect; a complaint is an example of one kind of petition.

petitioner—The person who files a petition. See petition. See also appellant.

plaintiff—The person who brings a civil action by filing a complaint in a court. There can be more than one plaintiff in a lawsuit. In a criminal action, the plaintiff is called the "prosecution" or "the government."

plaintiff in error—Another term for an appellant. See appellant.

pleading—The written statement containing a party's allegations about each point or issue involved in the lawsuit. In civil actions, the principal pleadings are the *complaint*, filed by the plaintiff, and the *answer*, which is filed by the defendant and which responds to the complaint. See allegation, answer, complaint.

plurality opinion—When a court has a panel of judges ruling on a single case and no opinion of any one judge in the case obtains the agreement of the majority of judges participating, the plurality opinion is the opinion with which most of the judges on the panel agree.

presentment—A statement issued by a grand jury without a prosecutor's participation and charging that a crime has been committed.

primary authority—See authority.

regulation—A directive issued by a government agency, pursuant to statutory authority, to implement and carry out a governmental policy or program. Unless invalidated by a court or rescinded by the agency, a regulation has the effect of law and binds those over whom the agency has regulatory power. Regulations are also referred to as "rules."

relief—Assistance or redress given to a party in a civil or criminal action when the court determines the party has a right to it. A temporary injunction is an example of the many kinds of relief a court has the power to grant. See, and compare with, remedy.

remand—To send back, as when an appellate court returns a case to a trial court for further proceedings.

remedy—Something that corrects a violation of civil or criminal law. Unlike relief, which can be given before, during, or after trial, a remedy is given only after an injury has been fully proved to a court. (In short, a remedy is always relief, but relief is not always a remedy.) Damages and permanent injunctions are two kinds of remedies in civil cases. Imprisonment, restitution, and fines are types of remedies available in criminal cases. See, and compare with, relief.

reply—A pleading sometimes made by a plaintiff in response to a defendant's answer. See pleading, answer.

reporters—Published volumes containing court decisions arranged chronologically by date of decision. See pages 10–13.

respondent—A term sometimes used interchangeably with "appellee." See appellee.

rule—See regulation.

secondary authority—See authority.

slip opinion—An individual court decision published separately from other opinions, and soon after it is rendered.

subpoena—A court order compelling a person to appear and give testimony on a certain matter. For a definition of "subpoena duces tecum," see Appendix M.

suit—See lawsuit.

summons—A notice delivered by a sheriff or other officer informing someone that a civil action has been commenced against him or her, and that he or she is required to appear as a defendant in court on a certain date to answer the complaint.

tort—A civil (*i.e.*, private) injury other than a breach of contract. It is different from a crime, which is considered an injury to the public even though just one person may be directly injured. A tort has three elements: (1) a legal duty that the defendant owes to the plaintiff; (2) a violation of that duty; and (3) an injury to the plaintiff resulting from that violation. Often, the same act that constitutes a tort is *also* a crime, and the person who commits it can be prosecuted both criminally by the government and civilly by or on behalf of the individual directly harmed. For example, if Doe deliberately shoots Roe, Doe has committed a battery that is both a tort and a crime. The government can prosecute Doe criminally, and Roe can sue Doe civilly to try to get money (*i.e.*, damages) for his injuries.

writ—A court order requiring the performance of a specified act, or giving authority to have it done.

APPENDIX M

Translations of Foreign Words and Maxims Frequently Encountered in Legal Research

A

ab antiquo—Of an ancient date; from antiquity.

ab initio—From the beginning or inception.

actio criminalis—Criminal act.

Actus non facit reum nisi mens sit rea—The intent and the act must both concur to constitute the crime.

ad damnum—To the damage. In a complaint, the name of a clause containing a statement of a plaintiff's money loss or other damage suffered.

addendum—Something that is added or to be added; a list or section of added material.

a fortiori—By a stronger reason. A term used in logic to denote an argument that a fact must exist because another fact exists which includes or is analogous to the first fact.

ad hoc—Pertaining to a particular purpose only.

ad idem—To the same effect.

ad interim—In the meantime.

ad litem—While the lawsuit is pending.

ad satisfaciendum—To satisfy.

ad valorem—According to value.

ad vitam—For life.

aliunde—From another place; from outside.

a mensa et thoro—From bed and board. Refers to a qualified divorce by which the parties are separated or live apart without affecting the marriage itself. Compare a vinculo matrimonii.

amicus curiae—Friend of the court. A person who has no absolute right to appear in a lawsuit, but who is allowed by the court to offer argument to protect his or her interest.

animus—Intention; disposition; design; will.

animus furandi—Intention to steal.

animus testandi—Intention to make a will.

a posteriori—From the effect to the cause. A term used in logic to denote an argument which takes ascertained facts and reasons backward or inductively to show their cause.

a priori—From the cause to the effect. A term used in logic to denote an argument that takes a principle as a cause and proceeds to deduce the effects that necessarily follow.

assumpsit—A promise to pay to or do something for another.

a vinculo matrimonii—From the bond of matrimony. Refers to a complete and unqualified divorce. Compare a mensa et thoro.

B

bona fide—In good faith. Compare mala fide.

C

capias ad satisfaciendum—A writ commanding a person to be taken and kept, so that he will appear in court on a certain day to satisfy damages or a debt.

causa mortis—In contemplation of approaching death.

caveat—Caution; warning; notice to beware.

caveat emptor—Buyer beware.

certiorari—The name of a writ of review (often abbreviated as "cert.") designed to secure the record of a lower court proceeding for review by a higher court.

cestui que trust—A person who has a beneficial or equitable interest (*e.g.*, the right to receive rents or profits) in property whose legal title is held by someone else.

cestui que vie—A person the length of whose life measures the duration of another person's estate.

cf.—Abbreviation for "conferre," meaning "to compare". A signal, used in connection with a citation, directing the reader's attention to an authority containing a point analogous to the point made by the person citing the authority. See Chapter 2 for a discussion of signals used with citations.

chose—A thing; an item of personal property.

chose in action—An item of personal property not presently in an individual's possession, but whose possession the individual has a right to recover through a legal proceeding; also refers to the right itself to bring an action for the recovery of the personal property or for some other remedy (*e.g.*, damages for loss) with respect to the property.

coram nobis—Before us. A writ of error directed to another branch of the same court.

coram non judice—A court without jurisdiction to make a particular determination.

corpus delicti—The body of a crime; the physical thing upon which a crime has been committed, *e.g.*, the corpse of a murdered person, the burned out shell of a stolen automobile.

corpus juris—The body of the law.

culpa—Civil fault, neglect, or negligence.

D

damnum absque injuria—Damage or loss that cannot be redressed by a proceeding in law.

d.b.e.—Abbreviation for "de bene esse." See below.

de bene esse—Conditionally; provisionally. Refers to proceedings that are allowed to stand in the interim, but which are subject to future modification, *e.g.*, allowing a witness who may not be available for trial to testify immediately, subject to possible future re-examination and exclusion of the earlier testimony at trial if the witness becomes available.

de facto—Actually; in fact. Compare de jure.

de jure—By operation of law. Compare de facto.

delict—A wrongful act; tort.

de minimis—Minimal; trivial; so trifling as to be of no consequence in the law.

De minimis non curat lex—The law does not concern itself with trifles.

de novo—Anew; from the start.

dicta—Plural of dictum.

dictum—Shortened form of "obiter dictum." See obiter dictum.

donatio mortis causa—Gift made upon contemplation of death, and conditioned upon the occurrence of the donor's death.

duces tecum—Bring with you. Refers to a directive instructing a person who has been summoned to appear to bring with him or her some document, piece of evidence, or other thing to be inspected. See subpoena duces tecum.

E

e.g.—Abbreviation for "exempli gratia," meaning "for example."

ejusdem generis—Of the same kind, class, or nature. A rule that is sometimes followed in construing the words of written documents: where general words are linked with enumerated examples of persons or things, the general words are not construed in their broadest meaning, but are construed as applying only to persons or things of the same kind, class, or nature as those specifically enumerated.

en banc—Refers to a session of court in which all the judges of the court (rather than a smaller panel of selected judges) participate in deciding a case.

ergo—Therefore.

et al.—Abbreviation for "et alii," meaning "and others."

et seq.—Abbreviation for "et sequentia," meaning "and the following."

et ux.—Abbreviation for "et uxor." See below.

et uxor—And wife.

ex curia—Out of court.

exempli gratia—For example (typically abbreviated as "e.g.").

ex officio—By virtue of an office or official position.

ex parte—By or for one party; pertaining to one party only.

ex post facto—After the fact.

Expressio unius est exclusio alterius—A rule that is sometimes followed in construing the words of written documents: the express mention of one thing implies the exclusion of others.

ex rel.—Abbreviation for "ex relatione," meaning "upon relation of." Refers to legal proceedings commenced on behalf of the United States or an individual state, but on the instigation of an individual who has a private interest in the matter (for example, *"United States ex rel. Smith v. Jones"*).

F

Falsus in uno, falsus in omnibus—False in one thing, false in everything.

ferae naturae—Of a wild nature.

fiat—Let it be done. An official proclamation.

flagrante delicto—In the very act of committing the wrong.

fructus industriales—Fruits of one's industry or labor, *e.g.,* cash crops produced through cultivation, such as tobacco. Compare fructus naturales.

fructus naturales—Products produced by nature alone, *e.g.,* milk, ore. Compare fructus industriales.

H

habeas corpus—You have the body. Refers to various writs whose object is to bring a person before a court, most commonly directing the release of a person from illegal confinement.

haec verba—See in haec verba.

heriditaments—Inheritable property.

I

ibidem—At the same place, *e.g.,* in the same book (typically abbreviated as "ibid."). See also idem.

id.—Abbreviation for "idem." See below.

idem—At the same place, *e.g.,* in the same book (typically abbreviated as "id."). In legal writing, the abbreviation for "idem" is preferred to "ibid." for referring to a previously cited reference.

id est—That is (typically abbreviated as "i.e.").

i.e.—Abbreviation for "id est." See above.

in custodia legis—In legal custody; in the keeping of the law.

indebitatus assumpsit—An action to recover on a debt. See assumpsit.

indicia—Signs or indications.

in forma pauperis—As a pauper. Refers to permission given to a poor person to sue without paying his or her own court costs.

infra—Below; appearing below. Compare supra.

in haec verba—In these precise words; in the same words.

in limine—At the beginning; preliminarily.

in loco parentis—In the place of a parent.

in pais—Refers to proceedings conducted outside of court; commonly used in contradistinction to written matters or matters of record.

in pari delicto—Equally at fault.

in pari materia—Pertaining to the same subject. A rule that is sometimes followed in construing statutes: statutes dealing with the same subject matter are construed together, *i.e.,* in relation to one another, or as a whole.

in personam—Against the person. Compare in rem.

in re—In the matter of; concerning; in regard to. The phrase is commonly used in the title of non-adversary judicial proceedings that revolve around a particular thing or person, such as a bankruptcy or guardianship proceeding (for example, *"In re John Doe"*).

in rem—Against the thing. Commonly used to describe legal proceedings taken against a thing or piece of property (for example, a property foreclosure action), as opposed to personal actions. Compare in personam.

in situ—In the original place.

inter alia—Among other things.

inter alios—Among other persons; among those who are strangers to the proceedings.

inter partes—Between or among the parties.

inter se—Among themselves.

inter vivos—Between the living. Frequently used to describe a transaction by which property is passed from one living person to another, as opposed to a transfer by will from a deceased person.

in toto—Completely.

intra vires—Within the scope of one's powers or authority. Compare ultra vires.

ipse dixit—A bare assertion that is made, but not proved.

ipso facto—In itself; by virtue of the fact itself.

J

j.n.o.v.—Abbreviation for "judgment non obstante veredicto," meaning "judgment notwithstanding the verdict." See non obstante veredicto.

L

lex domicilii—The law of the domicile.

lex fori—The law of the forum, *i.e.,* where the suit is brought.

lex loci—The law of the place.

lex loci contractus—Either the law of the place where the contract was made, or the law by which the contract is to be governed (which may or may not be the same place).

lis pendens—A pending lawsuit.

Locus Sigilli—The place of the seal. The place for the seal on a written document (usually abbreviated as "L.S.")

L.S.—See Locus Sigilli.

M

mala fide—In bad faith. Compare bona fide.

mala in se—Describes acts wrongful in themselves; unconscionable or morally wrong acts. Compare mala prohibita.

mala prohibita—Describes acts that are wrongful because prohibited by law. Compare mala in se.

mens rea—Criminal intent; a guilty mind.

mesne—Intermediate; intervening; the middle between two extremes.

modus operandi—Method of operating.

mutatis mutandis—With the necessary changes in detail.

N

N.B.—Abbreviation for "nota bene." See nota bene.

ne exeat—A writ prohibiting a person from leaving the jurisdiction of the court or some other specified place.

nisi prius—Denotes a court of first instance; a trial court, as opposed to an appellate court.

nolle prosequi—A declaration that one is unwilling further to prosecute part or all of a case against a defendant.

nolo contendere—I will not contest it. In a criminal proceeding, the name of a plea having the same effect as a plea of guilty.

non compos mentis—Not sound of mind or memory.

non constat—It does not follow. Commonly used to refer to conclusions that, although they may appear to follow, do not necessarily follow.

non obstante veredicto—Notwithstanding the verdict. Refers to a judgment entered by court order for a plaintiff or defendant, even though the jury has returned a verdict against that party.

non sequitur—Something that does not follow.

nota bene—An instruction to "note well" (frequently abbreviated as "N.B.").

nudum pactum—A promise made without legal consideration, such as a promise supported by mere good will or affection.

nunc pro tunc—Now for then. Refers to an action having retroactive effect.

O

obiter dictum—Statements by a court in an opinion that are not necessary to the decision of the case; gratuitous or incidental commentary by a judge.

P

pari materia—See in pari materia.

pari passu—On equal footing.

particeps criminis—A criminal accomplice; partner in crime.

pendente lite—During the progress of a lawsuit.

per curiam—By the court. When a court sits by a panel of judges, this term is used to designate an opinion written by the whole court, rather than by one particular judge.

per diem—By the day.

per se—In and of itself; inherently.

persona non grata—A person who is considered unacceptable.

posse comitatus—The power or force of the county; the populace of a county that a sheriff may summon in certain cases to help keep the peace, make arrests, etc.

prima facie—On the face of it; at first blush. Refers to something initially presumed to be true until the appearance of some evidence to the contrary.

pro bono publico—For the public good.

pro forma—As a matter of form.

profit a prendre—The right to take the fruits, or profits, from the land of another, such as the right to cut and remove timber from another's land.

pro hac vice—For this one particular occasion.

pro se—For himself; on one's own behalf (*i.e.,* without an attorney).

pro tanto—To that extent; as far as it goes.

pro tempore—For the time being; temporarily.

pur autre vie—For or during the life of another. Denotes an estate in land which a person holds during the lifetime of another designated person.

Q

q.c.f.—Abbreviation for "quare clausum fregit." See below.

quaere—A query; question; doubt. Frequently used to indicate that the point or statement that follows is open to question.

quare clausum fregit—Because he broke the close. Refers to a type of legal proceeding for trespass—specifically, "breaking a close," meaning unlawfully entering upon another person's land.

quantum meruit—The amount a person deserves as compensation for services rendered.

quid pro quo—Something for something. Refers to the giving of one thing of value for another thing of value.

quo warranto—By what authority? Refers to legal proceedings undertaken to ascertain whether an officer is acting within the scope of the authority granted him by law.

R

re—In regard to. Commonly used to designate legal proceedings in which there is only one party. See in re.

res—Thing; object; property.

res adjudicata—A common but less preferred spelling of "res judicata." See res judicata.

res gestae—The whole of a transaction, including all its incidental circumstances. In the law of evidence, the phrase is often used to denote one exception to the hearsay rule allowing the admission of evidence about acts and declarations surrounding the event under investigation.

res ipsa loquitur—The thing speaks for itself. Refers to the rebuttable presumption that a defendant who had the injury-causing instrumentality in his exclusive control must have been negligent because the accident in question would not normally have occurred without negligence in connection with the instrumentality.

res judicata—A thing adjudicated. A doctrine in civil law to the general effect that matters fully and finally adjudicated on their merits between or among parties to a lawsuit may not subsequently be re-litigated by or among those same parties, or their privies.

respondeat superior—Let the master answer. A doctrine in civil law by which a master (or principal) generally is liable or answerable for the wrongful acts of his servant (or agent).

S

scienter—Knowingly; guilty knowledge.

seriatim—One at a time; serially.

sic—Thus; in this manner. Frequently used to indicate a mistake in an original writing being quoted.

sine die—Without assigning a date for a further meeting or hearing. Frequently used to refer to a final adjournment.

stare decisis—To abide by decided cases. A fundamental policy of courts generally to follow principles of law laid down in earlier cases when deciding later cases with substantially similar facts, regardless of whether the parties are the same.

status quo—The existing state of things.

sua sponte—On a person's or court's own motion; voluntarily; without prompting.

subpoena duces tecum—A writ, process, or order directing a person to produce or deliver certain papers or things in his possession or control.

sui generis—In a class by itself; the only one of its kind.

supersedeas—Name of a writ ordering a stay in legal proceedings, such as the suspension of enforcement of a lower court judgment pending an appeal.

supra—Above; appearing above. Compare infra.

U

ultra vires—In excess of one's powers. Compare intra vires.

uxor—Wife.

V

vel non—Or not; whether or not.

venire—To appear in court. The name of a writ summoning a jury (also called a "venire facias"). "Venire" is also used to refer to the list of names of jurors thus summoned.

vi et armis—By force and arms.

viz.—To wit; that is to say.

voir dire—To speak the truth. A phrase used to refer to preliminary examination of jurors or witnesses, conducted to explore competency, conflict of interest, etc., which may be grounds for objection to their qualifications either to serve as jurors or give testimony as witnesses.

Volenti non fit injuria—One who consents to injury cannot sue for damage suffered.

INDEX